DISCARD

The Universalist Movement in America

1770–1880

Recent titles in
RELIGION IN AMERICA SERIES
Harry S. Stout, General Editor

The Universalist
Movement in America
1770–1880

Ann Lee Bressler

UNIVERSITY PRESS

2001

OXFORD
UNIVERSITY PRESS

Oxford   New York
Athens   Auckland   Bangkok   Bogotá   Bombay   Buenos Aires
Calcutta   Cape Town   Chennai   Dar es Salaam   Delhi   Florence   Hong Kong
Istanbul   Karachi   Kuala Lumpur   Madras   Madrid   Melbourne   Mexico City   Mumbai
Nairobi   Paris   São Paulo   Shanghai   Singapore   Taipei   Tokyo   Toronto   Warsaw

and associated companies in
Berlin   Ibadan

Copyright © 2001 by Ann Lee Bressler

Published by Oxford University Press, Inc.
198 Madison Avenue, New York, New York 10016

Oxford is a registered trademark of Oxford University Press.

Library of Congress Cataloging-in-Publication Data

Bressler, Ann Lee.
The Universalist movement in America, 1770–1880 / Ann Lee Bressler.
p. cm. — (Religion in America series)
Includes bibliographical references and index.
ISBN 0-19-512986-5
1. Universalist churches—United States—History—18th century.   2. United
States—Church history—18th century.   3. Universalism—History—18th century.   4. Universalist
churches—United States—History—19th century.   5. United States—Church
history—19th century.   6. Universalism—History—19th century.   I. Title.   II. Religion in
America series (Oxford University Press)

BX9933.B74   2000
289.l'73—dc21   99-058071

1 3 5 7 9 8 6 4 2

Printed in the United States of America
on acid-free paper

For Molly, Morgan, and Robin

Acknowledgments

My academic work on the Universalist movement was sparked by study of its pioneering women, Olympia Brown and Mary Livermore, during my first years as a graduate student. But I will have to admit that my interest has deep roots in a personal concern with soteriological and eschatological issues, a concern already in evidence when I was eleven or twelve, struggling with basic questions in a church confirmation class. It now seems natural that my historical research on Universalist women should have expanded into an examination of a movement that was based on the denial of hell and the assertion of universal salvation.

This study first took shape as a dissertation at the University of Virginia under the direction of Joseph Kett, who appreciated that American historians had largely bypassed the Universalists, and who also wisely prompted me to broaden the scope of the work. Robert Cross and Ira Brown kindly reviewed manuscript drafts. Joseph Conforti commented on several chapters. Ernest Cassara shared many discussions with me about the Universalists. Russell Snapp has listened patiently and perceptively as I have tried to articulate my historical understanding. All these scholars have been more helpful to me than they realize.

Alan Seaburg, curator of manuscripts at the Andover-Harvard Divinity School Library, guided me through the extensive collection of Universalist documents kept there. I have also made frequent use of the resources of the Pattee Library at my alma mater, Penn State. I am grateful to Leland Park, director of the E. H. Little Library at Davidson College, one of the best small-college libraries in the country, for many courtesies, large and small. His staff has been ever supportive; in particular, Joe Gutekanst went out of his way to locate obscure materials for me.

My parents always fully shared my interests in history and religion; they were a constant source of encouragement and support. My mother, Marion Bressler, a distinguished teacher of Advanced Placement American history, has been an inspiring model of the excitement that historical study can bring. My late father, Leo Bressler, a former professor of English at Penn State, gladly entertained my early musings on American religion and lent his skillful writer's hand to help me polish awkward prose. My editors at Oxford University Press have been patient and instructive as I have navigated the publication process.

My husband Robin Barnes has long shared my enthusiasm about the Universalists and has been my invaluable partner in this work. Beyond our countless informal and lively discussions, he has consistently devoted his time and talents to help me clarify concepts and edit drafts. Over the years he has come to know Hosea Ballou and Thomas Whittemore as well as I do. I cannot adequately express my gratitude to him.

Our children, Molly and Morgan, have grown up with this book. Almost every summer they have endured trips to historic Universalist sites and New England graveyards. The names and teachings of nineteenth-century Universalists must be lodged somewhere deep in their minds. As I complete this work, that is not an unhappy thought.

Davidson, North Carolina   A. L. B.
January 2001

Contents

The Universalist Movement in America

1770–1880

Introduction

In 1805, a thirty-four-year-old preacher unknown outside scattered church circles in New England published *A Treatise on Atonement*. Written some three and a half decades after John Murray had begun to spread the notion of universal salvation in America, the work was a straightforward and lively exposition of Universalist faith. His widely read *Treatise* established Hosea Ballou as the foremost theologian of a popular religious movement that was just then experiencing a rapid shift from reliance on itinerant preachers to the establishment of settled congregations.

Some fourteen years later, William Ellery Channing, the pastor of an elite congregation in Boston, delivered a sermon at the Baltimore ordination of Jared Sparks that became "the chief manifesto of American Unitarianism."[1] Outlining the major elements of the liberal faith that had grown up within Boston's Standing Order, Channing sought to explain Unitarian principles to a new audience. His willingness to state forthrightly the precepts of "Unitarian Christianity" confirmed him as the "prime embodiment" of the Unitarian movement.[2]

These key exponents of two branches of early nineteenth-century religious liberalism were, by 1817, the pastors of large, closely neighboring Boston churches. Channing was at the famous Federal Street Church, one of the oldest and most highly regarded congregations in the city. After an early career of itinerant preaching and brief ministries in Portsmouth and Salem, Ballou had become pastor at the fast-growing Second Universalist Society, only a few corners away on School Street. One might easily assume that the two men were acquainted and that they spoke to

3

one another about the many common themes of their writings. But this was not the case. Indeed, when Ballou moved to Boston, he was extended no ministerial courtesies or fellowship; it was reported that Channing, by then an eminent figure, treated him as though he were a leper.[3] Channing's most sympathetic biographer can find no real explanation for his "infuriating practice of treating Ballou as if he did not exist."[4]

Differences of social class surely played a role: the Harvard-trained son of a well-connected Newport family had little time for the self-taught minister of an undistinguished congregation. Ballou clearly felt this distance. In a commentary on one of Channing's discourses, he wrote that he did not "expect" Channing to "condescend" or "explain himself on the subject" any further.[5] Living, as his biographer observed, "amidst the embellishments and comforts of dowered wealth," Channing could show a striking lack of awareness about those not of his station, asserting in an 1833 sermon that "the poor are often over-worked, but they suffer less than many among the rich, who have no work to do, no interesting objects to fill up life . . . to satisfy the cravings of man for action." He referred to the Irish privately as "ignorant hordes" who "cannot but abuse" a citizenship granted on "too easy terms."[6]

Yet Channing's disdain for those of humble background cannot completely explain his lack of collegiality, indeed of civility, toward a neighboring minister whose doctrinal criticism, as we will see, often mirrored his own. There was an even deeper divide here than the important differences of social background. A brief comparison of the *Treatise* with the Baltimore sermon can offer broader insight into Channing's perception of Ballou. More important, it can help to show that while early Universalists and Unitarians shared significant elements of belief—and disbelief—they represented two quite different, even opposed, strains in American religious culture.

There are obvious differences in literary style and tone between these key Universalist and Unitarian documents. The excitedly punctuated *Treatise* is a passionate and polemical appeal that reflects the oral directness of a man whose life was devoted, above all, to preaching. The Baltimore sermon, on the other hand, is an elegant, restrained, "magisterial" statement of belief,[7] reflecting an attitude of calm self-assurance. Yet the two works do share some clear similarities in content. Both Ballou and Channing exposed major tenets of Calvinism to critical analysis, found them wanting, and proposed alternative beliefs that were, in some cases, nearly identical.

Both ministers began by endorsing rational scriptural interpretation, although Channing's eloquence contrasted sharply with the bluntness of Ballou's comment that, without reason, the Scriptures "would be of no more service to us than they are to brute creation."[8] Channing, like Ballou, dismissed the Anselmic view of atonement traditionally held by New England Calvinists by which the death of Christ paid the infinite penalty of human sin.[9] Ballou had insisted in 1805 that "God was not the unreconciled party"; indeed, he maintained that to argue "that God loved man any less, after his transgression, than before, denies his unchangeability." Man, rather, "was wanting in love towards God."[10] Channing, in 1819, similarly held that "the impression, that the death of Jesus produces a change in the mind of God towards man" was a pernicious error, which contradicted God's unchangeable love and led men to think "that Christ came to change God's mind, rather than their own."[11]

Discussing Christ's function as the messenger of "the divine grace of reconciliation," Ballou rejected the Trinity, jesting that, if the "Godhead consisted of three distinct persons, and each of these persons is infinite," then the whole Godhead was "infinity, multiplied by three!"[12] A more sober Channing also wondered how it was possible for the "weak and limited mind of man" to attach itself to "three divine agents, performing different offices"; the doctrine of the Trinity "sets before us three distinct objects of supreme adoration, three infinite persons."[13]

Ballou and Channing agreed, moreover, that the one indivisible deity was not to be conceived as an absolute monarch whose will simply defined the good. Christian faith was not inspired, wrote Ballou, by the image of "power moving on in front, exhibiting tyrannic majesty in every action, and meager justice in the rear, obsequiously pronouncing all right!"[14] God was not, Channing advised, raised by "greatness and superiority" to reign "tyrannically . . . over the principles of justice and morality."[15] Rather, both insisted that God possessed a "parental" character.[16]

These similarities are what usually have drawn notice. John White Chadwick, for example, maintained in his 1903 biography of Channing that the *Treatise* "anticipated the full-grown expression of Channing's thought on all its principal lines."[17] Chadwick's subtly condescending assertion, issued long after the Unitarians and Universalists had grown cozy, reflects a view about the relationship between the early histories of the two movements that remains prevalent nearly a century later. Unfortunately, it is based on a fundamental misreading of the *Treatise*. While many of the major ideas and arguments in the two works are strikingly similar, the central thrust of the Baltimore sermon differs greatly from that of Ballou's *Treatise*.

One commentator has observed that, in Channing's thought, we can see a "vast reversal in the orientation of the New England mind since the time of [Jonathan] Edwards," even "the triumph of Edwards's opponents."[18] Channing valued the gospel for its "aids," "motives," and "excitements" to a "generous and divine virtue" and insisted that virtue could not be "infused into us without our own moral activity."[19] It was in the human ability to oppose nature and history, not in human openness to God, that Channing saw the beauty of man.[20] As Ballou's biographer, Ernest Cassara, has pointed out, Channing's Arminianism was directly opposed to Ballou's belief.[21] The keynote of Ballou's message was the power of God's love in the face of human sinfulness and apparent intransigence. Man "experimentally becomes a child of God," and "by the spirit of the word, the soul is brought into sweet communion with God."[22] In this key respect, Ballou remained closer to Edwards than to Edwards's opponents.

Indeed, the disagreement between Channing and Ballou continued in important respects a conflict that had originated between Jonathan Edwards and the liberal clergy of Boston. Figures like Jonathan Mayhew and Charles Chauncy had developed what Henry May has called "a post-Calvinist adaptation of the Moderate English Enlightenment."[23] They held at more than arm's length the sort of intense concern with human sinfulness and the fate of souls that flared during the Great Awakening.

Channing was clearly an exponent of the outlook they had nurtured. Ultimately, he sought to furnish the rational structure for a religion of moral self-culture. For Channing, after all, virtue was rooted in human moral nature, with its likeness to God.[24] Andrew Delbanco has written that Channing's conception of virtue "as a property of individual insularity" made him uncomfortable with the "communitarian metaphysics of Edwards, who always conceived of virtue in terms of relation."[25]

We can see the basic incompatibility between Channing and Ballou when we recognize that Ballou's vision was essentially communitarian as well. Indeed, Ballou's understanding of the power of the doctrine of universal salvation is reminiscent of Edwards's expression of true virtue:

> In pure love to others i.e., love not arising from self-love, there is a union of the heart with others; a kind of enlargement of the mind, whereby it so extends itself as to take others into a man's self: and therefore it implies a disposition to feel, to desire, and to act as though others were one with ourselves.[26]

Ballou held that the heartfelt belief in universal salvation induced people to rise above the "natural moral sense," to act out of a higher and less purely selfish virtue. Faith in universal salvation severely discouraged the elevation of individual virtue as it celebrated the organic purpose and will of God.[27]

In the end, Ballou and Channing thus directed reason to very different purposes; Ballou put it in the service of fervent evangelical piety, while Channing used it to illuminate an urbane moralism. Channing's refusal to recognize Ballou, then, was probably far more than the snubbing of one who held a lower social station; it was also an expression of distaste for the broad implications of Ballou's teachings. Ballou had, in an important way, appropriated the legacy of Edwards, while Channing was socially and intellectually descended from his opponents. Imbuing the organic, egalitarian piety of Edwards with a heavy dose of Enlightenment rationality, Ballou challenged an Arminian individualism that implicitly reinforced a sense of social hierarchy. Intellectually as well as socially, this preacher from the hill country made William Ellery Channing uneasy.

The central point of belief in universal salvation clearly and deeply separated the teachings of Ballou from those of Channing. Ballou himself was long puzzled by Channing's refusal to admit a belief that appeared to grow logically out of his other convictions. It took time even for him to appreciate how fully his own faith in God's sovereignty differed in substance from Channing's emphasis on individual freedom and God's moral justice.

The belief that an all-good and all-powerful God saves all souls may be virtually as old as Christianity; in the view of some biblical scholars, Saint Paul himself preached a definite if often muted doctrine of universal salvation. But, despite the efforts of a small handful of interpreters to gain acceptance for the idea in later centuries, it never gained a secure place in Christian teaching. Its fate in the history of American Christianity was ultimately similar, yet the doctrine found unusually rich soil in which to grow in the early American republic. Indeed, here it experienced its most significant flowering and its moment of greatest potential.

That flowering, as well as the subsequent withering, can be reconstructed most clearly through a study of the Universalist denomination. To be sure, Universalist churches did not hold a monopoly on the idea of universal salvation in late eighteenth- and nineteenth-century America. But the denomination did become a home for the majority of those who consciously and openly adhered to the doctrine, so that to explore meaningfully the history of the Universalist church in America is to study a religious movement rather than merely to study the development of a sect or institution.

Students of this movement have often been lured into unwarranted assumptions by the tendency among American Protestants to view all of the main "liberal" religious groups through the same lens. Indeed, already in the early nineteenth century Universalists were commonly lumped together with Unitarians as "liberal religionists" who refused to be constrained by the beliefs of the major evangelical bodies. The eventual union of the two denominations in 1961 and their similar opposition to creeds and to many traditional Christian doctrines have led historians to conclude that fairly superficial differences kept them apart. According to this common view, Unitarianism was an elite, Enlightenment reaction to the harshness of Calvinist doctrine; Universalism was its rustic, less intellectual counterpart. The movements were thus separate but parallel challenges to New England Puritanism.[28]

This assessment has some validity. Particularly in the nineteenth century, social barriers certainly stood in the way of contact and cooperation between Unitarians and Universalists. But the linking of the two groups has clouded examination of the very different origins and development of each. Universalism has probably suffered more; it has too often been regarded as simply Unitarianism's poor relation, finally acknowledged and taken in with the creation of Unitarian-Universalism.

The tendency to portray Universalists as the unlettered (and therefore less significant) kin of Unitarians is partly responsible for the long-standing scholarly inattention to Universalist history. Older surveys of American religious history regularly treated the denomination as little more than a footnote to other liberal religious movements and rarely suggested that it had any independent religious significance. Even the most recent and broadly conceived surveys have had little to say about the role of the Universalists.[29] Yet the study of Universalism opens a wide window on the American religious scene from the 1770s to the 1880s.[30]

Under the forceful leadership of Hosea Ballou, Universalism became a major antagonist of the Second Great Awakening and the evangelical culture it spawned. In boldly affirming the doctrine of universal salvation, Universalists exposed and challenged the Protestant drift away from traditional Calvinist orthodoxy. Universalists sharply criticized the moralistic character of the dominant religious beliefs in the first decades of the nineteenth century and the theological contradictions underlying revivalism.[31] But, as I will show, by the second quarter of the century Universalists themselves began to argue that their view sustained the popular notion of the moral government of God. Meanwhile, the sense of a superintending God gradually dimmed in Protestant culture, and social reform efforts intensified. Like other Victorians, Universalists increasingly extolled moral seriousness and the cultivation of the self.[32]

A come-outer movement that preached a heretical and feared idea at the end of the eighteenth century, by the time of its official centennial celebration in 1870, Universalism was becoming a comfortably established and generally accepted form of liberal Protestantism. In no other religious movement do we witness so dramatically the shift from an eschatological and communally oriented faith to an open-ended, progressive sensibility centering on individual personality.

To examine the course of nineteenth-century Universalism is to encounter problems such as the relationship between reason and faith in a young, fast-growing but deeply uncertain society. The controversy over universal salvation, moreover, reveals much about the emerging emphasis on the individual and the freedom of the self in American society.[33] Finally, and perhaps most importantly, the study of nineteenth-century Universalism brings into focus the dramatic diminution of overt eschatological concerns in American culture.

Calvinism Improved

At first glance, American Universalism seems to have been one of the clearest manifestations of the rational spirit of the revolutionary era. With its bold assertion of salvation for all, the Universalist movement was shocking even in an atmosphere charged with challenges to orthodox Calvinist doctrines. In the nineteenth century, when they embraced a unitarian theology years before William Ellery Channing's classic 1819 expression of Unitarian Christianity, Universalists became even more closely identified with rationalistic dissent.

Universalism was, however, more than one small tree in the flowering orchard of liberal religion. The significance of Universalism for American religious history lies in the determination of its adherents to put reason in the service of piety. Drawing upon eighteenth-century evangelical Calvinism on the one hand and Enlightenment liberalism on the other, Universalism emerged as an attempt to nourish piety through rational conviction. Reason, Universalists argued, dictated that a benevolent God would redeem all of creation. The doctrine of universal salvation was God's way of influencing human affections and turning naturally self-centered human beings to the love of God and the greater creation. Hosea Ballou, the preeminent theologian of the growing movement in the era around 1800, described the belief in universal salvation as changing the heart in a way that was practically supernatural: although the doctrine was a rational belief, it had transcendent power over the feelings. Clearly a movement strongly associated with Enlightenment belief, Universalism also reflected the legacy of Edwardsean Calvinism.

Jonathan Edwards and the Human Family

Historians have long recognized that New England Calvinism was not monolithic but a precarious balance of a number of convictions. Seventeenth-century thought had, for example, accommodated two main forms of Calvinist covenantal belief. The covenantalism linked to Genevan Calvinism stressed God's conditional promise of salvation to a limited number of souls. Another interpretation focused on human obligation in the matter of salvation. Ministers tended to emphasize one view of the covenant over the other while adhering formally to both. The unraveling of this unstable synthesis during the eighteenth century exposed the variety of theological positions implicit in New England theology.[1]

A major division occurred in the wake of the growth of Arminianism and of the experimental piety of the Great Awakening. Often termed "Old Light" or "Old Side," the clerical opponents of the Awakening increasingly envisioned God as reasonable instead of arbitrary and allowed congregations to assume that those among them who met the conditions of the covenant were of the elect. They prepared the way for Arminians such as Charles Chauncy, who openly expressed the "inherently individualistic" aspect of covenantal theology.[2] The "experimental" preaching of the Great Awakening, on the other hand, portrayed human beings as united by their fallen nature and total spiritual inability. Evangelists who turned to a sovereign God for regeneration were not inclined to regard humanity as a collection of discrete and willful souls.

Jonathan Edwards's religious philosophy centered on his conviction that humanity was not an assemblage of autonomous persons. Bruce Kuklick reminds us that Edwards was really a "behaviorist" who rejected the Arminian notion of a freely acting soul. He did not believe that the individual, self-determining soul existed; rather, there was "only the series of conscious acts."[3] Edwards, therefore, philosophically opposed what was evolving into the Arminian creed: that "God never violates the human personality."[4] Edwards believed that God did not "save" souls and then gather them individually; grace broke through the jealous shell of the individual, opening him to the effulgence of God's love. Edwards's vision of human perfection, Robert Jenson observes, was "not first or last a vision of rescue, followed by self-achieved fulfillment, but of 'heaven,' of transfiguring absorption in Christ's glory."[5]

Edwards differed radically from the moralism of his Arminian opponents in his understanding of virtue as "love to being in general." Edwardsean Calvinists faulted liberal thinkers for conceiving the Newtonian system as merely mechanical. Understood properly, Newtonianism taught that "the gravity inherent in the atoms of creation was a type of love which alone could hold the beings of the spirit world together." Edwardseans understood this sort of attraction not metaphorically but in a literal scientific sense, and from it they derived their religious imperative: "to cement all men in the bonds of mutual affection." Thus, the saint was loved less for his individual excellence than for his harmony with the greater whole. "The Calvinist pursuit of happiness," Alan Heimert writes, "was, almost by definition, a quest for the great community." Despite the uncertainty of Edwards and other Calvinists as to whether the unregenerate could be truly loved, their definition of sainthood "allowed no man to rest content short of all mankind's being drawn up into beautiful union."[6]

In support of this notion, Edwards even acquiesced in the modification of the traditional Calvinist doctrine of atonement. His *Freedom of the Will* had stated that humans had not a natural but rather a moral inability to repent. Yet the concept of limited atonement implied natural inability. The New Divinity disciples of Edwards, who struggled self-consciously to uphold his legacy, solved this dilemma by asserting an unlimited atonement in which Christ died not to take upon himself the sins of humanity but rather to demonstrate God's power and hatred of sin. This notion of atonement theoretically allowed for the salvation of all. By writing the preface to Edward Bellamy's *True Religion Delineated* (1750), which argued for an unlimited atonement, Edwards implicitly endorsed this New Divinity doctrine.[7]

Edwards's apparent willingness to revise the traditional Calvinist belief in limited atonement testifies to his essentially organic vision of human union. For Edwards, the world is an active web of relationships. A being "drives toward a goal, which is union with other beings."[8] Individualism had no place in his social thought and social ethics; for him, society was "ideally an organic whole, in which persons treated each other as fellow members of the body of Christ," not in a contractual agreement but as a family.[9] As Edwards wrote in one work, "God has made of one blood all the nations of men to dwell on the face of the earth, hereby teaching us this moral lesson, that it becomes mankind all to be united as a family."[10]

Liberals and Evangelicals

Those who professed to follow Edwards were not as inclined to expound this organic spirituality. For Edwards, the love of God had been a positive expression of self-lessness, a giving of the self in a "consent to being," a "yearning to be constituted of the stuff of God's beauty." But, by the late eighteenth century, God seemed a more distant and abstract ordering principle instead of an immediate, magisterial, and awe-inspiring presence. God became, as Richard Rabinowitz observes, more an "explanation" than a "living force." The joy-filled yielding of self to God became, under Samuel Hopkins and others, essentially privative, the necessary submission to divine purpose and government. Many professed Calvinists tended to worship God's ultimate plan of salvation, rather than God himself.[11] An evangelical system driven by a sense of individual obligation and empowerment gained ground as the perception of God's immediate and fearful reality faded.[12]

Edwards's New Divinity followers, including Hopkins, Joseph Bellamy, and Jonathan Edwards, Jr., gave impetus to evangelicalism by insisting that only the selfish heart, not the understanding, needed renovation. They argued that sinners possessed the natural ability to repent. Opponents of the Awakening had maintained that, first, the understanding needed to be illuminated through various "means of grace"; the slow renovation of the heart would then follow. New Divinity believers rejected this gradualist view, saying that nothing stood in the way of a sinner's immediate repentance except the stoniness of his own heart.[13] Renovation of the heart was therefore not step-by-step; there was no middle ground between a regenerate and an unregenerate state.[14] Relentlessly preaching the necessity of conversion and acknowledging a universal instead of a limited atonement, New Divinity proponents shifted the onus to the individual.[15] Joseph Bellamy, who had argued that sinners imperiled their chances for salvation by not availing themselves of the means at hand, profoundly influenced his student Timothy Dwight. As Yale president, Dwight sanctioned the use of human means in pursuit of conversions. With the beliefs of Dwight and his students Lyman Beecher and Nathaniel Taylor, Calvinism acceded more fully than ever to the moral demands of the age: God as loving father desired human happiness and offered people a part in their own salvation.[16] Indeed, by small increments, and often in contradiction to their professed doctrine, even evangelical Calvinists came in some degree to accept the eminently reasonable God of the Arminians and liberals, who regarded humans as individual and responsible moral agents.[17]

Under the Boston leadership of Charles Chauncy at the First Church and Jonathan Mayhew at the West Church, the liberals held that people as moral agents experienced happiness when they followed the laws of God as expressed through both reason and revelation. Ebenezer Gay's 1757 publication, *Natural Religion*, captured the heart of liberal faith: the affirmation that Scripture only confirmed what man was constituted to learn through observation of the world.[18] Divine government was a rational, fair operation in which God did not arbitrarily save or condemn but presided over a regime of laws.[19]

Both Mayhew and Chauncy saw a symbiotic relationship between faith and works, and both rejected the notion of sudden, complete conversion. One gradually grew into the "object of God's love"; human striving was at least as important as the divine initiative.[20] Growing out of the sort of latter-day Puritan moralism embodied in Cotton Mather's *Essays to Do Good* (Boston, 1710) and strengthened by the philosophical moralism of the Enlightenment, Arminianism emphasized the moral striving of each person within the community, which served as a kind of proving ground of faith. Arminians first looked for evidence of a regenerate Christian life in the moral activity of the individual.[21]

Many liberals did adopt the idea of universal salvation, but among these thinkers it was never preached as a key theme. Chauncy warmed to the idea because of his great faith in the possibility of individual human reformation, not because he cherished a social vision of the universal regeneration of all souls. Mayhew argued, in somewhat contradictory fashion, that a paternal God would inflict discipline only as a reformatory measure and that the everlasting punishment of a limited number might be for the benefit of humanity in general. In his anonymously published 1784 work, *Mystery Hid from Ages and Generations; or, The Salvation of All Men*, Chauncy put forth a distinctly Arminian defense of universal salvation, which pictured a period of trial and discipline before a final restoration. He consciously sought to distance himself from what he regarded as the inflammatory preaching of the uneducated "father" of American Universalism, John Murray. He warned that Murray's concept of universal salvation ignored future punishment and could be an "encouragement to Libertinism."[22] Chauncy accepted universal salvation as logically following from God's benevolence. But his liberal vision of heaven, waggishly described by Heimert as "a sort of glorified Harvard graduate school," bore little resemblance to the egalitarian and communal ideal that would develop with the early Universalist movement.[23]

The "guiding spirit" of Arminian social thought was a basic individualism, which saw the community's welfare as best served by the individual pursuit of happiness. Such an emphasis on individualism was closely tied to a hierarchic social perspective, exemplified by the "great chain of being" in which, Chauncy noted, "a diversity of beings" were "duly subordinated to each other."[24] A certain snobbishness thus characterized eighteenth-century Arminians, who disdained the "unthinking multitude" and appealed to the "common conclusions of all educated men."[25] When Arminians became nineteenth-century Unitarians, this attitude did not change. Those liberal descendants of the Arminians who enshrined human moral perfectibility, such as William Ellery Channing, were distinctly uneager to embrace the notion of universal salvation, and many refused to acknowledge it as part of their faith.

Most Calvinists rejected the full-fledged individualism and implicit elitism embodied in the liberal social vision. But prominent Calvinist moderates, including Dwight and Jedidiah Morse, had actually come to resemble Arminian Jonathan Mayhew more than Jonathan Edwards.[26] By the 1830s, when Charles Grandison Finney was waging a holy war against the "cannot-ism" of the unconverted, Calvinist evangelicals were not concerned with elucidating God's majestic and eternal sovereignty. Most Protestants still looked askance at the Boston liberals, who, having evolved into Unitarians, seemed beyond the pale of Christianity. But evangelicals and liberals alike were united in a conception of the freedom and responsibility of souls to work out their own salvation.

The growing sense that God did not dispose of his creatures arbitrarily contributed to the eighteenth-century decline of eschatological anxiety among American Protestants generally. Indeed, the specter of hell that had haunted the seventeenth-century Puritans did not survive the Great Awakening. While many believers continued to worry over divine wrath and endless punishment, traditional visions of hell began to lose their immediacy. The idea of hell as an awesome aspect of God's justice and glory was fading in New England by the mid–eighteenth century. By the time of the American Revolution, few believers shared Michael Wigglesworth's hair-raising visions of "that dismal place, far from Christ's face, where death and darkness dwell."[27] As the Enlightenment emphasis on the goodness and benevolence of God gained ground, the tendency to depict eternal punishment as an essential element of God's sovereignty waned.

New England's Protestants had become far more sanguine about their ability to gain assurance of their salvation and thus broke down the distinctive Puritan tension surrounding death and dying.[28] By the mid–eighteenth century, a growing sentimentalism had colored the common attitude toward death as fearful anticipation of God's judgment receded. Sermons and poetry indicate this change, but tombstone carvings provide the most graphic evidence, as smiling winged cherubs replaced grim death's head images by the 1750s.[29] Belief in a just and forgiving God and the hope of a capacious heaven muted terror of an inscrutable deity. By the second half of the eighteenth century, the destiny of the soul appeared far more open-ended and conditional, hinging on individual human as well as divine action.

Preachers of a Rational Election

The emerging Universalist movement, with its insistent eschatological and communal emphasis, challenged the growing sense of the freedom and distinctiveness of souls. The notion of universal salvation had been introduced in America as early as the 1740s, when George de Benneville of Oley, Pennsylvania, had preached the doctrine among local settlers. The belief seems to have appeared more or less independently among a number of eighteenth-century churches and sects, including Anglicans and Congregationalists in New England and German pietist congregations, such as the Schwenkfelders in Pennsylvania.[30] Since none of these groups made the doctrine central to their creed, however, they should not be considered part of the Universalist movement.

When it did emerge as a popular movement in the late eighteenth century, Universalism represented a determined effort to "improve" Calvinism. Like Boston liberals, Universalists expressed an Enlightenment belief in God's rational benevolence. But the early movement was more significantly linked to the radical evangelicalism of the Great Awakening, with its emphasis on experimental religion and the reception of a new spiritual sense.[31] Universalists held that a new spirituality was kindled in the hearts of those who embraced the belief that no soul was eternally lost.

Universalists identified this single rational concept—the extension of salvation from a restricted group of elect to all of mankind—as the one point that distinguished them from Calvinists.[32] Early Universalists preached a change of heart that would enlarge the affections and evoke an understanding of salvation as a social and communal, rather than as a personal and individual, event. The acceptance of universal salvation came to mark the regeneration of the believer, who now perceived a benevolent divine will to redeem all humanity. Above all, in this emphasis on the social context of salvation, harking back to Edwards, Universalist views differed from those of prominent eighteenth-century liberals, who also found the idea of eternal damnation hard to reconcile with the rule of a reasonable and benevolent God.

Universalists traditionally have cited John Murray's arrival in North America in 1770 as the beginning of their denomination.[33] In the formative period between Murray's arrival and 1805, when Hosea Ballou published his *Treatise on Atonement,* itinerant preachers spread the message of universal salvation, and ministers established the first settled churches and conventions. Ballou's definitive statements on the nature of God, sin, and the meaning of atonement came only after earlier American Universalists had been wrestling with these issues for a generation.

Hosea Ballou 2nd, a great-nephew of Hosea Ballou and a scholar of the Universalist movement, explained in 1848 that, in the decades before 1800:

there seems to have risen up, simultaneously, in different parts of the country, a sense of unsatisfied wants, a longing for something more than the old system of religion could give. The fierce excitements of the great "revivals" had passed; their doctrinal elements were now left to their natural action on the living organism of the human heart, and what rest was there for the soul? Here and there were individuals, especially among the Separatists and new Lights, who, without concert, were painfully groping, each his solitary way, out of the stifling atmosphere of high Calvinism, to some freer issue.[34]

The basic perception was accurate: ideas about universal salvation first spread in a scattered and uncoordinated way in the later decades of the eighteenth century, as attitudes about traditional religion shifted at an accelerating pace. Yet, with remarkable consistency, early preachers of Universalism saw themselves as extending the basic Calvinist tenet of unconditional election. Appealing to those who strained under the strictures of traditional Calvinism, Universalism was a faith that sought to reconcile popular rationalist stirrings with a fervent pietism.

John Murray and Elhanan Winchester, two key figures of early Universalism, reflected in their differing styles and ideas the roles of piety and reason in the early movement. Murray, minister of the first established Universalist congregation in America, was born into a strict English Calvinist family. A member of George Whitefield's tabernacle in London, he tried to dissuade a young woman parishioner from her belief in universal salvation. But her main argument, that "if Jesus be not the savior of the *unbeliever* until he *believes*, the *unbeliever* is called upon to believe a lie," took cognizance of the implicit Arminianism in church teachings and had a strong effect on Murray.

Soon afterward, a London preacher named James Relly became Murray's mentor.[35] Also a Whitefield convert, Relly had preached universal salvation to a London congregation between 1757 and his death in 1778.[36] His *Union or, A Treatise on the Consanguinity and Affinity between Christ and His Church* proposed that because Christ bore the burden of human sin, his death was the salvation of all; humanity was one in redemption as well as in the fall. Both men believed that all souls were effectively "redeemed," but all had not yet come to the realization that brought salvation itself, and to effect this transforming realization was the purpose of preaching the gospel.[37]

Having suffered a series of personal misfortunes but fully convinced by Relly's theology, Murray emigrated to New Jersey in 1770 and embarked on a life of itinerant preaching along the northeastern seaboard, refusing any settled pastorate.[38] He found especially strong sympathy for Universalism on his trips to Gloucester, Massachusetts, and by 1779, dissenters from the First Church of Christ in Gloucester had organized the first Universalist church in America. The Independent Church of Christ consisted of thirty-one men and thirty women, with Murray as pastor.[39] The establishment took place despite strong local opposition and criticism from the prominent Newport minister Ezra Stiles, who termed Murray a "papist" who hoped to disrupt and divide Protestants.[40]

The other leading eighteenth-century proponent of Universalism, Elhanan Winchester, was born in 1751 in Brookline, Massachusetts, to a devout New Light family.

At nineteen, he became an itinerant Baptist minister and later settled for a time among a group of Calvinistic Baptists in Welsh Neck, South Carolina.[41] His conversion to Universalism was gradual, beginning in South Carolina with his reading of the *Everlasting Gospel* by Georg-Klein Nicolai of Friessdorf. Published in America in 1753 under the pseudonym of Paul Siegvolck, this work was particularly important in the spread of Universalist ideas in the mid-Atlantic regions.[42] After Winchester moved to Philadelphia to become minister of the Baptist church of that city, his Universalist convictions deepened with his reading of *The Restitution of All Things* by Sir George Stonehouse, an Oxford-educated English cleric and vicar to Charles Wesley.[43] Growing sympathy for Winchester's views resulted in a schism in the Philadelphia Baptist church and the founding in 1781 of the Society of Universal Baptists.[44] Among the prominent members of this new group was Benjamin Rush, physician, reformer, and signer of the Declaration of Independence.

Winchester moved to England in 1787 and did not return until 1794; he died in 1797. Despite this long absence and his relatively short career, his work gave important impetus to the propagation of Universalism. Like most other early Universalists, he was largely a self-educated man. Yet his knowledge of languages, particularly ancient tongues, was remarkable; his belief in universal restoration was rooted in extensive scholarship. A successful preacher, he also spread his ideas effectively through his printed writings, some of which were distributed by Rush.[45]

Unlike Murray, Winchester came to Universalism "from a very moderate Calvinism, if not downright Arminianism."[46] He held that universal salvation would occur only after the wicked had been punished—perhaps not for fifty thousand years.[47] According to Hosea Ballou 2nd, Winchester's immediate followers thought Murray's ideas were inimical to holiness. Opponents of Winchester's system, on the other hand, looked upon the system as a gospel of works. Ballou 2nd believed that, although both teachings ultimately reached the same result, it was "impossible" for the two views to coalesce; the 1780s and 1790s were thus a "transitional, chaotic" time for Universalists.[48]

It is clear that Universalism's first prominent leaders were drawn to the notion of universal salvation for somewhat different reasons.[49] Winchester appreciated the reasonableness of a belief that appeared to satisfy both justice and mercy; he stressed the intellectual case for Universalism. Rush, in fact, gave Winchester the "ultimate compliment of the eighteenth century" by terming him the "theological Newton."[50] Murray, a more humble intellect, discovered the potency of the doctrine to stir a deep piety in his listeners; his contemporaries likened his preaching style to that of the powerful George Whitefield.[51] Yet the two preachers managed to play down their differences for the sake of their common belief, and opponents seemed unaware of any confusion or disagreement among proponents of the doctrine.

Despite Winchester's important scholarly role, there can be no doubt that Murray had the greater immediate influence. Winchester's thought veered in an Arminian direction with his insistence on future punishment for sin, but this was not the general tendency of early Universalism. To be sure, Arminian tendencies would emerge strongly later in the movement. As we will see in chapter 2, by the mid–nineteenth century, a majority of the denomination agreed with Winchester's conviction that the faith required clear moral sanctions. Most commonly, however, early Universalism appealed to Calvinists who wished to satisfy some of the demands of rational religion while reasserting the piety they saw as central.[52]

Stephen Marini sees the emergence of rural New England Universalism as "one of the many theological byproducts of the breakdown of the Evangelical Calvinism held by New Divinity Congregationalists and Separate Baptists."[53] A representative figure is Caleb Rich (1750–1821), who had been a Baptist before becoming a preacher of universal salvation in frontier areas of Massachusetts and New Hampshire. Like Winchester, Rich focused on the Calvinist tenet of predestination, reconciling it with divine benevolence through the idea of universal, rather than partial, election. John Murray held a Christocentric view: he argued that Christ's atonement was not limited but universal.[54] Marini stresses that such variety in the early movement does not imply that Universalists were averse to theological argumentation, or that Universalism "was a product of popular 'common sense.' " Indeed, he asserts that "early Universalists engaged in sophisticated systematic theological reflection."[55]

Universalism's strong pietist roots are suggested by the appeal of the very early movement among New England Baptists. Adams Streeter was among the first teachers of universal salvation in the hinterlands of Massachusetts and New Hampshire; he had been a Baptist minister before becoming a preacher of the doctrine in 1777 or 1778. Noah Murray, formerly a Baptist preacher in Lanesboro, Massachusetts, became a Universalist minister in 1784, and David Evans, a Baptist deacon from New Britain, Pennsylvania, avowed universal salvation in 1785. Shippie Townsend, probably the first layman in New England to publish a defense of universal salvation, converted to the belief from the hyper-Calvinistic Sandemanian Baptists, a group that strenuously objected even to minor attempts to soften the doctrine of election.[56] In the 1780s and 1790s, Universalist preachers in New England found nearly all Baptist churches receptive to their belief, and they often acquired as many as twenty converts from a single church. Even Jonathan Maxcy, who became president of the Baptist Rhode Island College in 1792, was suspected of sympathy with Universalism; the prominent Baptist leader Isaac Backus scrutinized his works for evidence of this heresy.[57] For those who sought an alternative to the embattled Calvinist orthodoxy of the late eighteenth-century Baptists, Universalist teachings seem to have had a natural attraction.

The first adherents wanted to reconstitute what they perceived as a confused but basically sound Calvinist impulse. The title of Joseph Huntingdon's posthumously published tract, *Calvinism Improved* (1796), clearly reflects the attitude of many eighteenth- and nineteenth-century Universalists toward their movement. Brother of the governor of Connecticut (Samuel) and of a signer of the Declaration of Independence (Benjamin), Huntingdon, a Congregationalist clergyman from Coventry, maintained a "respectably" orthodox reputation during his life.[58]

His work, published two years after his death, was meant to improve Calvinism by demonstrating that terms such as "elect" and "decree" meant not the salvation of a part of humanity but rather a "firm and fixed purpose" or an "immutable determination of God."[59] Like Murray, he put forth the traditional view of vicarious atonement, the satisfaction of the law, but maintained that the intention was universal, not limited, salvation. Mankind was united not only in the fall but in redemption as well.[60]

For eighteenth-century Universalists, human beings were helpless creatures in need of divine grace: Murray, Winchester, and Huntingdon all professed belief in original sin. "By nature we are all born diseased," wrote Winchester.[61] The first generation of Universalists thus did not embrace a romantic anthropology; humanity did not enter the world innocent and pure but was rather clearly inclined toward sin.[62] But by balancing God's awesome sovereignty with the assurance of his benevolence in the salvation of all sinful souls, early Universalists sought to adapt Calvinism to the demands of a new era.

The early preachers of the movement came to take great delight in the role of traditional Calvinism's rationalistic gadfly, poking it in vulnerable areas and forcing it to face its own paradoxes. Joseph Young was among the early Universalists who attacked the increasingly exposed flanks of the prevailing theology. Calvinists were hypocritical, he charged, in their approach to the divine character:

> God forbid, says the Calvinist, that I should call God a tyrant! I can only affirm that he has brought millions of beings into a state of existence out of a state of non-existence, in which case they were incapable of offending him, or suffering any inconvenience whatever, *knowing*, and having predetermined that they should be *punished in hell flames* to the *endless ages of eternity*! Although I must confess it can not be called a very merciful dispensation of Providence, I dare not call it tyranny.[63]

Aware of the gradual acceptance by nominal Calvinists of a human role in salvation, Young accused them of trying to "flatter the Deity, affirming that he had the undoubted right to *create millions*, on purpose to damn them eternally for his own glory."[64] Essentially, Young tried to force Calvinism to come to terms with itself at a time when the growing embrace of Enlightenment humanitarianism made it difficult to preserve inherited assumptions. He reminded his readers again and again that, according to traditional teachings, God had, for whatever reasons, clearly decreed the damnation of some.[65]

Huntingdon, too, charged that many ministers deceived their congregations by preaching that all who believe would be saved. He pointed out that they should warn, "*if you are one of the number of the elect*, you have full warrant and ground to believe in salvation. Otherwise there is no foundation laid in Christ for your faith."[66] Huntingdon sought to demonstrate that the Calvinist concept of belief was quietly being invested with Arminian ideas about human capacity. The learned and pious divines, he joked, say:

> that all sinners are commanded to believe that which has no truth in it, antecedent to their believing in it; and in the devout and obedient exercise of their minds in believing, *that* is turned into a glorious and saving truth, which had no truth in it when their minds first began to work upon it. They say this is a most *inconceivable, astonishing mystery*. I think so, too, and can get no relief to my own mind in that way. If I could believe without previous truth, and make truth by believing, I should believe myself into the enjoyment of many agreeable things, temporal as well as spiritual.[67]

The efforts of Calvinist thinkers to adapt to changing attitudes were certainly made no easier by this sort of Universalist sniping.

Universalists charged, in particular, that the doctrine of election was implicitly antiegalitarian. In his *Calvinism and Universalism Contrasted*, Young chided Calvinists for their exclusiveness, noting, "They believe all the gracious promises made by God to mankind, are made to themselves only; that is, to the elect."[68] Huntingdon warned against any "qualification for" or "acceptance of" salvation. Whether one termed oneself a Calvinist, Arminian, or antinomian, such notions of conditional salvation could easily make one thank God "that I am not like other men."[69] As Calvinist believers who had taken to heart the rationalists' faith in the benevolence of the deity, early Universalists viewed the evangelical conception of a God who damned some — or many — souls as unnatural, offensive, and perhaps above all antiegalitarian.

Indeed, if any religious group warranted the epithet "spiritual republicans," which Alan Heimert adopts to apply to a broad variety of evangelicals, it was the Universalists.[70] Benjamin Rush, like Winchester, believed that Universalism was a faith that complemented republicanism, as the Calvinism of the Old World had suited absolutism and monarchism. For Rush, who had adopted Universalism by 1782, as for many other adherents of the movement, Universalism expressed in religious terms the millennial promise of the democratic revolution. As he wrote to Jeremy Belknap in 1791, "A belief in God's universal love to all his creatures . . . is a *polar* truth. It leads to truths upon all subjects, but especially upon the subject of government. It establishes the *equality* of mankind."[71]

Exceptionally learned and prominent, Rush was in many ways not a representative adherent of Universalism. Though a leading member of a Universalist society, he continued to belong to the Presbyterian church that had shaped his religious background. Yet this unusual mixture of church affiliations provides a striking illustration of the basic appeal of eighteenth-century Universalism. Rush had embraced a belief in the benevolence of the deity and in progress, but he remained a committed evangelical Calvinist. Though best known as a rational optimist and as an outstanding figure in the Philadelphia Enlightenment, Rush had been educated by leading Great Awakening figures, such as Samuel Finley and Samuel Davies, and he remained a believer in original sin and divine grace. In his determinism, moreover, he rivaled Edwards.[72] For Rush, belief in universal salvation created a more desirable Calvinism, a rational and ultimately cheerful faith well-suited to a free and democratic society.

Communal Redemption

In promoting their "improved" Calvinism, Universalists were concerned with more than overcoming abstract theological errors. The doctrine of universal salvation appealed to them more concretely as a rational means of building and maintaining a sense of community. Puritan society had been held together by a powerful feeling of mutual obligation within the Christian community. Central to this sense was the experience of conversion. Conversion was fundamental for Universalists as well; accepting that all were saved marked a change in a person's mind, heart, and relation to society.

In his study of the psychology of Puritan religious experience, Charles Cohen explains that conversion not only bound the soul to Christ, it also established the bonds of affection within the holy community as "saints felt they belonged to the Lord and to each other." The cohesiveness of the Puritan community, Cohen asserts, "arose from the psychological foundation laid down by the Lord's mercy in regeneration."[73] A major strain of early New England piety centered on "the communal fulfillment of all things in Christ at the end of time." The first Puritan generation embraced an eschatology of Christ's final triumph over death and the completion of the church in Christ. In this eschatology, conversion, not death, was the most significant event in a person's life.[74]

By the end of the seventeenth century, such a communal eschatology had waned considerably. An "individualized and spiritualized eschatology" reemerged with death, not conversion, "the most important eschatological boundary."[75] By the mid–eighteenth century, conversion had become for most New Englanders less an entry into a group on a holy mission than "a private act of supreme individual importance."[76] Indeed, there was a growing "idolatry of the isolated self," as one scholar puts it, a tendency to define oneself in opposition to others and to ignore one's consanguinity with them.[77]

Other studies have emphasized the loosening of social bonds that accompanied the eighteenth-century dissolution of Puritanism. Among colonial Americans in general, Helena Wall observes, the lines between public and private life had been kept deliberately weak. "Individual desires, personal relationships, family life: all gave way to the demands of the community."[78] In the second half of the eighteenth century, however, the foundations of traditional community life crumbled for a number of reasons: "the shattering of the religious consensus, the increasing complexity of economic relationships and the influence of the market, population growth, migration."[79]

By the end of the century, the inherited patterns of social relationships were rapidly giving way to a new emphasis on the private world of the family. Wall adopts the term "affective individualism" to refer to the emerging values of personal autonomy and powerful emotional links within the family, values particularly evident in New England culture. This shift involved every aspect of social life; traditional patriarchal conceptions of political authority, for example, were undermined by the newer sense of familial bonds as essentially voluntary, private, and serving the individual growth of each member.[80] This was the time, indeed, in which "the individual was taking shape as the conceptual building block of society."[81]

The rise of Universalism in the late eighteenth century was partly a reaction to the loss of an organic sense of a covenant society under divine judgment. Universalism was an attempt to maintain an objective, communal faith in opposition to the subjective individualism that increasingly characterized social and religious attitudes in New England. In the dominant religious attitudes of the era, Universalists saw a growing emphasis on personal salvation, a narrow view that excluded genuine concern for one's neighbors; they believed that faith had deteriorated and become contracted and selfish. Piety, they feared, was becoming an individual, private matter, more and more removed from an ideal of broad social cohesiveness and harmony reflecting the greater glory of God.

For early adherents of the movement, the rational embrace of the notion of universal salvation effectively took the place of the conversion experience. They believed this idea would establish an objective basis for social harmony that was more secure than the ultimately subjective ideal of conversion. The movement also adopted, and indeed sought to universalize, aspects of the new family ideal, preaching both the freedom and the essential brotherhood of all people under the loving and rational fatherhood of God. Lucy Barns, who published *The Female Christian* in 1809, explained that, when Universalists accept that all men are brethren to be loved, they know they "have passed from death unto life."[82]

The "common, coherent, Christian culture" of colonial America was giving way to the highly competitive environment of the nineteenth-century republic. Among the forces contributing to this transformation, none was more important than the rapidly growing print culture, which extended even to some of the poorest families in the rural Northeast. Richard Brown describes the shift from a society of scarcity, in which information and knowledge flowed from the higher echelons downward to the common people, to a society of information abundance, where popular and hierarchic elements meshed. Despite the general diversity of colonial America, Brown observes that "within rural communities scarcity had all but required conformity of perceptions since nearly everyone shared access to the same information and the same interpretive commentaries on it." But the beginning of mass communication "encouraged individualism among the many. Public opinion was acknowledged to be powerful, but there were numerous competing public opinions . . . a welter of competing alternatives." Whereas the face-to-face diffusion of information had onced helped to maintain social cohesion, the explosion of printed materials laid the foundation for social diversity, as people were able to select their own sources of public information.[83]

Again, the rise of the Universalist movement can be viewed partly as a reaction to this broad cultural change. Up through the mid–eighteenth century, many or even most colonists, living in small communities, could assume a certain universality for their religious beliefs, for they had limited exposure to competing doctrines. By the last decades of the century, as the diffusion of information through printed sources of all sorts accelerated rapidly, the competition and conflict among various teachings became evident to virtually everyone. One means of cultivating a sense of community in this situation was to look deliberately beyond competition, to concentrate on a religious message that ultimately reduced all human differences to insignificance and that was objectively graspable by all human beings. Universalism extended the ideal of the local community to a universal plane; however naively, it taught that the whole world could become one community as its central message gained adherents.[84] Emphasizing universality and nonsectarianism, Universalists hoped to diminish what they saw as ultimately unimportant differences in belief by focusing on a greater and unifying truth.

The development of such views was, as one well-known study has suggested, "congruent with the new realities" of back-country New England in the last decades of the eighteenth century. The subsistence farm societies of central, western, and northern New England provided fertile ground for fresh religious dissent in the 1780s, including the rise of Universalism. The simple, undeveloped economy of the hill country, which produced raw materials and imported finished goods, perpetuated an egalitarian social structure marked by minimal class distinctions. Hill country residents were especially likely to look at the world "through the prism of family values."[85] Unlike more settled regions, where the nonfamilial institutions of town, church, and business increasingly set societal norms, northern and western New England in the last two decades of the century still looked primarily to the family. Plentiful land and a scarcity of labor led to rising birthrates and magnified the importance of the lineal family. The family in this region tended to be "larger, more isolated, more economically necessary and more culturally self-reliant than nuclear units to the south"; it became a "social crucible" for a culture that was not only anti-Federalist but "localist, egalitarian, [and] tribal."[86] In this culture, the doctrine of universal salvation spread among small groups, often of extended kin, who were searching for a newly egalitarian understanding of the covenanted community.[87]

The imagery of the Universalist movement was in fact highly familial, calling on people to repent not as sinners in awe of an inscrutable God but as shame-faced children seeking the forgiveness of a loving father. Randolph Roth calls attention to the paternal imagery of Universalism in his study of the Connecticut River valley of Vermont in the early national period. He suggests that the faith "spoke to the moral experience of farm youths" who rarely went through early, difficult separations from the family but rather remained at home until their parents could help them obtain their own farms.[88] In these circumstances, the teaching of universal salvation, which included a strong conception of the brotherhood of all people under divine guidance, certainly played a role in helping to maintain a sense of godly community. From this perspective, it is not surprising that Universalist teachings showed strength in areas where close and lasting family ties were more common than early independence. It was perhaps a natural tendency for those remaining in familiar—and familial—territory to envision the entire world in terms of a large family.

Yet, even though back-country New England certainly proved receptive to the notion of universal salvation, early Universalism was by no means only a rural phenomenon. Whereas the idea of universal salvation was widely preached to approving back-country audiences in the late eighteenth century, formally organized Universalism tended to arise first in the towns. John Murray became minister of the First Universalist Church and Congregation in Boston in 1785, signifying the beginning of a notable Universalist presence in that city. Other towns in eastern Massachusetts, as well as larger urban centers like Philadelphia and New York, were also early homes to Universalist societies.

Universalism played a notable role in the formation of Philadelphia's working class in the late eighteenth and early nineteenth centuries. Unlike Methodists and evangelical Presbyterians, Universalists "spoke of a community of love in ways that echoed the solidarity of tight-knit journeymen's societies and the mutuality of the larger working-class community."[89] The leader of the Mechanics' Union of Trade Associations and the Workingman's Party, William Heighton, was a devoted Universalist who organized meetings in the city's Universalist churches. Loudly critical of those who would exploit the working classes, he stressed the need for the clergy to "teach the absolute necessity of undeviating justice between man and man."[90]

The evidence leaves little doubt that the conception of an objective, egalitarian, and communal faith exercised its appeal in cities and towns as well as in rural areas. In both settings, early Universalism gained followers largely among intently religious, eagerly literate people of relatively modest means. Roth notes Universalism's particular appeal to the "rural intelligentsia" of Vermont. Pamela Brown, a young schoolteacher from Plymouth who was alienated from evangelical religion, valued Universalism's rational theology, and Justin Morrill, a young clerk from Strafford, appreciated Universalism's tolerance of radical ideas.[91] Universalists such as Brown and Morrill were generally self-educated people who had developed enough intellectual tools to be broadly critical of established authorities and dogmas. They felt uncomfortable with any idea or institution that seemed to threaten either the freedom or the cohesiveness that they saw as natural to a truly Christian society.

Despite the desire to reassert a vision of all human beings as bound together under divine sovereignty, the basic message of early Universalism was anything but reactionary. In the generally unsophisticated but active minds attracted to this teaching, the seemingly endless promises of an immensely rich continent and a new republic evoked a combination of all that was most hopeful in both Christianity and the heritage of the Enlightenment. The result was an outlook that, to modern observers, is often breathtakingly naive. We need to keep in mind, however, that, especially in the decades before 1830, it took considerable strength of will and an ability to endure social isolation in order to be a Universalist; these were hardly conformists. Their broad ideal of human brotherhood was accompanied by an insistence upon the critical judgment of the individual.

Thus, the heavy familial and communal emphases of early Universalism did not imply a complete rejection of the political and economic individualism of the age. Although some members of the movement would later become involved in utopian communalism, Universalists in general were not inclined to withdraw from the hustle and bustle of American society. In the early nineteenth century, the movement appealed to entrepreneurs as well as to provincial farm boys and urban artisans. Thomas Whittemore (1800–1861) was the leading disciple of Hosea Ballou and one of Universalism's most vocal and active promoters in the period before 1860.[92] An editor, publisher, banker, railroad executive, and state legislator, Whittemore was the epitome of the self-made man. In his promotion of Universalism, he was as pugnacious a controversialist as any that age produced. In his eyes, belief in universal salvation functioned as a kind of social cement, an ultimate safeguard, both biblical and rational, against the disintegration of human bonds. By vigorously affirming God's ultimate determination to redeem all humanity, Universalists like Whittemore found an antidote to the mobility, loss of community, and atomism of their age.

Ballou's *Treatise on Atonement*

In 1805, when Hosea Ballou published his *Treatise on Atonement*, a unified and truly distinctive Universalist theology emerged, a full-fledged synthesis of evangelical piety and Enlightenment reason. In several respects, the work reflected a new insistence upon enlightened human reason as a necessary standard of theological truth. Yet Ballou's theology definitely remained a product of the early Universalist effort to improve Calvinism, especially in its heavy emphasis on the absolute sovereignty of God. Ballou laid the real intellectual cornerstone of the movement; his *Treatise* became virtually the testament of Universalism. Through at least the first half of the nineteenth century, most Universalists regarded the work as a necessary companion to the Bible. The *Treatise* provided a clear, focused explication of the ideas that were coming together, in the years around 1800, and giving rise to a growing and significant movement.

Born in a Richmond, New Hampshire, log cabin in 1771, Hosea Ballou was the eleventh and last child of hardscrabble farmers; his father was also a Baptist minister. His early life in the newly settled backwoods village on the Massachusetts border eventually became the stuff of Universalist legend, full as it was of Lincolnesque associations. With stripped birch bark for paper and coals for pencils, young Hosea had supposedly taught himself to read by a fire of flaming pine knots, as tallow candles were too great an expense. A Bible, an ancient dictionary, and an old scriptural pamphlet served as his library. Materially deprived as a boy, lacking even shoes in the harsh New England winter, he nevertheless grew into a healthy, physically active young man, over six feet tall, with a ruddy complexion, dark hair, and sparkling blue eyes. Before he was two, he had suffered the death of his mother, and although he soon acquired a stepmother, it was his father to whom he remained profoundly attached. His later, oft-expressed belief in the parental and especially fatherly love of God surely owed much to his childhood experience.[93]

Raised as a conservative Calvinist by his theologically strict father, Ballou was eighteen when he became converted and baptized, along with a hundred others, during a large Baptist revival in Richmond. Despite his profession of faith, he continued to be intensely bothered by the doctrine of eternal reprobation and attempted to reconcile it with his belief in God's goodness. Within months, he came to embrace universal salvation. Preachers of the doctrine had frequented his home territory, and Caleb Rich, one of the most notable, had influenced his older brother David Ballou to accept Universalism. Hosea, like David, quickly became a preacher of the doctrine, a decision that apparently created no rifts in the tightly knit Ballou clan.

Although his formal schooling was limited to brief academy training, Hosea Ballou prepared himself independently to preach and was ordained by the General Convention of Universalists in 1794. Serving as minister in a series of New England churches, including Portsmouth and Salem, Ballou became a prominent Universalist figure. By the time he moved to Boston in 1816 to become pastor of the School Street Church, Ballou had established himself as the leading Universalist minister of his day. Until his death in 1852, he served in his Boston pastorate and also supported his denomination as an editor and controversialist. The key intellectual shaper of the Universalist movement, Ballou made his most lasting contribution with his *Treatise*.

Written some forty-five years after Jonathan Edwards's death, the *Treatise* conserved an essentially Edwardsean piety even as it challenged fundamental tenets of Calvinist faith. Edwards's central concern had been the transcending of self-interest and self-love in the realization of God's universal love. Yet this was impossible, Ballou argued, with the traditional Calvinist vision of a God who could glorify himself by making any of his "rational, hoping, wanting creatures endlessly miserable."[94] In Edwards's understanding, the candidate for sainthood, at a moment of profound despair, yielded his constricting love of self and became receptive to the love of "universal existence."[95] Edwards had deliberately pushed people to the brink of terror and taught that the "idol of self-love" had to be abandoned through a personal, mystical confrontation with God's omnipotent power and purpose. Because it was never "mercenary" or "interested," grace had to be a "supernatural, internal principle of action." Grace, with its consequent "true virtue," was not rational; it did not come through the natural understanding.[96]

Ballou, however, insisted that the objective power of reason did contribute to a transforming experience of universal love. Our reason, he contended, helped to determine that universal salvation was a biblical doctrine. To embrace this doctrine was to be overtaken by the reasonable "spirit of benevolence" or the experience of "holiness."[97] Pulled from the mire of self-absorption by the reasonable recognition of universal love, the awakened soul was able to see "the brightness of God's glory."[98]

Ballou maintained that the opposing belief—that not all sinners would be redeemed—inevitably produced a sinful and selfish sense of preeminence on the part of the "converted." Ballou rejected Edwards's central conviction about the possibility of a wondrous and supernatural change of heart. Indeed, he remarked in one of his sermons on his inability to "conceive of anything so mysterious and unaccountable" as an instantaneous change in a person's nature. But he asserted that those who were "instructed in the nature and spirit of the gospel of God's unchangeable love" could realize "different affections and feelings." Here, he united reason and piety: rational understanding supported spiritual and emotional conversion.[99]

Ballou was dismayed by a growing conception of sin, conversion, and regeneration that, he believed, added up to little more than an outward manipulation of behavior. Christian belief, he warned, was being reduced to something necessary in order to avoid divine wrath.[100] Edwards had feared this development as well. For Edwards, a selfless, disinterested "love to being" marked the saint; conversion did not entail a sense of pardon or relief from the escape of punishment for wicked behavior.[101] Edwards insisted that Christianity would be degraded by such a view of salvation, which amounted to nothing more than a "religious insurance scheme."[102]

Along with the New Divinity followers of Edwards, Ballou despaired at what he saw as the withering of piety and the growth of a basically selfish faith, preoccupied with the process of individual salvation.[103] The New Divinity had responded by insisting that conversion must manifest itself in disinterested acts of holy love; this belief was expressed in extreme form in Samuel Hopkins's famous assertion that the authentically converted would even consent to be damned for God's glory. But Jonathan Edwards himself had never gone that far. " 'Tis impossible," he had maintained, "for any person to be perfectly and finally miserable for God's sake."[104] In *Charity and Its Fruits*, a work he wrote in 1738, Edwards asserted that a person's love of his own happiness "is as necessary to his nature as the faculty of the will is; and it is impossible that such a love should be destroyed in any other way than by destroying his being."[105] Ballou agreed, commenting in his usual commonsense terms: "Man's *main* object, in all that he does, is *happiness*; and if it were not for that, he would never have any other *particular* object."[106]

To believe humans capable of true disinterest was, Ballou contended, unreasonable and foolish. Spiritually awakened or not, human beings were always—indeed they were constitutionally—interested in their own happiness. To say that "we ought to love God for what he is and not what we receive from him" was absurd. A thirsty man loved water because of its benefits, not because it was water. And to presume a creature capable of disinterested love was to impute to him divine attributes. "Undoubtedly the Almighty loves without an influential object," Ballou observed. "But all created beings love because of influential objects; and they love according to the influence objects have on their minds and passions."[107]

Instead of disinterested benevolence, Ballou proposed the scriptural message of universal salvation as the challenging way through which God weaned humanity away from morally crippling selfishness to the love of holiness. Ballou did not propose that an immediate and radical change of heart would necessarily follow the adoption of a belief in universal salvation. But he did suggest that the doctrine possessed a kind of supernatural power over the affections and emotions to change the open-hearted believer.[108] If man sought happiness in "the heavenly system of *universal benevolence,* knowing that his own happiness is connected with that of his fellow men," he would be more just, merciful, and "no more selfish than he ought to be."[109]

Ballou's *Treatise* turned the New Divinity on its head by positing that we could fight selfishness only with an awareness of God's universal love and pardon of sin.[110] The *Treatise* argued that a dynamic unselfishness would be animated only with the acknowledgment and celebration of God's awesome power and purpose to rescue for eternity even the most insignificant and despised souls.[111] God's greater glory was not furthered through the self-abasement of his creatures, Ballou insisted, and religious leaders who preached this were rightly ignored.[112] The teaching of universal salvation, on the other hand, served as a constant warning against self-distinction and spiritual pride. To use Edwardsean terms, genuine belief in universal salvation prompted the exercise of true virtue; those who took it to heart were regenerated, substantially changed in their dispositions toward God and humanity.[113]

God remained ultimately transcendent, but his creatures could know his will to redeem all souls. Ballou's own thought rested on the classic Calvinist conviction that God was always in control of his creation. A frank necessitarianism undergirded his profoundly pious view of life. For him, as for Edwards, determinism and freedom were intertwined aspects of theism.[114] "I cannot but think it incorrect to suppose that God ever gave any creature agency to perform what he never intended should be done," he wrote with characteristic straightforwardness.[115] True piety meant complete trust in divine power and love because humanity could not always see the good in God's design.[116]

Ballou did not accept the biblical account of the fall of man or the doctrine of original sin, which seemed to him opposed to reason and common sense. He nevertheless declared that the disposition to sin was a key attribute of created human nature. Quoting Saint Paul's epistle to the Romans, Ballou characterized sin as the inevitable product of the conflicting laws of flesh and spirit. In their sin, people envisioned God as an enemy who needed to be pacified, who required "atonement."[117] Blinded to its own need for atonement, for reconciliation with God, humanity had imputed the human frailties of anger and vengeance to an infinitely good divinity. "Atonement signifies reconciliation," Ballou explained, and it was man who was the unreconciled party. "Where there is dissatisfaction, it presumes an injured party, and can it be hard to determine which is injured by sin, the Creator or the sinner?"[118] The unchangeable God of love did not require appeasement, Ballou asserted, but people did need to be reconciled to the loving rule of God. Ballou's understanding of atonement was what most clearly separated him from his eighteenth-century Universalist predecessors and what made his teaching not simply "Calvinism improved" but an original, full-fledged synthesis of Calvinist piety and Enlightenment rationalism.

Although Ballou portrayed the Trinity as an illogical notion ("it amounts to the amazing sum of infinity, multiplied by three!"), he explicitly proclaimed Jesus as the "Savior" of mankind. The "Almighty committed power into the hands of Christ," who, as "Mediator," is entrusted with "the work of reconciliation." For Ballou, Christ is a man, but he is, more importantly, God's representative, the "anointed" one. Jesus was no mere moral exemplar; he is "Lord" and the "Captain of our salvation."[119] Jesus brought to the world the spirit of God's love, revealing the victory of spirit over flesh and of love over sin.[120] The atoning grace bestowed through Jesus was the certain knowledge of God's love and its power over sin and death; it was redemption. To the extent that he emphasized the need for such grace in conversion and sanctification, Ballou clearly remained in the evangelical tradition.[121] He believed that, without divine redemption, men and women would engage endlessly in the pursuit of an elusive happiness, trapped and driven by their carnal state of being. "Atoning grace," he asserted, "produces all which the Bible means by conversion, or being born under the Spirit, and brings the mind from under the power and constitution of the earthly Adam to live by faith in the Son of God."[122]

Ballou acknowledged that God did not grant his grace equally to all in this life. His attempt to deal with such apparent divine partiality followed a well-worn path: one simply had to acknowledge that God works in his own time and way for the good. At death, all would experience a change from sin to holiness.[123] The assurance of God's grace, an assurance that Ballou believed to be at once rational and spiritual, allowed the converted to appreciate "God's divine beauties and excellencies" and to obey God's laws because they are "joyous and not grievous."[124] Again, Ballou's conception recalls in some respects early Puritan communal eschatology, in which "the most crucial event in the life of each person" is not death but "the effectual calling or conversion of each person which turned him once and for all from death to life."[125] For Ballou, conversion to the belief in universal salvation was the one true safeguard against mortal selfishness.

With his sanguine assertions that God wished to "happify" mankind and his often irreverent remarks about traditional religious beliefs, Ballou has often been interpreted as a rather typical turn-of-the-century enlightened believer. The influences of Ethan Allen's *Reason: the Only Oracle of Man* (1784) and of Thomas

Paine's *Age of Reason* (1776), for example, are clearly apparent in his *Treatise*. Ernest Cassara stresses these influences, placing Ballou "firmly on the side of the eighteenth-century cult of reason."[126] Certainly, Ballou's thought owed much to late-century popular rationalism. He admired deism's reasoned questioning of orthodoxy; he undoubtedly derived much from deist criticisms of the tyrannical image of God, the abstract notion of the Trinity, and intolerance of heterodox belief.[127]

Ballou nevertheless remained a committed believer in revelation, in the miraculous and the supernatural. Although he rejected what was offensive to his reason, he did not doubt that much was above his reason. Abounding with scriptural references, the *Treatise* reveals Ballou as a devoted biblical Christian. His faith in the transforming power of love and his essential egalitarianism, furthermore, link him more properly with evangelical Calvinism than with enlightened Arminianism. Ballou firmly rejected the hierarchical social vision of the Arminian liberals. Following the lead of earlier Universalist thinkers, he observed that many people opposed universal salvation because of its temporal implications. Some people, he reflected, resembled the Pharisees of old, who did not expect to see publicans and harlots in heaven. They could not tolerate the thought that, whatever distinctions they achieved, they were, in the end, on a perfectly equal plane with all other people.[128]

Ballou's work is thus most notable not as an example of popular enlightened thought and anti-Calvinist criticism but as a concerted effort to generate and defend piety with reason. His effort to revive the social dimension of providential Calvinism was a protest against the incipient moralism of his age. "What is morality," Ballou asked, but the "natural effects of our love" for our Creator and our fellow beings? The understanding of God's universal love and his plan of universal salvation uniquely compelled moral behavior on the part of the pious. It stands to reason, he concluded, that we will be more moral to our neighbors if we truly love them and more important, "if we believe our Father loves them as well."[129]

In his effort to integrate piety and reason, Ballou remained, in Rabinowitz's term, a "doctrinalist"; the understanding, not the will or the feelings, was most important to him. Indeed, at the turn of the nineteenth century, when even orthodox Calvinists did not take their own theological doctrines literally, Ballou's aim was to make doctrine meaningful to reasonable creatures.[130] He agreed with his New Divinity foes that right doctrine confirmed the New Birth, not the other way around.[131] Reasserting the power and necessity of doctrinal belief, Ballou implicitly denied the growing glorification of the self and the individual conscience.[132] A product of the same rural New England that had given birth to and sustained the New Divinity, he shared its "idealized corporate perspective."[133]

Ballou's dearest hope was the revitalization of a demanding corporate vision, and his major fear was the growth of an overly subjective faith.[134] Like Edwards before him, Ballou faced a widening division between the objective and the subjective elements in Christian belief. At one pole lay the tendency to an abstract, even deistic, view of the transcendent God. At the other was an increasingly personal, sentimental affection for Jesus.[135] In the nineteenth century, the latter tendency came to dominate in American Protestantism, as Jesus became more of a benign, approachable friend; the transcendent God, meanwhile, appeared more and more as simply the source of natural law. Ballou's Universalist theology reflected his desire to cultivate a sense of God as both transcendent ruler and loving, caring father. To be sure, Ballou's talk of the loving and paternal nature of God hardly echoed Edwards's expressions of awe at divine beauty; the two thinkers presented the personal experience of God in very different terms. Like Edwards, however, Ballou readily admitted the stark facts of injustice and human suffering in what he nevertheless believed was a divinely governed world.[136] Even as he denied the eternal damnation that Edwards had so graphically upheld, Ballou unhesitatingly affirmed God's eschatological purpose in allowing evil and earthly misery. He preached neither God as a rational principle nor emotional refuge in Jesus but faith in a Christ who bestowed the knowledge of atoning grace.

Scholasticism for the Unschooled

The goal of establishing a satisfying synthesis of faith and reason had been present from the beginning in New England religion. Perry Miller observes that the seventeenth-century Puritans were "first and foremost the heirs of Augustine, but also . . . among the heirs of Thomas Aquinas and pupils of Erasmus." In later generations, there remained strong elements of the belief that "faith can never remain mere spiritual conviction; it must be made articulate."[137] Jonathan Edwards notably refused to follow the tendency of revivalism, as described by Henry May, to "set the religious spirit over against learning and intellect."[138]

Hence, Ballou and the early Universalists were hardly alone in their efforts to promote a viable synthesis of reason and religious belief. As we will see more fully in the next chapter, the flowering religious moralism of the decades around 1800 had its own arsenal of rational arguments. In America, the school of Scottish Common Sense, with its claim of the authority of conscience and its emphasis on the "moral sense," led to the development of moral philosophy as a highly influential academic discipline parallel to theology. John Witherspoon, who became president of the College of New Jersey (later Princeton) in 1768, used such moral philosophy to further a "Protestant scholasticism." When he was studied scientifically and objectively, man became a moral being, equipped by God with a moral sense to oversee his pursuit of virtue.[139] The Calvinism taught by learned theologians and their followers now called for an instructed conscience as well as a converted soul.[140]

But Ballou had little interest in the self's pursuit of virtue. His *Treatise*, and the Universalism to which it gave direction, represented a different form of Protestant scholasticism, a popular effort to cultivate a truly communal piety through reasoned argument. The significance of Universalism lies not in its protest against Calvinism but in its attempt to establish a reasonable form of the piety that once marked that system. This popular Protestant scholasticism was anything but an academic movement. Commonsensical rather than learned, blending homely rationalism with a long-standing New England piety, and appearing to complement the political egalitarianism of the new republic, Ballou's Universalism arose largely from humble native roots. In its effort to oppose what it saw as the spiritually shallow but spreading individualism and moralism of the age, it was both profoundly conservative and radically nonconformist.

As rationalism and piety appeared increasingly at odds within American religious culture, evangelical Protestants grew deeply distrustful of intellectualized religion.[141] Those more inclined to a rational approach, meanwhile, saw in much of popular religion little more than emotional excess. Universalists in the eighteenth century had sought to shape a new piety within the strong currents of rationalism and humanitarianism. But not until the early nineteenth century would the full synthesis of Calvinist piety and Enlightenment reason appear in Ballou's *Treatise*, a kind of scholasticism for the common man. Ballou tried to steer evangelical Protestantism away from the path of anti-intellectualism and, at the same time, to protect reasonable religion from the lure of moralism and humanism. As we will see, the history of Universalism in nineteenth-century America is essentially the story of the largely unsuccessful struggle to maintain the synthesis that gave the early movement definition and purpose.

The Challenge of Communal Piety

In the first decades of the nineteenth century, the Universalist movement gained both momentum and attention. Although still a small minority in the vast spiritual scene of the age, Universalists stirred up widespread controversy with their improved version of Calvinism, the "reasonable" faith that all human souls were linked together under an infinitely benevolent and powerful providence. They faced massive opposition, even persecution; their opponents included everyone from leading academic theologians to extreme dissidents and sectarians. Almost all who denounced them were united in a single fundamental criticism: their teaching ignored the basic lesson that all people were responsible before God for their actions, that goodness would be rewarded and evil punished. Universalists responded by trying to show that "the larger hope" of their faith transcended such "carnal" concerns and was most conducive to social concord. Within Calvinist churches, church discipline was quickly brought to bear against those who voiced "universalist sentiments."[1] On its face, Universalism seemed a prescription for social chaos, since it appeared to remove all sanctions against sin.

Americans in the nineteenth century increasingly embraced the Methodist message of "individual freedom, autonomy, responsibility and achievement."[2] By the second decade of the century, even the New Divinity was being swept into what David Kling calls a "generic form of Protestantism,"a broad, nondoctrinal, moralistic evangelicalism.[3] As God's fearful presence faded, character became the self-written ticket to eternity. People were participants in the moral government of God, who became a distant governor instead of an immediate judge. A sense of open-endedness superseded traditional eschatological categories. Romantic ideas of the endless possibilities for individual growth blossomed, and the boundary of death was effaced. But Universalism made death the only boundary and God the only way of salvation. One's lot was cast with the rest of the human race; personal will and character, in the end, mattered not at all. These were not entirely glad tidings for an age of self-made men.

For at least a generation after the turn of the century, the Universalist vision represented a genuine challenge to the religious and moral norms that accommodated the needs of a burgeoning capitalist society. As we will see, however, the movement as a whole would not continue to sustain and develop the sort of spirituality that was reflected in Ballou's teaching. The communal piety of early Universalism would prove an unsatisfactory foundation for a denomination, and the movement would ultimately move toward the moralism against which its early adherents had struggled so vigorously. Ironically, the form of nonmoralistic spirituality that would gain lasting recognition in American religious history would not be the popular preaching of Universalism but the largely literary preoccupation of a comfortably domesticated cultural elite. The Transcendentalism of Ralph Waldo Emerson, while sharing certain themes with early Universalism, ultimately reflected a profoundly different orientation that was more closely in line with the broader tendencies of nineteenth-century American culture.

The Priesthood of Humankind

The appearance of Ballou's *Treatise on Atonement* marked the beginning of a new phase of popular Universalism; the work seems to have erased lingering ambiguities, and it was widely hailed as a definitive manifesto. By this time, the movement had taken root among scattered communities throughout rural and small-town New England; there were quickly growing congregations in a number of eastern urban centers as well, including Boston, Gloucester, Philadelphia, New York City, Providence, Portsmouth, and Baltimore. Although Universalism would always remain strongest in the Northeast, over the next three to four decades, it would expand south to Georgia and Alabama and west to Michigan; by 1833, there were some 300 more or less official preachers and some 600 societies; leaders claimed more than 300,000 adherents.[4] To a large extent, this growth was the accomplishment of itinerant and circuit-riding preachers. Farmers and mechanics, equipped with little more than a common school education, a Bible, a copy of Ballou's *Treatise*, and perhaps a few other Universalist tracts, began preaching, sometimes full time, often part time, as their responsibilities allowed. The goal of these humble but zealous folk was to communicate a single, crucial message; as Sydney Ahlstrom recognized, the movement was "far more evangelical than is generally realized."[5]

It would be difficult to overemphasize the idealism that pervaded early Universalist preaching. Ballou and his followers sincerely believed that humankind was a single community and that their own reasonable faith would sooner or later be shared by all. George Rogers, who traveled many thousands of miles during his remarkable itinerant career in the 1820s and 1830s, described his experience at Universalist gatherings: "All were on a parity; all distinctions of caste were lost sight of; all individualities were merged in the mass: and as one family all rejoiced in a common and glorious hope."[6]

Universalist ministers stressed the rationality of their doctrine to people who were now applying new ideas of fairness and benevolence to their notion of God's rule. God won respect for his law, Rogers explained, through a belief "so reasonable in itself—so just—so pure—so benevolent . . . that the mind truly enlightened in regard to its nature and claims, cannot but choose to obey its dictates."[7] Stephen R. Smith, a pioneering Universalist preacher in upstate and western New York, extolled the "simplicity and intelligibility" of Universalism to bring about "mighty and growing change."[8] Smith, Rogers, and their fellow preachers saw themselves as evangelicals bringing the good news of universal salvation by removing the scales of irrationality from the eyes of the unenlightened. However naive they may appear in retrospect, Universalists were convinced that they were the heralds of a grand, unifying, and cosmopolitan faith.

From the beginning, adherents paid less attention to the institutional problem of building a church than to spreading their version of rational, universal truth. The brotherhood of man clearly took precedence over the fellowship of professed Universalists. Russell Miller, the major institutional historian of Universalism, emphasized that the early denomination evolved in a "casual, uncoordinated, and almost accidental way, reflecting the individualism and suspicion of centralized organization shared by most Universalists." Indeed, Miller found that Universalists expressed their independence and localism with "an almost perverse pride."[9]

This attitude was directly related to the naive cosmopolitanism we have noted. Among common folk whose experience was strongly shaped by family and community values, but who were increasingly exposed to the universal ideals of the Enlightenment, any structure that placed barriers between the individual and the universal brotherhood of man seemed suspect. Popular Universalism turned the Protestant priesthood of all believers into a priesthood of all rational creatures, but the ideal retained its grounding in the eschatological outlook of a Bible-oriented, traditionally Calvinist culture.

Thus, throughout the early nineteenth century, the movement remained averse to anything but minimal organizational efforts. The Philadelphia Convention of Universalists, which met for the first time in 1790, was an early but unsuccessful attempt to gather Universalists nationally. It was the New England Convention, initiated in 1793, that eventually developed into the U.S. Convention of Universalists (1833), but even then it was hardly a centralized organ in any more than name; local congregations communicated mostly through loose state associations. The growth of the New England Convention itself has been attributed primarily to the need to provide legal authority for itinerant clergy; in 1800, the convention officially began ordaining preachers. Meeting in 1803 at Winchester, New Hampshire, the New England Convention drew up a Plan of General Association in an effort to give the movement some form of legally recognizable organization and unity. The

Winchester Profession, adopted at the same meeting, was at least in part an effort to strengthen the legal status of Universalism. It deliberately left open all but the most crucial points:

> Article I. We believe that the Holy Scriptures of the Old and New Testament contain a revelation of the character of God, and of the duty, interest and final destination of mankind.
>
> Article II. We believe that there is one God, whose nature is Love, revealed in one Lord Jesus Christ, by one Holy Spirit of Grace, who will finally restore the whole family of mankind to holiness and happiness.
>
> Article III. We believe that holiness and true happiness are inseparably connected, and that believers ought to be careful to maintain order and practice good works; for these things are good and profitable unto men.

From the beginning, the movement had attracted independent thinkers who differed on countless points of interpretation. Indeed, to the Profession was appended a "liberty clause," which allowed additions as individual churches or associations saw fit.[10]

Despite its vagueness, however, the Profession revealed a belief in the overriding power of its central point. Early adherents clearly saw the integrating force of their movement in the idea of God's will to redeem all souls; they felt united in the mission of spreading this best of all possible news. A single, crucial doctrine, Universalists insisted, supplied the objective basis and framework for all theology and for social life itself. Articulated most clearly in Ballou's *Treatise*, it was a doctrine directly at odds with the surging emphasis of the age on the ultimate independence and responsibility of the individual.

Organic Order

The aim of Ballou and his fellow Universalists to promote a communal piety is manifest in the debate over the proper nature of piety, which arose in the decades after 1800. By the late eighteenth century, American religious leaders had been attempting to determine whether piety was, as William McLoughlin has expressed it, "an individual or a social concern."[11] In New England, corporate religious life was in precipitous decline as the system of state support known as the Standing Order broke apart, and dissenters went their separate ways. But the Standing Order had its vocal defenders, who pointed out the social dangers inherent in the splintering of religious beliefs and practices.

The debate that began in 1780 over the proposed Article Three of the Massachusetts constitution, which retained religious taxation but gave equal status to all Protestant denominations, illustrated increasing public unrest with governmental regulation of the moral and civil order. For its sponsors, Article Three was, in effect, a way of maintaining the principle of the Standing Order—or the Puritan ideal of the corporate Christian state—while attempting to satisfy dissenting groups, such as the Baptists. While declaring no one religious body as "standing," Article Three rearticulated the state's interest in and support of religious instruction as essential to the civil good.

Far from placating the pietistic Baptists, led by the vocal Isaac Backus, Article Three aroused their anger and fear. Dissenting groups would, it appeared, find it more difficult than ever to obtain tax exemption. Even more significant for Baptists was the principle that they believed Article Three mistakenly furthered. Morality was certainly necessary to the proper functioning of civil government, Baptists admitted, but piety was the concern of the individual; the state should not be in the business of promoting "gospel piety" and "heart religion." God had provided ample means for spiritual regeneration, they averred, and did not require governmental assistance.[12]

Universalists embraced what was essentially a mediating position in this debate: they saw their mission as the maintenance of an organic religious aspect in a society increasingly attracted to principles of individualism and competition. They hoped that a belief in universal salvation would generate a communal faith that avoided both the corporate coercion of the Standing Order and the atomistic individualism that was replacing it. In Universalist eyes, such a communal faith, linking an individual's religious experience to a feeling of unity with all other human beings, was a natural outgrowth of faith in the ultimate benevolence of the Creator.

In the Universalist understanding, genuine faith was necessarily double-sided, including both individual and social aspects. Since a large proportion of their membership had come out of the Separate Baptist movement, Universalists were highly sympathetic to the idea of an individualistic, experimental piety. Nevertheless, they could not envision how a faith that assumed the salvation of only a part of humanity—the belief of most dissenting groups, including the Baptists—promoted the social welfare. Universalists could agree with Standing Order supporters of Article Three such as Samuel West of Dartmouth, who argued that the forms of belief that had spread in the eighteenth century tended toward selfishness, self-interest, and a pre-occupation with one's own salvation over the good of other men.[13] What Universalists sought was a new brand of "unselfish" faith, a faith that encouraged the believer to think of his own interests as inseparably linked with the eternal welfare of the whole body of humanity. "What can be a stronger restraint on the passions," asked Ballou, "than a belief in God's universal goodness and that all men are objects of his mercy?" Such a belief, he pointed out, "raises a supreme affection for God, and kindles the sacred fire of love and unbounded benevolence to mankind."[14]

Dissenting pietists trusted that individual conversion would ensure the social good. Supporters of established religions, many of whom had gradually turned to a moralistic view, were loath to give up religious taxation as a way of preserving the welfare of the community. The Universalist alternative was a faith that demanded that one think of one's own salvation as no more important to God than the salvation of any other human being, and that therefore evoked a natural and all-inclusive social concern.

To be sure, Universalists were vocal proponents of disestablishment; by the 1820s, they had taken over leadership of the campaign in Massachusetts from the Baptists.[15] But their ideal of communal faith differed from the so-called liberal teaching epitomized by the maverick Baptist John Leland, whose views pointed directly to the nineteenth-century growth of individualism, atomism, and secularism.[16] Religious populists like Leland regarded the pursuit of self-reliance as a godly crusade. Leland's individualism called for people to throw off the authority of church, state, college, seminary, even family. Dismissing "polemical divinity" and opposing creeds and confessions, Leland delivered a message of complete personal autonomy.[17] The "Christian" sect of the nineteenth century similarly rejected all doctrine as spiritual "tyranny." Prominent Christians Alexander Campbell and Elias Smith condemned "abstract" theology as antithetical to egalitarianism.[18]

In the case of Universalism, however, religious populism and the search for gospel liberty did not result in a similar rejection of theology. In opposition to groups such as the Methodists, Free Will Baptists, and Christians, Universalists held that the elimination of all creedal forms would only intensify the disturbing emphasis on the individual in isolation from the greater society.[19] They asserted that the "rational" application of the traditional doctrine of election—the idea of universal salvation—was not only an absolute bulwark of egalitarian values but also the long-hidden key to social harmony. Universalists believed that a strong eschatological faith, rooted in the assurance that no soul was eternally condemned, would both foster social concern and protect an organic view of society that was in danger of disintegrating along with the established church.

Whenever Universalists reflected on the practical implications of their teaching, this sense of wholeness and harmony appeared. In a kind of popular guide to the faith, for example, Universalist editor and controversialist Thomas Whittemore pointed out what necessarily followed from the realization that "God is no less the Father of others, than himself":

> See then, that there is a common bond—a tie—uniting the vast family of man. No national boundary can dissolve this tie, no distance—no circumstance of birth, or of color—no misfortune, no oppression; neither poverty, nor vice, nor disgrace, nor death can sunder it. It is as indissoluble as the love of God. . . . Who, believing and realizing this, can be unkind? Who can be entirely engrossed in his own welfare? Who can be the oppressor of his brethren? Who can be deaf to the moan of the sufferer? to the plaintive entreaty of the poor?[20]

Whittemore reflected the long-standing conviction of Universalists that their belief was a uniquely powerful stimulus to the betterment of society. More obscure but no less typical in his views was a writer for the *Candid Examiner* (Montrose, Pa.), who explained in 1826 that the faith of the Universalist leads him to "love the world of mankind" because he believes that "all [persons] are regarded by their heavenly father, and that they are objects of our love." Universalism taught man to "live in love and harmony with the world of mankind."[21]

George Williams finds a parallel between the remarkable energy the Universalists exhibited in furthering their central belief and the first Protestant generations, heady with the belief in *sola fide* salvation.[22] The comparison is apt, even though Universalists saw new and somewhat different dangers threatening Christendom. With their single-minded and notably idealistic emphasis on one crucial teaching, Universalists spoke out against what they saw as a religiously inspired individualism. Their views were based on assumptions different from those that motivated other antiestablishmentarians of the era: Unitarians, frontier "anti-mission" Baptists, followers of Alexander Campbell, and Jacksonian Democrats. Such groups shared a transcendent respect for the individual and a rejection of all ecclesiasticism; they also deliberately left God out of the "corporate life of the race."[23] Universalists, however, praised the doctrine of universal salvation for the social responsibility it inspired and demanded. With their characterization of the universe as absolutely interdependent, egalitarian, and benevolent, they stood apart from the prevailing culture's exaltation of the individual.

Safety for Sinners (and Infidels?)

Universalism was the only genuinely popular teaching that sought explicitly to anchor itself against the tidal religious movement of the age — the glorification of the free individual under the moral government of God.[24] To be sure, evangelicals shared certain common egalitarian leanings with Universalism, but they consistently condemned the movement over the years of the Second Great Awakening.[25] This is not surprising. As J. R. Pole remarks, the "one unifying theme of the period" was "equality of opportunity."[26] Universalists preached an egalitarianism that ran counter to this prevailing ideology; it was an egalitarianism not of opportunity but of desert. Human will and character could easily be seen as irrelevant in the Universalist scheme. To the evangelical mind, Universalism discouraged activity and achievement; it sanctioned passivity, even sloth, and blamed God for the existence of sin. In short, the movement directly contradicted the main tendency of the age.

While often formally adhering to Calvinist doctrine, evangelicals increasingly emphasized individual initiative in the government of a morally just God. The eighteenth-century movement from the contemplation of God to contemplation of his highest creation was manifest in the growing preoccupation with the cultivation of "virtue." By the end of the century, courses in moral philosophy, which were aimed at the construction of a "republic of virtue," had become the "capstone" of American college education.[27]

Donald Meyer points out that moral philosophers stressed human freedom and responsibility in order to encourage humanity to pursue righteousness. As the free society's "public moralists," they replaced outmoded doctrines of moral inability with a new philosophy of human nature more appropriate to the demands of a commercial and democratic society.[28] Samuel Stanhope Smith, Princeton's president in the early decades of the nineteenth century, rejected Jonathan Edwards's arguments against the freedom of the will. Mark Noll notes that Smith, instead, turned to the Scottish Common Sense philosopher Thomas Reid and "merely repeated that moral free agency is among the *first truths*, or axioms in science."[29]

By the early nineteenth century, Americans had come to enshrine human free agency.[30] The prominent Congregational theologian Nathaniel Taylor expressed increasingly prevalent views with his contention that "man is a self-determining force in nature; that is the essence of his humanness and his divinity."[31] With greater openness by the 1820s and 1830s, popular evangelical Calvinism directed attention to the human role in salvation.[32] God provided a moral system and gave all sinners the chance for salvation by providing a savior. But if a man refused to repent and believe, a just God could not save him. James F. Davis, a strident opponent of

Universalism, argued that God has no choice but to damn men when he "cannot consistently save them."[33] The final choice was thus man's, not God's.

Universalism's seeming denial of a divine system rooted in individual moral freedom outraged evangelical believers. As a critic argued in 1836, God could not operate with "veracity, goodness and justice" unless his creatures were free.[34] For some, Universalism was only the other side of the fatalistic coin of Calvinism, which, according to Seth Crowell's *Strictures on the Doctrine of Universal Salvation*, made people "passive machines in the hands of the universal agent." Crowell willingly yielded divine omnipotence, rejecting the idea that God was the source of moral evil, in order to preserve the deity's pure goodness. "In this world, we are all probationers," he asserted, and "God judges all according to their works."[35] Such Arminian arguments against Universalism had a broad appeal, and any version of predestinarian teaching faced increasingly formidable opposition. Jacob Tidd predicted in 1823 that "as minds grow more enlightened, Calvinism is sinking into obscurity; so also the doctrine of Universalism that is predicated on the same foundation and rising out of its ruins will surely share the same fate."[36]

Clearly, Americans in the antebellum period had difficulty with a teaching that seemed to diminish, if not ignore, the role of will and character. Moral advisors of youth, after all, spoke in clearly Arminian terms when they argued that character formation and religion were the same thing. The cultural assumption became ever clearer that in life, both here and hereafter, one became what one willed and labored to become. Universalism flew in the face of the central concern with free will and earned reputation.[37]

Anti-Universalist evangelicals were alarmed by a system that not only seemed to disdain the importance of character but also flouted the human need to see justice satisfied. By the second and third decades of the century, attacks on Universalism almost invariably invoked considerations of justice to condemn the faith. Universalism seemed to be built on an outmoded Calvinist base; it appeared to be the epitome of religious injustice. The belief that all were ultimately saved, no matter how monstrous their sins or great their infidelity, was antithetical to the human sense of justice and so had to be false. The renowned revivalist Charles G. Finney boasted that he had defeated a Universalist in an 1824 debate by denying the tenets of predestination and passive regeneration of the elect and asserting a universal atonement and invitation to repentance. In contrast to the Universalist God, who rewarded the righteous and wicked alike, Finney's God respected more mundane ideas of justice.[38]

By midcentury, anti-Universalist writings propounded even more forcefully the necessity for an understanding of divine rule that emphasized God's just and consistent judgment. The unnamed writer of an 1851 tract titled *Endless Punishment, a Result of Character* dwelled on "the great law of God's moral government," which "binds the moral universe together." This was the law that made "the conduct of the present mould the character and destiny of the future." After discoursing at some length about the chaos that would result without such a law, the author got to the heart of the matter:

> The doctrine . . . may also help to relieve the perplexity occasioned by the unequal manner in which the blessings of life are distributed. It must be admitted

that, in the distribution of temporal blessings, little regard seems to be paid to character; the good are depressed, the wicked prospered.[39]

Humanity needed the reassurance that the divine moral system would rectify such conditions.[40]

To its evangelical critics, Universalism seemed even worse than the Calvinism they had discarded. However unreasonably, Calvinism had at least allowed that the unregenerate would be punished. Universalism paid little heed to the human longing for justice or fairness; the belief that God redeemed even the most hardened and unrepentant sinner seemed perverse theology, too far removed from the realities of human experience.

To most evangelicals, the traditional forms of piety that had suited the close-knit Puritan community were simply not appropriate for the nineteenth century's mobile, restless, and expansive society. Whereas now a faith with clearer moral guidelines was called for, Universalism, by insisting that all would be saved, appeared to deny the need for moral sanctions. Philemon Russell reminded his readers that, in Universalism, God was responsible for all things, and "among this *all* things, *sin* holds a place." In fact, this doctrine "*makes God the only sinner in the Universe,*" he wrote in his 1842 *Letters to a Universalist.*[41]

Along with many others, Presbyterian Edwin Hatfield pounced on the common Universalist acknowledgment that God was ultimately responsible for sin. He complained that Universalists believed men sinned only because of their God-given carnal attributes; sin therefore became "not 'exceedingly sinful' " because it resulted merely from the victory of the "animal appetites." Since God created these, the victory should "be regarded as a fulfillment of his will"; Universalists "thus converted sin into righteousness."[42] Their belief seemed to promote both sloth and criminality. To the evangelical mind, Universalists seemed oddly out of step with the age and as blithely unconcerned as atheists about the vital role of religion in maintaining the moral order of society.

The Universalist view of sin, John Borland complained in 1848, was akin to "Jesuitism," for sin could easily be rationalized away in such a casuistic system.[43] It was not uncommon for anti-Universalists to charge the faith with Jesuitism, or craftily avoiding moral responsibility. Congregational minister Parsons Cooke, who "exposed" Universalism in 1834, also asserted that Universalists employed a "Jesuitical" doctrine.[44] He echoed Timothy Dwight, who had warned that Universalism "is calculated only to foster the love of sinning and provide safety for the sinner."[45] A later critic agreed and compared the doctrine to the pope's offering of indulgences, because it "offers *beforehand* a security of safety to transgressors, though they commit heinous crimes."[46]

Critics of Universalism argued that, without the threat of retribution, human beings were left morally adrift, fell victim to the baser passions, and doomed society. They frequently charged that Universalism attracted or, indeed, produced hardened, degraded sinners. A Presbyterian tract titled *The Universalist* related the transformation of a "shockingly profane" man, a Universalist, who had the good fortune to meet a Presbyterian missionary. After the man cast off Universalism and his sinful ways, he reflected that "while there are *some* moral men who are Universalists, the mass of them are immoral persons."[47] Even this denunciation was relatively mild. Lyman Beecher alleged that "nearly all the loose livers in the land are Universalists" and that "the wicked and depraved" were the first to join new congregations.[48]

Such opponents considered the denomination to be simply a convenient and pleasant rest stop along the road to infidelity. Methodist minister N. Levings was one of many who pointed to the famous case of Abner Kneeland, a Universalist minister who defected in 1829, eventually declared his atheism, and was convicted of blasphemy in 1838.[49] Kneeland had been a close friend of Hosea Ballou himself. His wildly checkered career as a religious thinker and preacher, especially his explicit rejection of Christianity, certainly helped to perpetuate the common tendency to equate Universalism and infidelity. But Kneeland came to attack the denomination for its backward Christian outlook.[50] By its nature as a liberal, popular movement, Universalism attracted numerous religious seekers who later adopted other heresies or turned against Christianity altogether. It is hardly surprising that its critics often compared Universalism to deism or dismissed it as a "mere modification of infidelity."[51]

Many critics, indeed, thought Universalism even more despicable than atheism in that it made people sin all the more boldly and take greater risks, for they looked forward not to the void but to endless glory.[52] The orthodox journal *Quarterly Christian Spectator* argued that, as a system of faith, Universalism was "decidedly worse" in its influence than the infidelity of "simple deism." Because he does "not *deny* the punishment of sin in the hereafter," the deist is still prompted by the possibility.[53] Universalism seemed to be the first cousin of atheism, masquerading in Christian dress.

Humbling Human Vanity

Universalists charged their critics with exposing their own pervasive religious cynicism. John S. Thompson, editor of the Universalist *Rochester Magazine and Theological Review*, responded in 1825 to the prediction of Methodist minister Lewis Covell that belief in universal salvation would open the floodgates of pleasure seeking:

> What are these the lovers of God, who are so willing to be damned for his glory, who tell us, if it were not for the dread of an endless hell, they would plunge into all manner of vice and extravagance, and even insult him with the greatest contempt? They have no relish for the pleasures of religion, are enemies of the cross of Christ, strangers to their own mercies. . . . [Among them], all the ceremonies of the sanctuary are a ridiculous mockery; the offspring of superstitious fear![54]

Universalist minister Abel Thomas echoed Thompson's sentiments. Acclaimed as one of the founders of the *Lowell Offering*, a magazine featuring the literary efforts of young female mill workers, Thomas argued that ministers who proclaimed endless rewards for virtue and endless punishment for vice clearly implied that the wicked had the best of it in this life.[55] No longer an insidious, gnawing, universal human affliction, sin had become an inherently pleasurable activity that humans were free to pursue or avoid. The Reverend J. Aiken, in reviewing the anti-Universalist tract titled *The Serpent Uncoiled*, joked that "if there is pleasure in sin, as hell is a place of endless sinning according to Orthodoxy, hell will not be such a miserable place after all!" On a more sober note, he attacked the common anti-Universalist assertion that fear of an endless hell was absolutely necessary to prompt remorse of conscience; such thinking only showed the extent to which true piety had waned.[56]

Expressions of concern for the welfare of society, Universalists believed, often merely disguised the selfishness and antiegalitarianism of evangelical moralism. Universalist educator Hosea Ballou 2nd maintained that opponents could not tolerate the idea that all men were of equal importance in the eyes of divinity and wondered why people should oppose "impartial grace and equal favor."[57] True social harm resulted, Universalists argued, when people were convinced that all would not be saved. Those who rejected universal salvation, Abel Thomas asserted, encouraged the most dangerous form of depravity—the often unconscious pleasure that the unredeemed, carnal spirit took in the misery of others.[58]

Because Universalists generally regarded their doctrine as the best religious expression of egalitarian ideals, they were highly sensitive to critics such as Philemon Russell, who lamented in 1843 that the faith "regards death as a leveller. . . . It sweeps away all the distinctions between the virtuous and the wicked."[59] The popular Universalist preacher Thomas Sawyer took issue with a similar sentiment expressed in Edwin Hatfield's *Universalism as It Is*. The realization that one could do nothing to curry divine favor humbled human pride, he noted. Yet people always wished to discharge just one "meritorious act," which would distinguish them as morally superior and deserving of better treatment than others. Sawyer impugned the motives behind Hatfield's attack, declaring, "If all our fellow beings shall be *equal* with us we trust we shall have such modicum of grace as will enable us rather to rejoice in their felicity than to murmur at it. Mr. Hatfield . . . seems to have his eye on the 'uppermost seats.' "[60]

Only a vain and unchristian spirit, Hosea Ballou charged in 1844, would conclude that there were different stations in heaven from the biblical passage "In My Father's house there are many mansions."[61] Everyone agreed that, strictly speaking, no one could merit salvation, so it was an exercise in human arrogance to speculate about who could or could not be saved. Universalists believed it was an exercise that demonstrated a disturbing need to find people unequal in the eyes of God. They suspected that those who held that only a certain segment of humanity would be saved similarly supported earthly conditions of inequality and feared Universalism's central tenet, which represented the "Democracy of Christianity."[62] In Universalist eyes, this fear explained the especially strong opposition to their movement in the South, where religion served to buttress the system of slavery.[63]

Clearly, Universalism was a movement different in kind, not merely in degree, from the Methodists, Campbellites, and other dissenting groups that "democratized" American Christianity in the early nineteenth century.[64] Universalism effectively set aside the traditional psychological foci of religious belief—sin, guilt, repentance, and judgment—that absorbed and channeled human anxiety. A sovereign God, a common humanity, and especially universal regeneration at death were its major reference points. Its message of God's universal love notwithstanding, Universalism was not for the faint-hearted, for it dismantled the common mental structures of faith and the security found therein.

Restorationism

While they gave spirited responses to their critics, nineteenth-century Universalists themselves wrestled with the moral implications of their doctrine. The growing appeal of restorationism, or the notion of limited discipline or punishment after death and before salvation, even led to a schism within the movement during the 1830s. A departure from Ballou's radically egalitarian emphasis, restorationism was an attempt to give the faith a more explicit moral dimension. But the eventual adoption of a restorationist position by a majority of Universalists would seriously undermine the development of the movement as a distinctive expression of liberal piety. The rise of restorationism during the second quarter of the century helped ensure that the common characterization of Universalism would be as Unitarianism's poor relation, a form of liberalism that shared Unitarianism's view of a benevolent divinity and perfectable humanity but lacked its intellectual base and social standing.

In the eighteenth century, Universalists had concentrated on eliminating the idea of endless punishment; the subject of a possible limited retribution beyond death was of secondary concern. To be sure, many early Universalists subscribed to a belief in discipline after death, but adherents entertained a number of views, most prominently the conviction that all punishment ceased at life's end, or what came to be known as "ultra-Universalism." In a typical effort to accommodate all views, the denomination decided against the endorsement of a doctrinal position on the issue beyond the simple avowal of universal salvation.

Russell Miller suggests that it is "next to impossible" to determine how many Universalists in the early nineteenth century leaned toward a belief in future punishment.[65] But a survey of Universalist clergy by Thomas Whittemore in the late 1820s, part of his research for his *Modern History of Universalism*, turned up overwhelming sentiment for an ultra-Universalist position. Whittemore's sampling of Universalist clergy from New England to North Carolina indicated little support for a restorationist view among clergy or the laity they served.[66]

Edward Turner of Gloucester, Massachusetts, first brought the topic of future retribution into the open in a newspaper debate with Hosea Ballou from 1817 to 1818. Initially unsure of his views, Ballou came during the course of the argument strenuously to deny future retribution. His stance outraged the Unitarian editor of the *Boston Kaleidoscope*, who promptly proceeded to lump Universalists together with Roman Catholics, Calvinists, and deists as opposed to "rational and liberal Christianity." More significant, the debate began to call attention to an issue that had not been important earlier. Identifying himself as a "restorationist," Universalist minister Jacob Wood kept the controversy alive and met with six other Universalist ministers, including the prominent Bostonian Paul Dean, in Shirley, Massachusetts, in 1823. Wood failed in his efforts: the New England Convention refused explicitly to endorse future retribution, and an attempt to organize a separate restorationist association did not get off the ground. Hosea Ballou 2nd leaned toward the restorationist position, but he believed that the controversy had more to do with personal jealousy of the highly influential Hosea Ballou than with genuine theological differences.[67]

Within a few years, though, restorationists in southern Massachusetts were organizing again. In 1831, after several years of bitter intradenominational debate, some of the restorationists formed a separate association, the Massachusetts Association of Universal Restorationists, which lasted until 1841. Adherents thereafter either drifted back to the Universalist denomination or joined other movements, particularly Unitarianism.[68]

The restorationist controversy, though confined mostly to eastern New England and involving a relatively small number of Universalists, nonetheless greatly influenced the evolution of the denomination by forcing it to face the moral and social implications of its chief tenet, implications that had long worried the evangelical opponents of Universalism. Although they failed to make the denomination modify its formal doctrinal profession to include a belief in future discipline, restorationists would win the larger battle.

Restorationists were uneasy with the denomination's refusal to take a stand on such an important subject. They pointed out that ultra-Universalism, which simply expanded the Calvinist concept of the elect to include all of humanity, eliminated all human responsibility for salvation. Restorationist and Waltham, Massachusetts, Unitarian minister Bernard Whitman charged that Calvinists and Universalists were equally guilty of permitting people to hope or believe that they could escape punishment for their sins. "There is but one step from the sublime to the ridiculous; and but half a step from Calvinism to Universalism," he declared in *Friendly Letters to a Universalist* (1833). Both were "irrational and unscriptural."[69] To uphold the impartial nature of the divine character, it was essential to teach that the inequalities and sins of the present life would be punished in the hereafter. Restorationists believed that Universalists had emphasized the mercy of God at the expense of his justice.[70]

Ultra-Universalists, restorationists also contended, made death the savior. Charles Hudson, a prominent restorationist minister, pointed out that death was, after all, only a physical operation, but ultra-Universalists ascribed to it the power to affect and reform character.[71] Repentance did not come about "instantaneously, like an electric shock, without any agency on the part of the creature" but as a gradual transformation of moral character. Regeneration had to be evident in conduct.[72]

Restorationists thus attempted to solve two prominent objections to Universalism—that it left justice unsatisfied and that it ignored human free agency. Moreover, they sought to preserve God's omnipotence and to explain sin and evil by promising rectification in the afterlife. Yet restorationists were probably most concerned with the pragmatic implications of doctrine. Calvinism led to anxiety, they charged, but ultra-Universalism engendered apathy and vice; fear was undesirable but so was moral sloth. Restorationism, its adherents asserted, struck the proper balance by emphasizing individual accountability. As Hudson explained, "We value our system on account of the excellent piety and morality which it enforces."[73]

Ballou despaired at such talk. Throughout the period of the restorationist controversy, Ballou's general sentiment against limited retribution hardened into a conviction that he expressed in 1834 in *An Examination of the Doctrine of Future Retribution*. Prompted in part by the schism in the denomination, Ballou's last major volume served as an important sequel to his *Treatise on Atonement*, reaffirming the pietistic view of the earlier work and rejecting again the growing moralism of popular religious belief. Hatred of sin and love of God, Ballou insisted, could not be induced by fear of future punishment. Moreover, he pointed out, the specter of delayed punishment had done little to deter immoral practices in this world.[74]

Ballou continued throughout his later life to argue against what he saw as the growing moralism of Universalism. From the 1830s on, he voiced stern opposition to the "modern theory of liberal Christianity" in which man was a moral agent in a world of probation. This belief, he emphasized, was a poor alternative to the old, faded Calvinism.[75] The true Christian, he asserted, forgot his own merits in the sight of God and did not "wrap the drapery of his goodness around him, as the old Roman gathered his drapery around him to die nobly." Humanity needed to form conceptions of God's love that "radically and utterly forbid any dependence for eternal glory to rest on what the soul has done."[76]

In an article for the *Universalist Quarterly* in 1845, he acknowledged the human desire to see justice done. But he maintained that the key message of Christianity—the foundation on which Universalism was built—was love of one's enemies and the hope that all would share equally in the redemption. Without this spirit, "we may be loud and even clamorous about distinctions in the immortal state." Discussions of the effect of our present conduct on our future state, Ballou suggested, did nothing to encourage piety. He asked:

> Does Christianity teach us that all men, who have sinned and come short of the glory of God, will be, on account of sin, less happy in the immortal state than they would have been if sin had never existed? Here we have the whole question before us. If we answer the question in the affirmative, we impeach both the wisdom and the goodness of God. If we answer the question as we ought, in the negative, we necessarily repudiate the belief that sin committed in the mortal state will lessen the enjoyment of the immortal.[77]

He expanded on this theme several months later in a commentary on an essay by William Ellery Channing, who had suggested that our "present" character had a bearing on our future weal or woe. Even granting that we do carry our character into the future state, he asked, would not the "utterly incomprehensible change, the resurrection into an immortal state" be attended by a similar incomprehensible change of mind?[78]

It is noteworthy that the 1831 restorationist manifesto, which defined "regeneration" as consisting of a "general Judgement, Future Rewards and Punishments, to be followed by a Final Restoration of all mankind to holiness and happiness," pointedly condemned "modern sentiments of no future accountability, connected with materialism."[79] We know that at least in his later years Ballou was influenced by the work of the English Unitarian and materialist Joseph Priestley (who emigrated to the United States in 1796).[80] Priestley's philosophical necessitarianism complemented his own necessitarian views. More significant, Priestley enlisted materialist philosophy in the service of piety and in his emphasis on resurrection.

Priestley had argued that man is not "naturally" immortal but becomes immortal only because, as Revelation teaches, God chooses to resurrect him.[81] This argument was implicit also in Ballou's 1834 work in opposition to future punishment. Key to Ballou's evolving thought on restorationism was his emphasis on resurrection, the so-called death and glory aspect of his theology. Ballou concentrated on the biblical teaching of "our resurrection into an immortal state"; he was less interested in extended theological or philosophical defenses of the mortality of the soul.[82] But his ardent disciple, the Scottish immigrant Walter Balfour, invoked detailed arguments against the natural immortality of the soul in his long campaign against restorationism.

Arguing against a Platonic view of the soul's immortality, Balfour maintained that "The immortality of the soul supersedes the necessity of Christ's resurrection, or ours, through him, for according to this doctrine, we are immortal creatures, and must live forever if Christ had never risen from the grave." Balfour insisted that Martin Luther had "rejected the doctrine of the soul's immortality and its punishment in a disembodied state" but that he had found these ideas too deeply rooted to eradicate. Balfour expressed the hope that another Luther might "lash the popery of Protestants, and scourge this and other heathen doctrines out of Protestant churches."[83] The Universalist clergyman C. F. Lefevre voiced similar ideas in his discussion with John Kendall, a Presbyterian minister:

> I read nothing in the scriptures of an *immortal* soul. I read as much about the death and destruction of the soul as of the body. If it were immortal in its nature this could not be the case. . . . I read of immortality through resurrection of the dead and in no other way.[84]

Ultra-Universalism thus implied a form of "Christian mortalism," the belief, based on Scripture, that bodily death is accompanied by the death of the soul as an independent, conscious entity. In the sixteenth century, Christian mortalism had "appealed to the more radical temperaments . . . who were convinced that Holy Scripture contained yet undiscovered truths that must be searched out diligently without human prejudgments."[85] This theological tradition had remained at least marginally alive in nineteenth-century American Protestantism, and some ultra-Universalists took it up when they termed the spreading Platonic ideas of the soul's immortality "pagan" and called for a return to the more Protestant, Hebraic idea of the resurrection of the body. For these Universalists, the idea of an immortal soul—and the acceptance of restorationism—reduced God to a supporting player in the drama of salvation.

Critics believed that those Universalists who questioned the idea of an immortal soul disclosed the movement's dangerous theological radicalism. Citing the works of Ballou, Balfour, and Lefevre, one opponent concluded in 1844 that "[t]here seems to be no difference between these Universalist ministers . . . and the Infidel Materialists of France, who . . . pronounced death to be an eternal 'sleep,' or rather an extinction of being." The only distinction, he argued, was that Universalists mis-leadingly professed belief in resurrection; in fact, they believed in an entirely new creation.[86] In an 1845 debate L. N. Rice, a Cincinnati Presbyterian minister, con-stantly assailed Universalist minister E. M. Pingree of Louisville with the charge that Universalism "teaches the *materiality and mortality* of the soul." Clearly on the defensive in a public forum, Pingree insisted that, while a few Universalist writers had espoused this doctrine, "the great mass of Universalist Ministers and people believe man *not* to be entirely mortal. Materialism, I repeat, is NOT one of the premises of Universalism."[87]

It it difficult to gauge the extent to which even ultra-Universalists embraced Christian mortalism, for it was not a widely discussed element of Universalist belief. A much more common focus of debate remained the question of future discipline, an issue that occupied Hosea Ballou to the end of his life. In 1849 Ballou offered advice to young men about to enter the Universalist ministry.

He warned them against speculating about the "particulars" of the future state, especially the notion that a process of purgation awaited. It is to be feared, he wrote, that some entered the Universalist ministry with an eye toward "rendering their labors acceptable to the Unitarians" by "adopting such like opinions and holding them forth in public."[88] During his last years, Ballou sensed ever more strongly that restorationist moralism threatened to destroy the distinctive liberal theology of Uni-versalism.

Despite the efforts of Ballou and many of his fellow preachers, it appears that, by the 1850s, most Universalists were rejecting an ultra-Universalist position in favor of a belief in some form of limited future punishment.[89] Increasingly, adherents called for the recognition of the "moral connection" between the present and the future. Ballou 2nd insisted in 1847 that the notion that there was no moral or intellectual link between the present and the future was utterly "incongruous with our forms of thought"; man recoiled at the idea of being cut off from his developed "character," an integral part of his being. It was also important to recognize that man was a "substantive agent," who was not only influenced by but could also control his circumstances. People would be changed through "the workings of the will and the affections," in other words, through moral means.[90]

Numerous contributions to the *Universalist Quarterly* indicate that a growing number of Universalist thinkers agreed with Ballou 2nd. Typical was an 1847 article maintaining that in heaven, man would not be changed like a machine. God, the writer believed, would not treat man as a potter did clay, without "our agency or cooperation," for this would destroy the "whole moral purpose of our life." It would make life a "farce."[91] Nothing could be more absurd, another commentator for the *Quarterly* agreed, than the idea of a sudden, mysterious change in which man was made perfect in Christian knowledge and righteousness.[92]

By 1853, Ballou 2nd was arguing still more stridently about the effect of conduct in the present life on the immortal state. Invoking arguments from Common Sense and Scripture, he presented the case for rewards and punishments and for the connection of the present life to the future. In a revealing conclusion, he warned his Universalist readers that the vital, distinguishing message of their movement was imperiled. As soon as we have gotten people to accept the truth of universal salvation, he wrote, "We have begun to make the worldings among them indifferent, and to send the religiously disposed on a search for something more satisfactory to their profoundest wants."[93] These words reflect a growing nervousness about the state of the denomination and the movement by midcentury, a subject to which we will return in chapter 3.

Certainly, Ballou 2nd was not alone in his fear that ultra-Universalism could produce apathy in some adherents and fail to satisfy the cravings for justice in others. It is difficult to determine the extent to which the adoption of restorationist views was an unconscious response by the majority of Universalists to evangelical criticism or even a bid for greater public acceptance of universal salvation. It seems more than coincidental, however, that restorationism arose concurrently with attacks on Universalism as a force for immorality; to the defenders of the notion of hell, restorationism clearly seemed less threatening than ultra-Universalism. Methodist minister Wilbur Fisk, for instance, was "encouraged" by the new movement.[94] Ultra-Universalist Walter Balfour believed that the spread of restorationism was certain to please believers in endless hell, who could assume that the acceptance of limited future punishment was only the first step in the demise of the whole idea of universal salvation.[95]

While restorationism was undoubtedly greeted as a salutary modification of an extreme doctrine by Universalism's traditional evangelical opponents, it was perhaps most welcomed by certain Unitarians, who, as Hosea Ballou understood, envisioned greater cooperation among liberal groups. Henry Bellows of New York City, one of Unitarianism's most distinguished clergymen, found restorationism to be a most auspicious development indeed. In 1847, he asserted that ultra-Universalism barely existed, at least in New York state. He regarded the gradual refinement of Universalism into restorationism as a promising sign of a possible eventual union of Universalism with Unitarianism.[96] To some extent, Ballou's perspective did remain influential within the denomination, since thoughtful defenses of ultra-Universalism continued to appear. Indeed, the decades around midcentury saw a great deal of heated debate over these issues. In 1847, for instance, Ballou's views were echoed by several writers who advised believers not to concern themselves with questions of God's justice or human merit. A believer needed to have faith that God's design was "wise and benevolent," stressed one contributor to the *Quarterly*, and should not worry about keeping score.[97] God does not look to punish sin in the future, another suggested, but to educate man about it in the present. Sin was something foreseen and controlled by the Creator, who desired man to learn that, just as happiness resulted from obedience to moral laws, so did misery result from sin.

But it is clear that, by this time, ultra-Universalism was already a minority position, defended mostly by an older generation of preachers and writers. The editor of the *Universalist Quarterly* added a revealing disclaimer to the latter article. This writing, he noted, did not present the views of the editor; it was rather "an ingenious systematic expression of the philosophy held wholly or in part, by some of our most distinguished writers." To the editors, this view appeared to "deny the reality of moral principles as distinguished from mere sensuous emotions." More disturbingly, it could lead to "naked" utilitarianism.[98] The weight of such objections continued to grow among Universalist writers. By 1870, a highly laudatory sketch of Ballou's life observed that Universalists now took a "juster" view of the immortal state than Ballou's "extreme" belief in no future punishment.[99]

Although certain Universalist thinkers would attempt to sustain what they believed was a distinctive nonmoralistic spirituality into the latter half of the nineteenth century, Ballou's pietistic Universalism largely belonged to an earlier age. The quiet modification of Universalism wrought by restorationism represented the movement's unspoken compromise with the moralism of the age and its unwillingness to defend Ballou's brand of piety. Restorationism gradually undermined Ballou's whole emphasis on the solidarity of humankind; it drew attention away from the essential fact of human brotherhood toward distinctions based on virtue and sin.

With its emphasis on a fundamental continuity between this life and the next, it led its adherents toward distinctly humanistic conceptions of individual growth and progress. The increasing prevalence of restorationist views made the denomination more acceptable to evangelicals as well as to many religious liberals, and it clearly paved the way for the Universalist rush into various moral and social reform projects in the decades around midcentury.[100] But restorationist beliefs also helped to doom the movement as a unique expression of liberal piety. To the great sadness of Hosea Ballou's disciples, Universalist teachings appeared more and more over the course of the nineteenth century to be simply a popular reflection of the sort of moralism espoused by the Unitarians.

Transcendental Flight

As Ballou unsuccessfully attempted to stem the moralistic tide that swept over Universalism in his later years, another nineteenth-century universal optimist, Ralph Waldo Emerson, chafed against the confining moralism of Unitarianism and became the movement's most famous apostate. In light of the efforts of both Ballou and Emerson to nourish a nonmoralistic liberal faith, we can hardly avoid wondering whether Emerson recorded comments about Universalism or whether his Transcendentalism shared anything with the antimoralistic teachings of Ballou. A brief exploration of the common ground, and of the key divergences, can help us understand the flowering and withering of the early Universalist ideal in a broad historical context.

Although Universalism was experiencing its most dramatic growth as he came into maturity, Emerson had strikingly little to say about the faith. Certainly he was aware of the movement, which was much in evidence in Boston and the surrounding regions and which shared important ideas with his own inherited Unitarianism. By the time Emerson entered Harvard, "Father Ballou" was esteemed far beyond his School Street Church as Universalism's outstanding figure. Oddly, though, Emerson appears to have had virtually no interest in the controversial, locally important denomination or its most prominent leader. One searches Emerson's voluminous works in vain for comments on either, except for a brief but telling reference in a sermon to the "vulgar views of God's benevolence expressed in Universalism."[101]

His condescendingly dismissive attitude is reminiscent of the view of William Ellery Channing, who, as we have seen, had no time for Ballou and the lowly Universalists.

Nevertheless, it is difficult to ignore certain fundamental similarities between Emerson and Ballou. As a nineteenth-century Unitarian scholar recognized, Emerson's important essay "Compensation" (1841), despite its nonbiblical, even nonchristian tone, echoed Ballou in the assertion that "you cannot do wrong without suffering wrong." Emerson lamented, as Ballou had, the "base tone in popular religion," which included the beliefs that the wicked often prosper in this life and that "justice is not done now."[102] Like Ballou, Emerson rejected the notion that God was a moral referee; both believed that actions carried their own "unmediated" consequences, which were not always obvious. Although he admitted that evil-doers often seemed to elude retribution, Ballou shared with Emerson the confidence that "against all appearances the nature of things works for truth and right forever."[103]

The agreement between Ballou and Emerson extended beyond their mutual distaste for the moral calculus of prevailing Christian belief. For both thinkers, "the first quality of religiousness was universality."[104] Emerson's assertion that "the exclusionist in religion does not see that he shuts the door of heaven on himself in striving to keep out others" succinctly expressed a central message of Ballou's faith.[105]

Stephen Whicher finds it possible to argue that Emerson's faith "resembled unmistakably the Calvinist pietism that Unitarian moralism left behind." The cultivation of character was not enough; Emerson sought the experience of living, ravishing Being. He wanted *assured salvation, not simply moral capacity.*" Henry Parks, moreover, asserts that Transcendentalism extended the "divine and supernatural light," which, for Jonathan Edwards, had brought this assurance from an "elect minority to the human race as a whole."[106] In Emerson's early writings, this concept of election was rooted mainly in a new vision of human capacity. While still concerned with the experience of human freedom, however, by the 1840s Emerson was also emphasizing the laws of universal necessity. In the famous essay "Fate," he pointed to *"the eternal tendency to the good of the whole, active in every atom, every moment."*[107] "The last lesson of life," Emerson concluded in "Worship," "is a voluntary obedience, a necessitated freedom."[108]

Indeed, as he modified his conception of freedom to recognize "fate," Emerson increasingly regarded the individual human being as inseparable from the wholeness of divinity. The "Genius of Destiny," he wrote in 1844, was a

> cruel kindness, serving the whole even to the ruin of the member; a terrible communist, reserving all profits to the community, without dividend to individuals. Its law is, you shall have everything as a member, nothing to yourself.

Thus, as Whicher shows, Emerson made an "unconditional surrender of his first radical egoism."[109]

Emerson's biographer Robert Richardson emphasizes his "remarkably complete critique of romantic individualism."[110] "Nothing but God is self-dependent," Emerson wrote. "Every being in nature has its existence so connected with other beings that if set apart from them it would instantly perish."[111] Like Ballou, Emerson taught the impotence of the human will to violate eternal beneficence, and he saw the self's good as indivisible from that of the greater whole. Both men shared an orientation clearly at odds with prevailing evangelical Christian as well as Unitarian views.

The differences separating the outlooks of Ballou and Emerson are, to be sure, as significant as the points of convergence in their attitudes. Most obvious and important, Ballou was comfortable in a world of traditional Christian categories, and his thought, though certainly filtered through Enlightenment ideals, was closely tied to biblical forms and respectful of historical wisdom. Emerson, in touch not only with the broadest lines of Western thought but also with a variety of world cultures, sought by contrast spiritual experience that could not be formulated in terms of particular revelations or human reason. Sydney Ahlstrom remarks that Emerson viewed the past not as "a building to be renovated for present living" but as "a quarry to be pillaged."[112] The novelty of Transcendentalism was, after all, its denial of any authority outside the individual.[113]

For Ballou, the fatherlike personality of God, expressed in the doctrine of universal salvation, was paramount. The soul experienced redemption as it came to understand and rationally to acknowledge the most basic religious truth—that all souls were equally dear to a paternal God. But Emerson tended toward pantheism; he could not ascribe personality to infinite divinity. These opposed attitudes were related to deeper differences in outlook regarding time and history. Ballou stayed within the fundamentally eschatological tradition of Western Christianity, looking forward in time to a final divine resolution, and, significantly, to God's resurrection of the individual soul. Emerson, on the other hand, looked for ecstatic experience and was concerned less with future-directed hope than with directing the soul to timeless truths. Even the sudden death of his young son did not change his denial of personal immortality.[114]

In its attempt to reconcile the Bible and reason, as well as in its culturally naive appeal to the sense of human community, Ballou's conception of universal faith no doubt reflected its relatively parochial origins. Emerson's outlook, though in many respects more urbane, was also less energetic in the effort to realize human brotherhood; it was essentially mystical and individualistic. For even though Emerson came to argue that persons had to transcend egoism, his gaze remained squarely on the individual as the locus of spiritual development. David Robinson has noted that, for Emerson, "the cultivation of the self" was also "the exploration of the nature of divinity." The universal soul invited the individual "to be and to grow" without limit.[115]

Emerson did seek to infuse liberal faith with a sense of the pervasive power of the divine; yet this effort, far from reducing concern with the development of the individual soul, actually redoubled his attention to the limitless self. He echoed that concern frequently in phrases that would be enshrined in American culture, including "Nothing is at last sacred but the integrity of your own mind." Although he did repeat several themes that had been prominent in early Universalism, he veered away from the ideal of an objectively supportable, communal, and eschatological faith. Whereas Ballou had placed great emphasis upon the necessity for a biblical and reasonable belief that could be shared by all, Emerson showed a typically Romantic desire to see the individual soul totally freed from the limitations of both reason and particular revelations and lifted toward the infinite. Ahlstrom views Emerson as a "romantic pagan," "the theologian of something we may almost term 'the American religion.' "[116]

Because he sought direct, ecstatic spiritual experience, Emerson was not unappreciative of popular evangelical Christianity. He maintained a friendship with Edward Taylor, a "shouting Methodist" and preacher at Seaman's Bethel in the North End of Boston near Emerson's first church. Emerson "loved Taylor's heady, vigorous speech, and he called Taylor one of the two great poets of America."[117] He was captivated by the power of Taylor's language, by the forcefulness of this Methodist preacher.

One might expect that Emerson, called by Walt Whitman a "born democrat," would also have paid attention to the populist, self-consciously tolerant Universalist movement flowering in his own backyard.[118] But Emerson's concern with direct religious feeling made him unlikely to welcome Universalism's eschatological vision as comprehending God's relationship with the individual. Moreover, his uneasiness with Universalism was prophetic. Nineteenth-century American liberal Protestants would find Emerson's humanism, his concern with religious experience, and his Platonic view of the immortality of the soul far more palatable than Ballou's unrelenting focus on God's resurrection of all souls to immortality.

Not all of Emerson's fellow Transcendentalists were quite as dismissive of Universalism. For example, Theodore Parker praised Universalists for fighting "manfully against Eternal Damnation — the foulest doctrine which defiles the pages of man's theologic history." He continued, "Alone of all Christian sects, they professedly taught the Immortality of man in such a form that it is no curse to the race to find it true."[119]

Parker, a mainly self-educated farmer's son, could acknowledge the critical importance of Ballou's teaching in the evolution of liberal religion. Speaking to his Twenty-eighth Congregational Society shortly after the Universalist leader's death in 1852, Parker lauded Ballou as the main cultivator of the sentiment that "God is the Father and Friend of the whole race of man, that it was the will of our Heavenly Father that 'not one of his little ones would perish.' " In preaching this "great truth" for over a half century, Ballou had "wrought a revolution in the thoughts and minds of men more mighty than any which has been accomplished during the same time by all the politicians in the nation." When he had begun his labors, there were probably fewer than five thousand persons who accepted this truth, while now there were "probably five million!"[120] More in touch than Emerson with the actual workings of religious sentiment among the people, Parker was able to see that a popular and biblical teaching did not exclude, and indeed had produced, a faith that in key respects was truly universal.

While Parker did not share the Christian doctrinal orientation of Ballou, he clearly appreciated, in a way that Emerson never could, Ballou's appeal to "the objective ground of universals." Emerson's was a subjective concern with the intensely personal insights of the individual soul. But Parker looked for the experience of absolute and universal truth within the universal community. Critical of Transcendentalists who took "all their facts from their own consciousness," Parker emphasized the importance of the rational understanding. He could therefore whole-heartedly approve of Ballou's widespread and reasonable preaching of a "great truth."[121]

Most Universalists, for their part, had little comment on Emerson or Parker. They worried that the Transcendentalist movement was hostile to revealed religion and the authority of the Bible. Rationally interpreting the Bible was one thing; rejecting its authoritative revelation was something else again.[122] Universalist spokesmen were deeply disturbed that these "metaphysicians," by substituting a "lofty spirituality" for the fatherly nature of God, cut away the grounds for a vigorous piety. Do we feel any profound reverence, Hosea Ballou 2nd asked, for the human philanthropist who "contents himself with wishing well to his dependents and with giving them an open field for improvement, but who does not exert all the means at his command to accomplish their welfare?" "Pantheism and Philosophical Christianity" would not "answer the demands of the living, practical earnest men, who have hearts to feel for the everlasting interests of their race." The doctrine of man's final condition, he insisted, had to hold the "forward place" in liberal Christianity.[123]

While Universalists could also occasionally express admiration for the ideas of Emerson and his colleagues, it is clear that the universal vision of the majority of the Transcendentalists diverged sharply from that of Ballou's movement. Emerson's desire to escape the smallness of Unitarian moralism contributed less to a renewed idea of human wholeness than to an exaltation of the limitless potential of the individual.[124] Certainly, this is what popular audiences believed they heard from him: at midcentury, on the lyceum circuit, Emerson was even regarded as a prophet of economic individualism. The midwestern, mercantile audiences for Emerson's "young men's lectures" in the 1850s took away a mandate for hard work and financial self-improvement.[125] Much later, popular mind-cure advocates like Orison Swett Marden drew great inspiration from Emerson, especially from *The Conduct of Life*, which voiced "faith in the capacity of man to 'flux' the universe according to his needs."[126]

Nothing could have been farther from Ballou's radical eschatological vision, which had roots in the egalitarian idealism of the post revolutionary years. Throughout the first half of the nineteenth century, that vision could continue to find sustenance in the general culture. Opera, drama, instrumental music, painting, and sculpture drew heterogeneous audiences that crossed social and economic lines.[127] American museums were, at this time, not "segregated temples of the fine arts," Neil Harris reminds us, but "repositories of information, collections of strange or doubtful data."[128] As late as 1853, *Putnam's* magazine was suggesting P. T. Barnum, the arranger of Jenny Lind's U.S. tour, as the manager of the New York Opera, observing that he understood that "with us, the opera need not necessarily be the luxury of the few, but the recreation of the many."[129] Reflecting public culture, where the many were routinely brought together, the Universalist faith expressed the hope that all would be brought together into communion with God. As the ultimate expression of an egalitarian ideal, Universalism assumed that redeemed souls would want to be united in salvation.

But, like Emerson, most Americans found themselves less and less inclined toward such idealistic visions of human community. We will see that, while many

American Protestants in the second half of the nineteenth century granted that all might be saved, they were not particularly interested in Universalism's communal eschatological vision. It was one thing to acknowledge that God could manage to redeem the most hardened sinner, especially as Protestants increasingly accepted a form of purgatory. It was quite another to hope for eternal, undifferentiated human communion.

THREE

Controversy and Identity

What gave Universalists identity as a group in the early decades of the nineteenth century was primarily their acceptance of a single controversial doctrine. Beyond this, Universalists were united mostly by a sense of what they opposed: all that appeared unreasonable, superstitious, arbitrary, and oppressive in traditional and prevailing religious teachings. Precisely because its central teaching was so controversial, Universalism attracted members who were not afraid of disputation; indeed, their rationalist streak made many Universalists positively eager for debate about religious questions.[1] During the ferment of the Second Great Awakening, this aspect of Universalist identity came to the fore; the period between 1820 and 1840, when Universalists were most openly and consistently engaged in battle with other religious groups, was also the period of the denomination's most rapid growth and greatest overall vitality. We will see that, when the intense controversy of that era began to ebb, Universalists showed growing confusion about the proper direction of their movement.

A look at the volume of eighteenth- and nineteenth-century publications regarding Universalism or Universalist teachings offers a simple but helpful gauge of the movement's appeal and the denomination's vitality (see figure 3.1). It is clear that the first significant spurt of publication came in the years following the War of Independence; the figure of well over a hundred works before 1800 attests to the early preaching of John Murray and his contemporaries in the movement. The really dramatic expansion, however, came a bit later; from around 1810 through the

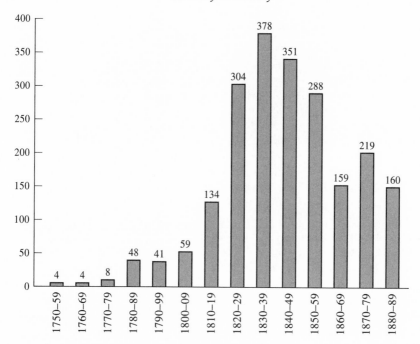

Figure 3.1. American Publications Related to Universalism, 1750–1889. *Source*: Richard Eddy. *Universalism in America: A History* (2 vols., Boston, 1884–1886)

1830s, we see a rapid and consistent rise in literature concerning Universalism. This period of high visibility and widespread controversy was, by all accounts, marked by the denomination's most significant expansion.

There was a slight drop-off in publications through the 1840s, which witnessed the beginnings of serious denominational debate over the direction of the movement, and the 1850s saw even fewer new writings published on Universalism. It is no surprise to see a sharp decline in the volume of publication during the wartorn 1860s, yet the following decades show no striking recovery. The general trend relative to the earlier era is clear. From at least one perspective, these figures are more revealing than the total number of Universalist congregations, which peaked in the 1880s.[2]

A Yearning for Spiritual Combat

Especially in the early decades of the century, when it was still a fledgling movement, Universalism attracted anyone but pious and respectful types. Supporters as well as detractors of the movement described common folk, often halfhearted churchgoers, gathered around some itinerant Universalist preacher, chortling as he held up "orthodox" theology to ridicule. An opponent asserted in 1834 that Universalist ministers "philosophise and speculate" and make their hearers doubt until "nothing is left *undoubted* to them, except that *priestcraft* is the principal evil in the world!" Admirers of Universalist preachers "laugh at their wit" and "chuckle at their [characterization of the orthodox] perversions of scripture."[3] Universalist preaching, another critic charged, brought out "gamblers, scoffers, infidels, blasphemers and topers."[4]

While Nathaniel Stacy, one of the first to preach the doctrine in central and western New York, would hardly have agreed with such a description of his listeners, he nevertheless made it clear that those sympathetic to the movement were nonconformists. He observed that converts to Universalism warmly welcomed "investigation and discussion of doctrinal tenets." Itinerant Universalist preachers were almost always engaged in "expositions and defenses of Universalism" in front of "many inquiring minds." While those drawn to the faith were generally uneducated themselves, he noted, they tended to revere learning and rationality.[5]

Seekers of a rational approach to religion thus attended discussions of Universalism in much the same way as those wanting an experimental piety turned to revivalism. Trying to make sense of the paradoxes of Calvinism, which loomed ever larger in the age of a benevolent deity, they were ripe for Universalist preachers anxious to tell about a "reasonable" and "liberal" faith. Stephen R. Smith, another early Universalist preacher in New York, told of hearing his first Universalist sermon, delivered by Hosea Ballou at a schoolhouse in Utica, a "meagre and muddy village." The sermon, Smith recalled, was the first he had ever heard that involved "neither a contradiction nor an absurdity"; Universalism seemed a completely "consistent" system.[6] Similarly, Thomas Whittemore, whose "moderate Calvinist" family attended the Charlestown church of Jedidiah Morse, began to embrace Universalism as a teenager, finding it a "very rational doctrine."[7] Preacher George Rogers had left a position as a Methodist minister and "stood before the winds of free inquiry" until he discovered Universalism, "religion in a rational form."[8]

Already in the late eighteenth century, Universalists had condemned the traditional Calvinist God as "tyrannical" and "depraved."[9] Orthodox Calvinists had responded with a barrage of counterarguments, dismissing Universalists as naive upstarts who avoided the basic theological issues of human sin and guilt and underplayed the necessity of repentance.[10] Increasingly by the 1820s, however, Universalists were confronted not by orthodox Calvinists but by their evangelical successors. Evangelicalism, and the culture it spawned, became the much more vulnerable targets of Universalist criticism. In the blazing fires of evangelical religion, Universalists saw the utter sacrifice of reason in religious belief; exposing what they saw as theological degeneration and restoring rationality to popular faith became their movement's raison d'être. Universalists thus tended to become ever more combative in defense of rational religion.

Their opponents complained constantly about the contentiousness of Universalists.[11] Andrew Royce, a Congregationalist pastor from Williamstown, Vermont, expressed a common concern that Universalism "wished to make war upon all religious organizations in the land."[12] As late as 1856, Samuel Bartlett was prompted to ask whether Universalists were against "*iniquity* or *orthodoxy*." Did they wish to make men "love God or hate Calvinism?"[13] Nathan George, a Methodist from Maine, angrily denounced the unrelenting attacks of Universalists on "priestcraft." He criticized their characterization of revivalist preachers as "soul hunters" and "mad sectaries" and voiced outrage about charges that revivals were held at night because people were more easily frightened in the dark.[14] Another opponent lamented that even ladies' missionary societies were not immune to such vicious and vulgar assaults; it was clear that Universalists simply treated other Christian denominations with contempt.[15] Critics contended as well that Universalists deliberately used crude sarcasm as a way to build their ranks. This approach, noted Parsons Cooke, Congregational minister in Lynn, Massachusetts, appealed especially "to the young and unreflecting," who were "particularly sensitive to the voice of ridicule."[16]

Former Universalists pointed to such rude combativeness as a disturbing aspect of the faith, which had helped drive them away. Lewis Todd, a Universalist minister who became a Methodist, charged that Universalists loved to "burlesque others" for their teachings; in his eyes, such attacks had grown tiresome.[17] One of the most notorious defectors from Universalism, Matthew Hale Smith, agreed with Todd's assessment of the movement. Although most Universalists regarded Smith as a rather pathetic and "naturally unstable" religious seeker, the publication of his lengthy anti-Universalist tomes did cause them consternation.[18] In *Universalism Examined, Renounced, Exposed* (1842), Smith maintained that the purpose of Universalism was not to reform people or make them holy but rather to "put down orthodoxy."[19] And he complained in *Universalism, Not of God* (1847) that "universalism breathes nothing but bitter hostility and hatred to all who differ from its communion."[20]

A more celebrated Universalist apostate, Orestes Brownson, perhaps the most famous antebellum religious seeker, brought such reactions to a sharp point by maintaining that, since the primary aim of Universalism was to "combat Orthodoxy," it was the embodiment of religious negativism. Indeed, Universalism was nothing more than extreme Protestantism, for Protestantism itself was "simple negativism," according to Brownson, who based his conclusions in part on his experiences as a Presbyterian, Universalist, Unitarian, and, ultimately, a Roman Catholic.[21]

Universalists were not unaware of the common perception that they were eager to foment religious discord. Perhaps the most feisty of all the denomination's publicists, Whittemore freely admitted in his autobiography that, as a young preacher, he had "rather yearned for spiritual combat." He defended the need for controversial discourses, arguing that many abhorred the doctrine he preached and needed to have it explicated and defended.[22] But Stephen Smith, who recounted his experiences as an itinerant minister in New York in the second and third decades of the century, decried the polemical approach of many preachers, who harped on the "weakness and absurdity" of dominant creeds and were "unmercifully severe" to the other sects.[23] In lengthy analysis published in the *Expositor and Universalist Review* in 1839 Hosea Ballou 2nd warned that the "constant practice of doctrinal controversy" was dangerous to the movement and was apt "to turn the very love of the truth itself into a regard for it only as a means of combat." An organization founded not on positive principle, but mainly on antagonism, would eventually be composed of "only the contentious." And even these people would sooner or later tire of the same old arguments and would go off in search of new challenges.[24]

Such testimony from the period of the movement's most rapid and widespread growth suggests that, at this time, the negative dynamic of Universalism—the attempt to portray classic Calvinism as perverse and its latter-day version as hopelessly senile—was at least as strong as, if not stronger than, its positive thrust, the effort to express God's all-encompassing love and omnipotent will. The evident tendency of Universalism to attract a contentious crowd, only too ready to point out the deficiencies of popular religious belief, did not bode well for the formation of a strong denominational identity. Indeed, many of those who joined the movement in the first half of the nineteenth century did not really think in denominational terms at all. They were interested in the propagation and defense of a "rational" faith, not in the organization and administration of an ecclesiastical body.

Rescuers of Sound Theology

Especially before the 1840s, Universalist polemicists seemed to believe that the best way to advance their cause was by demonstrating that popular evangelicalism had no viable theological base. Sniffing out the theological vulnerabilities of evangelicals like hounds after game, they pounced on inconsistencies and ripped at them single-mindedly. Again, the pleasure with which they attacked their opponents tells us something about the appeal of the early movement.

The highly active preacher Russell Streeter was typically tireless in this regard. Streeter pointed to A *Solemn Protest against Universal Salvation,* an 1816 work of Stephen Farley, a Congregational minister in Claremont, New Hampshire, as a hopeless attempt to straddle Calvinism and a kind of works righteousness. Most amazing to Streeter was that Farley's audience apparently perceived no contradictions in the sermon and asked that it be printed.[25] In an 1835 discussion, Streeter concluded that, although the skeleton of orthodox Calvinism remained, "the alterations and additions have been so great that what was rank heresy forty, thirty or even twenty years ago is reckoned Calvinism today."[26]

Whittemore was even blunter in his assaults on Calvinism's "latest improvements." Responding in 1830 to a sermon against Universalism by Lyman Beecher, he accused the famous preacher of being "so intent . . . in conforming his creed to the present taste, that but little of the original is left." He asserted that Beecher in effect denied predestination in order to allow for free agency, even though he supposedly subscribed to the teaching of the eternal decree. Asked Whittemore, "Does not the Dr. have one doctrine for his creed and another for his pulpit?"[27]

Universalists never tired of analyzing such "prevarications" or alterations in standard Calvinist doctrine. Their chronicles of the dilution of Calvinist tenets paralleled the work of the eminent New Divinity pastor Nathanael Emmons, who disparaged the Arminian-tainted teachings of Nathaniel W. Taylor and Lyman Beecher, among others.[28] Well before the 1820s, Universalists charged that election and reprobation had lost all significance for most preachers, that hell had become little more than a prison for a few incorrigibles, and that infant damnation had been quietly dropped as a relic of a crueler age.[29] To be sure, Universalists applauded the tendency of Calvinism to become less severe and more humane. But they regretted what they saw as the loss of intellectual rigor and the growing willingness to settle for obviously contradictory beliefs.

Contemporary revivalism was so successful, Universalists continually alleged, because congregations had gradually come to accept convoluted theology or to ignore doctrine altogether. Sylvanus Cobb, Universalist minister, editor, and antislavery reformer, illustrated the state of theology by recalling a conversation he had had in 1823, at the impressionable age of sixteen. He had asked what he must do to be saved.

Minister: Believe the truth.
S: What is the truth?
M: It is the gospel.
S: What is the gospel?
M: Why, this is the gospel: "He that believeth and is baptized shall be saved; but he that believeth not shall be damned."
S: He that believeth *what* shall be saved?
M: The truth.
S: What is the truth?
M: It is the gospel.
S: What *is* the gospel?
M: Why, I have told you. "He that believeth shall be saved," etc.
S: He that believeth *what*?[30]

An 1809 address from the Berean Society of Universalists in Boston to the Congregational Church in Weymouth took the Reverend Jacob Norton to task for appearing to be, alternately, a Calvinist and an Arminian "as may best suit his purpose, though we understand that he professes to be a Calvinist."[31] It was not the "ranting" of revivalists that primarily upset Universalists but rather the lack of a solid theology, which made it possible.[32]

One of the most thorough treatments of revivalism, Russell Streeter's *Latest News from Heaven, Earth and Hell,* focused on a four-day revival held in Shirley, Massachusetts, in 1832 and analyzed the performances of the various revival leaders. What was orthodoxy at New Haven was heterodoxy at Andover, Streeter observed, and the "New Measures" used at the Shirley revival were denounced as "mere tricks" at Williamstown. Even worse, those who studied Calvinism at Andover blithely preached *"ultra-arminianism"* at revivals. The typical sermon of self-styled Calvinist ministers, Streeter complained, was nothing but a "boisterous tirade of rank, uncultivated Arminianism." According to such clerics, God had no "will, purpose, or plan of grace" but only wishes and an *"anxious willingness* that free agents be saved from his own wrath." The Reverend George Fisher, a professedly Calvinist minister of Harvard, Massachusetts, had been less blatant in his contradiction of orthodox doctrine, Streeter acknowledged, but Fisher had been deliberately vague. If Fisher could not avow the traditional Calvinist doctrines, Streeter wrote, he owed it to his church to admit it and to stop calling himself a Calvinist.[33]

Only a weak and therefore easily twisted theology, Universalists believed, permitted acceptance of the prevailing revivalist mentality. Revivals in themselves were not necessarily bad; Streeter spoke favorably of the *"great revival"* of Jonathan Edwards's day: after their conversions, subjects had "a still *deeper sense* of their *guilt* and ruin as sinners than before. Their salvation was wholly of God." Today, though, subjects hoped to be saved before experiencing a change of heart.[34] Universalists constantly lamented the theological degeneration that allowed clergymen to dictate the terms of the revival and to forecast the operations of the deity.[35]

Menzies Rayner's 1834 lectures on religious revivals ridiculed the common assumption that the Supreme Being visited certain places for short periods. Rayner, a Universalist pastor in Hartford, reported the warning of a revival preacher in Connecticut that "God had not been in town in fifty years! and that he did not expect he would stay in the place but a very short time!" Rayner was outraged at the portrayal of "the Father of the Spirits of all Flesh — as a sort of travelling Deity," but he observed that this was a frighteningly popular notion.[36] Salvation had been turned into a straightforward mercenary transaction, a limited-time offer by a busy God available through revivalist-agents, who presumably worked on commission for every soul delivered. Once theological thinking had reached this point, Universalists concluded, any number of doctrinal perversions could be expected.[37]

With truly impressive persistence, Universalists sounded the warning that all rationality was being driven out of religion and that superstition, even a kind of madness, was taking its place. In an 1829 sermon on revivals delivered at Pawtucket, Rhode Island, Jacob Frieze asked how a man could believe that "his salvation depends *entirely* on God and *partly* on *himself?*" Rational people could not accept this notion, so in modern revivals subjects had to be "driven out of their senses, before they could consent to such preposterous absurdities." Successful revivalists set the right atmosphere and made declamatory assertions with no arguments, reasoning, or proof; they sought only to arouse the passions of the audience.[38] Another Universalist averred that, instead of appealing to reason or the testimony of the Bible, revivalists relied on "cant phrases," such as "getting religion," to win converts. Religion was thus reduced to superstition, resulting in a fearful, bigoted, persecuting spirit.[39] At revivals, the "credulous and timid" souls reacted to the prospect of God's spirit among them with "the sort of blind alarm once inspired by Salem witches or legions of demons," Russell Streeter complained.[40]

In Universalist eyes, the dangerous effects of revivalism were nowhere more manifest than in the immediate aftermath of such irrational outbursts. Revivalists, they maintained, were "fomenters of fanaticism," who stirred up a frightening religious mania.[41] Before midcentury, hardly a Universalist paper was complete without the obligatory story of the latest suicide provoked by religious frenzy. A man who attempted to murder his wife with an ax following a revival meeting was only bearing the "legitimate fruits of revivals."[42] After a four-day meeting in New Canaan, Connecticut, it was reported that a participant had killed his two children while in a state of "aberration of mind."[43] Thomas Whittemore, long-time editor of the Universalist *Trumpet*, diligently recounted the numbers of people who committed suicide or became insane after attending revivals.[44] A man named Calvin Easton from Pennsylvania, driven insane by the conviction that he was a reprobate, was merely "another among the many instances, which daily occur, of the awful consequences of the violent mode of conversion."[45] The authenticity of many of these tales is, of course, questionable, but Universalists believed they illustrated the folly of revivalism and saw them as an effective way to cast doubt on an evangelicalism that seemed to flee from all rationality in religious belief.

Menzies Rayner, more tolerant of the evangelical spirit than most of his Universalist brethren, admitted that some good could come out of revivals, since people were moved at least to think about religious questions and perhaps to join churches. But, in general, he believed the negative aspects far outweighed the positive, with a decided increase in "infidelity and skepticism." Religion was made to consist of "alternating paroxisms [*sic*] of despair and horror and ecstacy [*sic*] and rapture." Was it any wonder, then, that those with neither the time nor inclination to consider the subject "should conclude that the whole of religion is but a farce, in which the priests are the chief actors?"[46] Jacob Frieze concluded hopefully, if prematurely, in 1829 that revivalism was on the wane, since people had now begun to examine religious issues on their own.[47] Certainly, Frieze was much more optimistic than most Universalists, who feared that the collapse of a rationally defensible theology spelled the rise of ignorant zealotry, increasing apathy, and even hostility to religion.

Universalists believed that the rapid growth of Methodism epitomized the rise of utterly "mindless" religion, and they took frequent swipes at the movement. As an itinerant preacher during the first decade of the century, Nathaniel Stacy was among those who often competed with Methodists. Since the doctrine of universal salvation addressed itself to the rational understanding and not, like Methodism, to the animal passions, Universalists could not employ the fear of endless woe to "make those rapid and sweeping strides which Methodism was then making."[48] Methodism, he stated, was antithetical to the intelligent discussion of religious ideas. Recalling an 1809 Methodist sermon, Stacy summed up the ability of the minister by calling him "the most ignorant blockhead I have ever heard attempt to address a congregation." This man's main goal had been to "blackguard Calvinism, but the poor fellow knew no more about Calvinism than he did about the man in the moon. He stamped, raved and foamed a long time about 'lection,' but finally contented himself by saying, 'but I don't believe that.' "[49]

Similarly, George Rogers, who commonly encountered Methodists on his broad travels in the 1820s and 1830s, declared that "the mass of Methodists do not know what they believe or why." Methodist theology was a "bunch of tangled yarn, full of knots and kinks"; the movement itself was characterized mostly "by the wild rant and extravagance of its advocates."[50] D. J. Mandell, a pastor at Westbrook, Maine, reflected the common Universalist opinion that Methodism had replaced worn-out dogma with enthusiasm. The hero of Mandell's "Bunyanic narrative" did not venture into the "Halls of Methodism," having been warned that the place was designed "chiefly to make proselytes—to enfetter and enfeeble the mind and confine it to thralldom."[51] The idea that a movement lacking a clear belief could become so popular was immensely disturbing to Universalists.

Revivalism, as Bernard Weisberger recognizes, tended to reduce the differences between denominations to the point of unrecognizability, as serious discussion of religious issues retreated to the seminaries. Few people, and especially few revivalists, he notes, cared to ask whether this lessened theological concern involved a "cheapening process."[52] Universalists, though, refused to accept the assumption that specific tenets of belief were unimportant. Viewing themselves as inheritors of the Reformation, articulating anew a long-obscured insight, they insisted on the continuing need for rationality in religion.

Thus, it was the need to rescue coherent theology from what they saw as the mangling efforts of the evangelicals that gave Universalist leaders such a sense of purpose and mission in the 1830s. While they took on the role of gadflies attacking the massive organism of evangelicalism, most did not envision a permanently negative role. They were convinced that, after evangelical theology had been exposed and defeated, the acceptance of Universalism would follow; they assumed that, once the grip of evangelical tyranny had been broken, Universalism would be revealed naturally as the embodiment of Christian truth. Criticism of evangelical theology thus became a Universalist form of evangelism; rarely did Universalists consider what they would do if and when revivalism cooled.

Exposing Evangelical Priestcraft

Universalist fears about burgeoning evangelical growth focused particularly on what seemed to be the expanding power of the clergy over the minds and lives of Americans. Advocates of Universalism warned that a perverse evangelical culture, in which ministers exercised enormous power, was quickly taking root. Not only did evangelical religion lack solid theological underpinnings, it also unabashedly employed the tactics of fear and intimidation to bring about conversion. The main trends in American religion thus appeared profoundly unsuited to a free and rational people. While Universalists in general showed confidence in the ultimate triumph of theological rationality, they worried openly about the spiritual damage they saw in their own day.

Shameless emotional and psychological manipulation were the revivalists' tools in trade, Universalists charged: "innocent and harmless" people suffered from the terror inflicted by "theatrical preachers." Because of weak-mindedness or intellectual cowardice, common folk remained cowed by crafty ministers, who were interested mostly in accumulating great numbers of converts. Universalist writers liked to point to the typical postrevival rush to gather converts and the evangelical obsession with the number of souls saved. In one particular competition with the Presbyterians, a Universalist journal noted, the Baptists had garnered more members by promising an especially exalted Baptist heaven.[53]

According to such Universalist critiques, revivalism demonstrated the boundlessness of human guile and the endless possibilities for emotional manipulation. A two-part article in the 1825 *Gospel Advocate* entitled "The Way to Get Up a Revival" sought to depict the cynical attitude that Universalists believed lay behind revivalism. A revival leader needed to persuade his audience that, despite common assumptions to the contrary, people were free to control their own destiny, while God was "tolerably anxious to save man." A good, violent storm could always help to start things rolling, but barring that, a revivalist could create his own atmosphere with images of fire, smoke, brimstone, and the wrath of God. Easily frightened, women were the first to become "awakened." Those already under conviction could "stand within the fold and watch the farce played off upon others."[54]

Hosea Ballou elaborated on the charge that revival leaders deliberately worked on women, who seemed more susceptible to "gloomy fears"; some ministers, he claimed, acknowledged the expectation that, in many cases, more women than men would be saved.[55] Revivalists used "weak and credulous females," a Universalist paper contended in 1826, to influence other family members. Even children were "regularly cheated out of their gingerbread money" to support religious causes of which they were barely aware.[56] Another writer insisted that evangelical clergymen sought to entrap people by deliberately waiting until families were made vulnerable by sickness or the absence of male members, "since females are less acquainted with theological investigation." He related the story of a Unitarian woman whose sister had just died and who was informed by a minister that the death was a chastisement for her own false faith.[57]

Since ministers now attributed at least as much responsibility to themselves as to God for rescuing souls from the brink of hell, it was not surprising that they used such "arrogant" methods, Universalists concluded. But evangelicals went about their duties almost blithely, the Universalist preacher and journalist Abel Thomas asserted, considering that they thought they could help determine the eternal fate of millions of people. If they really believed their theory of endless punishment, "they would either preach it with more burning words or go mad or both," he insisted.[58] Universalist critics predicted that clerical efforts to assume spiritual authority were likely to backfire altogether, leading to a rejection of all religious sentiment. Reflecting on his confrontation with revivalists in the early 1830s, George Rogers declared that contemporary Protestantism had led to an atmosphere not only of oppressiveness but also of demoralization. People did not reject religion because of any innate antipathy toward it, he instructed his readers, but because of the "corruptions with which it has been mixed up, and the oppressions which have been practiced under its alleged sanction."[59]

Universalist critics were concerned with more than simple doctrinal brainwashing; they worried about the actual social power of ministers over their congregations. As Donald Scott notes, many nineteenth-century evangelicals thought that the "whole fabric of life outside specific institutions surrounding the church" was completely hostile to the sacred. Unlike colonial churchmen, who saw "the sacred and the profane entwined in all things," some evangelicals commonly saw it as their duty to "encourage a kind of quarantine against the world"; not incidentally, their own authority was thus enhanced.[60] In some cases, evangelical churches reserved the right to supervise practically all aspects of their members' behavior, from political activity to the use of leisure time and even to the choice of friends and acquaintances.[61] Among Universalists, this effort to protect the godly regenerate from the ungodly influences of the world smacked of further arrogance. Russell Streeter claimed that revivalists pressured converts to "give up the rose-bud of innocent amusement for the bramblebush of dread superstition"; females, he believed, were particularly vulnerable to control through the "deformities of sub-Calvinism."[62] Universalists could abide neither the evangelical clergy's vision of social guardianship nor its avowed goal to seek the salvation of those still outside its dominion.[63]

In Universalist eyes, the Bible and Tract societies and the missionary efforts that were well established by the 1820s and 1830s were ominous evidence of the increasing power of evangelical leaders. Universalists regarded missions, rapidly becoming the most popular of evangelical causes, as "cunning devices . . . designed to fleece

the ignorant of their hard earnings."[64] Mission societies, "insinuating themselves
into houses, as the fibres of a cancer do into a body," would even plunder a poor
woman for her bed ticking, a Universalist magazine charged.[65] Universalist critics
condemned most American missionary work as both a logical by-product of twisted
theological thinking and as the highest form of clerical arrogance. Hosea Ballou
made caustic comments on the theological assumptions behind missions, noting
that "money is far better now than it was in the sixteenth century." Then, it had
only released a soul from purgatory, but now a few pennies in the mission box
would "save a soul from hell, the dreadful state of the eternally miserable. What a
wonderful discovery this!"[66]

Universalists did not object to attempts to spread Christianity to foreign lands.
But their perception of the evangelical zeal for missions was somewhat akin to
Lenin's view of capitalism's imperialist lust for expanding markets. Evangelicals,
Universalists contended, needed the prospect of the unsaved heathen to stir the
hearts of the faithful; the missionary enterprises supplied fresh converts to feed a
growing operation. The Reverend T. G. Farnsworth, pastor of the First Universalist
Society of Haverhill, Massachusetts, spoke for many of his colleagues when he
wondered in 1829 how anyone could doubt that, through missions, many ministers
were pursuing not the salvation of the heathen but their own "aggrandizement and
power."[67]

Suspicious of the motives of evangelical leaders and convinced of the power of
their own rational doctrine to transform both the individual and society, Universalists demonstrated little insight into the appeal of evangelical culture. It has been
argued that revivalism harnessed the "collective psychic energy" of the new and
ever-expanding nation.[68] Evangelical Protestantism became a kind of national
church, charged with maintaining the moral order.[69] Perry Miller thought that when
revivalists summoned sinners to conversion they were at the same time "asserting
the unity of a culture in pressing danger of fragmentation."[70] The extent to which
evangelicalism really did foster a kind of cultural unity has been disputed.[71] Universalists, for their part, believed that it was a fragile, even illusory, unity built out
of fear on a theology of shifting sand. Even in an era made anxious by the nature
of free government, sectional tensions, a lawless frontier, increased mobility, and
the specter of deism and rationalism, Universalists left little room for emotional or
social sanctuary.[72] Universalism remained a movement for the intellectually vigorous, the confident, the buoyant.

The Threat of (Presbyterian) Theocracy

Universalist preachers and writers identified the self-styled orthodox as the most
ambitious and probably the most dangerous of the evangelicals. By the 1830s, their
fears were focused especially on the Presbyterians and Congregationalists, formidable groups that appeared guilty of trying to establish and extend political power
through the imposition of Calvinism. Beneath a veil of egregious theological inconsistencies, the forces of orthodoxy were working to achieve total social and religious control, Universalists feared. The willingness of the orthodox to profess Ar-

minianism in order to compete in the evangelical fray betrayed their thirst for power. Universalists worried that the "Presbygational" clergy, threatened by disestablishment and frightened by the new currents of thought that had arisen in the wake of the Revolution, were attempting to erect a new structure of dominance on the ruins of Calvinist doctrine.

Universalists were by no means alone in their fears over "Calvinist designs for social control"; the same concerns were widespread among groups such as the Methodists, Christians, and Baptists.[73] But Universalists had a particularly pressing reason to sound an alarm about the growth of church-state connections, for the profession of belief in universal salvation could have serious legal consequences in the first half of the nineteenth century. The common law borrowed from England required that those who participated in legal proceedings avow belief in a Supreme Being and a system of rewards and punishments; thus, Universalists were often lumped legally with nonbelievers. The Judiciary Act of 1789 had left the determination of the competency of a witness to testify up to the states; more often than not, Universalists were disqualified. In a famous 1827 case, Justice Joseph Story of the U.S. Circuit Court in Providence (later, of the Supreme Court) excluded a witness because he was a Universalist. A Unitarian, Story followed the recommendation of Moses Stuart of the Andover Theological School that Universalists should not testify. Stuart further asserted that no Universalist should hold public office.[74] In matters such as this, Universalist concern went far beyond polemical sport.

Universalists worried that a new "clerical aristocracy" would find a vulnerable population willing to acquiesce in its control, out of either latent religious fear or a desire for the moral regulation of society.[75] As one Universalist journal warned in 1831, a clerical elite was employing numerous means to "enslave our country"; liberty and independence were now more endangered by "priestcraft" than at any time since the Revolution.[76] The organization of the National Tract Society in New York (1825) was powerful evidence of an intention to impose a pernicious Calvinism upon the whole country. "None but Calvinists" comprised the publishing committee, despite the public notice that the society would serve all denominations.[77] The society, according to a Universalist newspaper, aimed for a *"national religious establishment and test."*[78] In light of such fears, it is hardly surprising that some Universalists, despite their harsh indictment of most evangelical religious groups on theological grounds, could occasionally express a sense of common cause with other popular movements, including Methodism.[79]

The threat to freedom posed by powerful clerical forces seemed increasingly real. Universalists reported that the secretary of state for New York, working in conjunction with the New York State Tract Society, had arranged to have Calvinist tracts distributed to schools and read at annual celebrations. Such widespread propagandizing in the common schools was a key part of an effort to join church and state.[80] Similarly, the Sunday school movement had become an instrument of "clerical aggrandizement,"[81] a form of "juvenile conscription," and a tool of indoctrination.[82] The American Sunday School Union was, in Universalist eyes, a "mammoth establishment for uniting Church and State," with leaders fattened on the "credulity of the public."[83] As with revivals and missions, it was not the principle that Universalists opposed; they had always advocated religious instruction for youth, had established their first Sunday school in Philadelphia in 1816, and continued to develop materials for religious education.[84] Rather, they feared what they saw as the sectarian emphasis and political goals of orthodox schools. Those goals were evident as well in the move to end Sunday mails. As a front-page article in one denominational newspaper announced, the ultimate aim was "ecclesiastical supremacy in all our concerns, public and private, temporal as well as spiritual."[85]

By the early 1830s, some Universalists had come to regard Presbyterian expansion with the same intense suspicion that other Protestants reserved for Catholic activity. A long series of articles in the *Sentinel and Star in the West*, a major western Universalist organ published in Cincinnati, elaborated on the Presbyterian plot, under the direction of Philadelphian Ezra Stiles Ely, "to establish Presbyterianism by law, to the exclusion of all other modes of worship." The writer attempted to prove that the Presbyterian clergy had formed a "secret combination" at the time of the adoption of the federal Constitution and were determined to force all citizens to submit to their form of worship. The "aristocratic and exclusive spirit" of the Presbyterian form of church government, he argued, was directly opposed to republicanism.[86]

The dangerous connection between church and state, another Universalist writer maintained, had begun in ancient times under Emperor Constantine, who was hailed by the clergy as a great leader and protector of the church. In the United States, a similar spirit now prevailed as candidates for office found it necessary to align themselves with a prominent sect.[87] Zelotes Fuller warned that great sums of money were being used to effect a union between church and state. In discourses delivered at the Second Universalist Church in Philadelphia in 1828 and 1829, he predicted that the "vast machinery of orthodoxy" aimed to monopolize the printing presses of the country and take control of institutions of learning. Those who wished to preserve religious liberty had to rise up against the "ecclesiastical tyranny" of Ely and the "Christian" political party.[88]

The same preacher spoke for many Universalists in charging that, among the established churches, the doctrine of eternal punishment was now most significant as a political tool, not as a deeply held religious belief. The threat of hell still appeared to be a frighteningly effective device for maintaining clerical authority. Johnson Mewhinney, a Universalist from Huntsville, Ohio, recalled that it was "the fear of hell" that had enabled the Catholic priests of Europe to "appropriate to themselves the fat of the land." In a country like the United States, the new "priests"—specifically, the Presbyterians under the command of Ely—were more dangerous than the political demagogues because people were far more hesitant to question the motives of clerical leaders. But the specter of endless hell that these leaders invoked was a withering remnant of the ages of European darkness and oppression, Mewhinney declared; it did not belong in a country of "Republican simplicity."[89]

P. T. Barnum agreed with this perspective. One of the lesser known aspects of the famous showman's life was his early role as a religious controversialist on the side of the Universalists. His biographer notes that Barnum "brooded about aristocratic combinations and overzealous Christians." Indeed, it was partly this concern about the drift of the age that prompted him in 1831 to begin a newspaper, the

Herald of Freedom, to "oppose all combinations against the liberties of our country." Living in conservative Connecticut as a Jacksonian Democrat, Barnum became something of a "backwoods Voltaire" in his crusade against churchly power.[90]

The growth of theocratic tendencies, like the other evils of the day, was for Universalists ultimately traceable to the disregard for theological meaning that accompanied evangelicalism. Only the adoption of coherent and reasonable theological beliefs, they insisted, would protect the country from such a contagion. Universalists thus distinguished themselves from those who had "cut themselves loose from all restraints and rejected all guides," those "who are perpetually crying *Liberty! Liberty!*"[91] While religious populists, such as the Christians and Baptists, condemned as oppressive the entire doctrinal orientation of Calvinism, Universalists believed that the main problem was wrong doctrine, not doctrine itself. O. A. Skinner declared positively that "doctrine is the omnipotent agent by which the world is to be carried forward to its glorious destiny, and by which every reform is to be effected."[92] A reasoned, objective faith was the essential safeguard of true Christian freedom.

Fellow Sufferers (of Bigotry)

In light of the intense aversion of most Universalists to ecclesiastical authority of any sort, the relative tolerance they showed toward Roman Catholicism is likely to be surprising at first glance. Indeed, as anti-Catholic forces began to gather strength in the late 1820s and 1830s, Universalists seemed less disturbed by Catholic expansion than by the course of American Protestantism.[93] This comparatively accepting attitude toward Catholics can be understood by referring both to broader attitudes and to more immediate concerns.

Although Catholicism certainly represented a form of priestcraft in Universalist eyes, it was a relatively old and weak one, hardly as powerful a threat as the new Protestant orthodoxy. Moreover, it hardly made sense to be especially wary of an influx of Catholics at a time when the overwhelmingly predominant Protestant theology increasingly resembled Catholic teaching. Thus, for instance, several articles in the *Gospel Advocate* argued forcefully that, while Protestants still formally affirmed Calvinist doctrine, only their name separated them from Catholicism and the outward acknowledgment of the role of human merit. One had only to observe that "the taste for Bible and Mission Societies had increased to a *mania*" to appreciate that Protestants aimed to attain heaven through their works. A more recent development, the *Advocate* noted, was the "Catholicizing" of the Protestant attitude toward church membership. Catholics held that there was no salvation outside the church, a belief Protestants had once clearly rejected. Yet a current publication from the American Tract Society strongly implied that acceptance of Calvinist dogma was essential for salvation.[94]

While Universalists could not be called supporters of Catholicism, their criticisms of it were often muted, and they were at times defenders of Catholic rights against overly zealous Protestants. Compared with militant Presbyterianism, Catholicism could often seem a distant and fairly irrelevant European relic. Universalists could even identify with Catholics as fellow sufferers of intolerance. Universalist minister Thomas J. Sawyer agreed that Roman Catholics in New York and Philadelphia had valid reasons for opposing the reading of the Protestant King James version of the Bible in public schools. Many Universalists believed that colleges, as well as public and private schools, practiced blatant religious discrimination. Universalists criticized every New England college between 1830 and 1850 for sectarian bias; they charged that institutions such as Dartmouth, Brown, Williams, and Amherst were but thinly veiled theological schools. And when, in 1849, the Massachusetts legislature denied a charter to the Roman Catholic Holy Cross College because it would be sectarian, Thomas Whittemore suggested that Harvard, Amherst, and Williams should, to be fair, yield their charters as well.[95]

Any religious group that was so reviled by the orthodox was sure to receive some sympathy from Universalists, whose own sense of identity was closely tied to their experience of struggle against intolerance and persecution. In 1831, a Universalist writer called attention to the fact that the influential Lyman Beecher was now focusing his "copious outpourings of sectarian malice and orthodox bigotry on the Catholics," having vented his rage fully against the Unitarians, Universalists, and Quakers. The author predicted that such warfare would promote rather than injure the Catholic cause. "I am far from being a Catholic," he remarked, but he could not "stand by and hear with indifference, that whole denomination proscribed as *anti-Christian* and not worthy to be called '*American citizens*.' "[96] The editor of the Universalist *Christian Intelligencer*, William Drew, lauded the 1833 election of a Roman Catholic priest as chaplain of the U.S. Senate because it showed "evidence of a republican and liberal spirit . . . which would treat all sects with equal courtesy and exclude none on account of its peculiar religious sentiments."[97]

Some Universalists showed even greater tolerance, arguing that the Roman Catholic idea of purgatory was more Christian than orthodox Protestantism's view of the afterlife. This view might be expected in a denomination that was moving toward restorationism. Catholicism's inclusion of a large middle ground between heaven and hell could appeal to those who, while rejecting the notion of endless punishment, were increasingly open to the idea of retribution in the hereafter. Abel Thomas believed that purgatory fostered sympathy and hope and encouraged people to pursue strenuous moral efforts for the good of their souls; by contrast, Protestant theology offered only "appalling desolation."[98]

Perhaps the "Occasional Sermon" delivered in 1846 before the Maine Convention of Universalists at Bangor illustrates Universalism in its most expansive mood toward Catholicism. We complain of Catholic corruptions, the orator reflected, but need to consider that such problems developed in a dark age. The seemingly perverse notion of clerical celibacy may well have been necessary to stamp out licentiousness. We do not care for the idea of a pope but need to recognize the one important truth underlying the office: the church is ultimately subject to a single divine head, whose gospel is infallible and authoritative. This anonymous speaker was clearly willing to acknowledge that Catholicism had made substantial contributions to the understanding of Christian truth.[99] His remarks were another reflection of the common Universalist interest in Christian history; this preacher was unprepared simply to dismiss a thousand years or more of religious experience. The contributions of evangelical contemporaries rarely fared so well in Universalist critiques.

To be sure, Universalists were by no means consistent supporters of Catholic rights, and some did succumb to the popular paranoia over the spread of Catholicism. Prominent Universalist editors like Whittemore and Sylvanus Cobb expressed their fears about Catholic influence in America.[100] To the extent that Universalists did defend the Catholic cause, it was at least in part a self-conscious demonstration of the tolerance and fair-mindedness of the denomination. But it also appears that Universalists, ever eager for controversy, had few surer ways of stirring up thundering debate on crucial issues than by coming to the defense of the hated and feared Catholics; there was perhaps no better way of jabbing at their evangelical opponents. Here again, they showed the vitality of their movement by their refusal to echo the common line and by their comparative indifference to popularity.

Lightening Up

Universalists continued to attack evangelical culture throughout the nineteenth century, but their criticisms were becoming less acerbic by the 1840s. Part of the reason was that revivalism itself was clearly in decline. As manuals instructed potential leaders on effective tactics, the revival process gradually became standardized and formalized. Moreover, as revivalist John Woodbridge noted in 1841, the pursuit of a nondoctrinal evangelical unity through a variety of benevolent and religious associations had produced a "homogeneous mass of neutrality and insipidity" regarding spiritual matters.[101] Evangelicalism, though still a powerful social force, was beginning to lose its hold over the national psyche. As a result, its Universalist critics, having experienced remarkable growth in the 1820s and 1830s, seemed to relax somewhat. One sign of this change is the rise of more openly humorous and satirical polemics.

The writings of itinerant minister George Rogers reflect the partial relaxation of Universalist attitudes. In 1837, Rogers published a serious and exhaustive answer to Universalist critics, *The Pros and Cons of Universalism*. But, by the 1840s, he had turned to humor to show why Universalists believed evangelicals were giving religion a bad name and why they were convinced that a mongrel Calvinism would eventually yield to a more rationally acceptable religious belief. In his eighteen forty-one *Tales from Life, Designed to Illustrate Certain Religious Doctrines Which Prevail at the Present Day*, Rogers wryly observed that, in one typical town, "although the *souls* of sinners were professedly the main objects of solicitude," much strife followed conversion "as to which [minister] should have the body. It may be owing to the body's superior tangibility." Moreover, he noted that, as farms rose in value, "souls of sinners became more precious in the estimation of the clergy." A Mr. Lumpkin, who was "young, lazy and foolish," was typical of those recruited to be revivalists. Even his clerical brethren admitted that he was a "pitiful lackbrain." But he was tall and gaunt and possessed a sepulchral voice with which to "frighten people of small intellect into a reunion with the church"; other ministers could take it from there.[102]

Five years later, in 1846, Rogers turned to full-blown satire to demonstrate his conviction that evangelicalism was fast exposing its own vulnerabilities. His *Adventures of Triptolemus Tub* related conversations between Tub, "a very pious man," and Shadrach Paddle, a goblin from hell. Moderately honest "as times go," Tub had one all-redeeming quality: he was "most orthodox in faith," particularly in respect to the article of endless damnation. This teaching did not imply his own damnation, of course: "none but fools, or very nervous people, believe in their own damnation." His smug certainties about hell and damnation were shaken by the appearance of Paddle, who informed him that his mother, a most inoffensive sort, had ended up in hell because of her failure to be born again. But hell was "far more respectable than most people imagine," Paddle assured Tub. A great many virtuous people now resided there because "they did not also get religion—a thing they might have got very cheaply—and at the last extremity."

True, ministers now admitted people could get to heaven without believing in Christ or being born again, added Paddle, but only if they had not heard the gospel and had "lived pretty decently." In the good old days, he reminded Tub, it was one saved to every thousand damned. Then, a Methodist or a Socinian or a papist had no chance, but now either heaven had become more capacious "or the gatekeeper had become remiss in examining the passports." Devil's advocate that he was, Paddle could not restrain himself:

> He he! At this rate, Mr. Tub, we shall all be in heaven by and by, the devil himself will be saved, and the great bonfire put out, which at the expense of so much sulfur, has been kept burning so long for the accommodation of wicked and heretical spirits. Only keep on improving your theology and that will be the upshot of it someday.

With the observation that "your theology is all in a snarl . . . an inextricably tangled affair," Paddle departed.[103]

Universalists believed that popular theology had tied itself in knots, but as the *Tub* stories attest, they were now able to indulge in lighthearted needling rather than consistently heated and serious disputation. Indeed, the sort of mocking tone employed in Rogers's writings grows notably more prevalent in literature from the 1840s. A comical piece in an 1847 *Gospel Banner*, published in Augusta, Maine, typifies the trend. Declaring in a funeral sermon that any man who died in an unregenerate state would be condemned to hell, the minister went on to exhort his mourning listeners to make their salvation sure and pleaded especially for the soul of the widow, asking that she be reunited with her husband. "Parson, parson," the widow shouted, "would you send me to hell also?"[104]

Such uses of humor and satire, however, were still essentially negative; they did little to further a shared sense of the practical purpose and direction of the Universalist movement. And even if many Universalists did develop a more relaxed attitude as revivalism declined, the general penchant for ridicule of others' teachings did not disappear. Even in the 1850s, with their denomination well established and finally gaining acceptance, Universalists were often quicker to denounce error in others than to elaborate on the meaning of their own teachings. The publication in 1853 of Edward Beecher's *The Conflict of Ages* afforded them the perfect chance to continue their critique of efforts to revise and update orthodox teachings.[105]

With five printings in three months, Beecher's book created a significant theological and commercial splash. Like Origen in the third century, Beecher looked to the idea of preexistence of souls to resolve the disjunction between evident human depravity and the belief in God's honor and justice. He posited that free individuals had chosen sin in a previous existence but were granted the opportunity for recovery and redemption in the "moral hospital" of the world. By reconciling conflicting Christian doctrines, Beecher hoped to become a kind of "moral Copernicus."[106] Universalist critics could not resist using the appearance of his book to underscore what they saw as the sad, even desperate, state of mainline theology. They ridiculed the work mercilessly as Calvinism confused and grasping for meaning.[107]

While some Universalist publicists criticized Beecher in serious and systematic fashion, many still relished the opportunity to do what they did best: make orthodoxy look absurd. They could not resist poking fun at a member of the illustrious Beecher clan, a prime target for their instinctive egalitarianism. Characteristically, they were more eager to fault Beecher for trying to save orthodoxy than to explore, in clear fashion, the practical ramifications of their own doctrine. By the 1850s, when it was necessary to beat the bushes to find a real orthodox Calvinist, at least in the North, such polemics were becoming almost superfluous and were hardly testimony to the development of a distinctive and coherent Universalist movement.

A Movement or a Church?

Universalism probably reached its high point in relative strength around 1847–1848. The seventh U.S. Census (1850) listed Universalists among twenty-one major sects and reported 529 churches in twenty-two states, but after 1850, Universalism seems to have lost ground in relation to other denominations and total population growth.[108] By the late 1840s and early 1850s, prominent Universalists had begun to sense that their movement had reached a critical stage. But in calling for stronger denominational development, Universalist clergy and scholars were not necessarily reflecting the desires of most Universalist laymen. For many of its traditionally cantankerous and independent adherents, Universalism remained more significant as a theological movement than as an organized church.

Around midcentury, a number of Universalist thinkers took to warning their fellows that they needed to reform their contentious ways. Thomas J. Sawyer, a well-known minister, warned in 1849 against the continuing tendency to unite "for the negative purpose of opposing some prevalent opinion or practice."[109] A writer for the *Universalist Quarterly* commented in 1850 that Universalism had entered a "calmer era"; he advised ministers to do less "controversial preaching" and avoid a single-minded and potentially counterproductive dwelling on universal salvation.[110]

Leaders could point to other factors that they believed were limiting or even retarding the denomination. Otis A. Skinner singled out the lack of insistence upon a profession of faith for membership in a Universalist church; Universalism seemed to be without any solid foundation. Universalists did not have to become "mere sectarists" or "surrender truth," Skinner advised, but church members did need to settle on a definite creed in order to join together in a "harmony of effort."[111] Another writer agreed that Universalists demonstrated a decided lack of "Christian confidence" in their hesitancy to embrace religious professions. They were guilty of "inconclusiveness" and "always heaping up materials but never building the house."[112] Skinner also expressed a growing perception among Universalist ministers that the denomination's churches needed to enter into a more definite system of organization; such a system would allow for a "concert of action" that was unobtainable under mere congregationalism.[113] The prominent minister Elbridge Gerry Brooks was among those who worried about the movement's lack of organization, discipline, and direction, and he called for the "orderly exercise of liberty."[114]

Historically averse both to creedal forms and to centralization, however, Universalists throughout the 1850s generally resisted such exhortations. Universalist laymen, especially, opposed more centralized administrative power; the "antifederalism" of the early movement was still much in evidence. Most congregations still openly balked at giving the General Convention, the national governing body, greater authority over teachings or practice. Thus, even as Universalism achieved such outward successes as the chartering of colleges and a more stable, educated clergy, most of its leaders were far from sanguine about the future of the denomination. They were convinced that theirs was the appropriate religious movement for the times: it had neither the "offensive dogmas of orthodoxy" nor the "hesitating indecision of the Unitarians."[115] Yet, as a group, Universalists seemed to know better what they were not than what they were.

From the 1840s on, denominational presses issued a widening stream of writings that expressed discomfort with and even hostility to various trends in Universalist thought and action. Many works reflected the concern that an eager embrace of humanitarianism and the ideals of moral reform demonstrated popular religion's increasing spiritual shallowness. An 1846 *Universalist Quarterly* article noted the popularity of great reform organizations, which attacked socially corrosive sins. Yet sin took innumerable and constantly changing forms, the author observed, and reformers only succeeded in reducing its outward manifestations. An inordinate faith in reform movements, he believed, indicated theological decline.[116] In an 1847 article, Hosea Ballou 2nd condemned the "common expectation" of earthly blessedness and blamed both the religious millennialists and the "speculatists," who saw human effort bringing on a golden age. Such a vision was the product of our "languor-loving, sickly, sentimental taste," he charged. Mortal life was "suffering and temptation."[117]

The flowering of humanitarian reform prompted a number of Universalist thinkers to reflect on the deleterious effects of the erosion of traditional Calvinism. Such writers, in fact, began to attribute whatever success their movement had enjoyed to its preservation of traditional Calvinist insights. After decades during which most Universalists had condemned the older form of Calvinism as a perverse, malevolent, and even blasphemous system, a significant group of denominational thinkers now showed a growing appreciation for their own Calvinist roots. They found less value than had earlier generations of Universalists in being perceived as religious outsiders, critics, and mavericks, waging war against a corrupt establishment; instead, they proved increasingly ready to locate themselves within the mainline of American religion. As a writer in the *Universalist Quarterly* recognized in 1849, "It might not be strictly correct to say, that Universalism is a natural offshoot of Calvinism; it may be more proper to call it a scion that was engrafted upon a Calvinist stock." The article recalled, for those who had forgotten or perhaps never knew, that Universalism had originally been defended on modified Calvinist principles: Christ died for the elect, meaning all people, not just a portion of mankind. Early Universalists had argued that God's justice was served in Christ, and they had managed to spread their doctrine because it was presented in an orthodox context.[118]

Several prominent Universalists suggested that their movement should now be a counterweight to the growing sentimentality in religion, the common tendency of the age, as E. A. Branch later described it, to sink into the "gentle delights of melancholia."[119] The denomination should act to repress the "grossest passions" and build bonds of sympathy among people, instead of engaging in "mawkishness."[120] The editors of the *Universalist Quarterly* expressed "deep interest," therefore, in what they viewed as "The Movement to Revive Calvinism." They saw in the new *American Theological Review*, edited by H. B. Smith and Joseph Tracy, a healthy assault on the exponents of "a diluted and mystified Calvinism." Many theologically minded Universalists were cheered by this effort to reestablish serious religion and to reassert belief in the absolute sovereignty of God.[121]

Thomas Thayer's widely used *Theology of Universalism* (1862) referred several times to Jonathan Edwards and the "great good sense" he demonstrated in *Freedom of the Will*.[122] Indeed, by this time, Edwards's reputation was undergoing an explicit rehabilitation among Universalists. While during the years of the Second Great Awakening Universalists had depicted him as the supreme fire-and-brimstone preacher, an 1866 *Universalist Quarterly* article described Edwards as the "St. Francis of New England," a "soul rapt with divine love." Calvinism taught that certain souls were immeasurably dear to God. "By dwelling on this theme, and stirring up the heavenly gratitude it was sure to awaken," Edwards and Samuel Hopkins had "profoundly influenced the theology of New England." Their "sainted spirits might not disdain to be called the father and promoter of American Universalism."[123] Such sentiments reflected a growing desire to throw off the common perception of Universalists as a disgruntled sect of antiorthodox agitators and a desire to be seen instead as the inheritors and defenders of the best elements not only of Christian thought generally but also of New England religion.

Historically, Calvinism had produced "vast benefits" by checking the tendency to mysticism and emphasizing logical understanding, a contributor to the *Quarterly* argued. "With iron hand, it has beaten the brains of a sickly sentimentality that would be wiser than Deity and more merciful than nature," he wrote. It provided necessary "veins of flint" even though it hardened the religious character.[124] A reviewer of Theodore Parker's *Sermons on Theism* appreciated the liberal religionist's theology but believed that he made a poor critic of Calvinism because he could not "estimate the secret life and hidden truths in creeds or sects whose verbal symbols are false or repulsive." Unlike current liberal forms of faith, Calvinism had "fed the ground-tier of religious emotions." Beneath the "barbarities" of its dogma, it understood that religion was more than "cheerfulness and joy."[125]

With the decline of Calvinism, Baltimore Universalist minister Otis Skinner lamented in 1856, God had been robbed of his supreme sway. In popular religious belief, there was no awe or majesty, no sense of irresistible power pervading the material and spiritual worlds; God was no more than a very amiable being. Belief in such a being did not engender positive faith or hope or quicken the soul; the religious spirit it awakened was "mere sentimentality," without true fervor or courage. Puritan piety, born of strong faith in God's sovereignty, was foreign in the new understanding.[126] But such piety was the foundation upon which Universalism had been erected, Skinner and numerous colleagues now argued. Universalism's distinctiveness as a movement, they implied, depended on the preservation of its historic orientation.

Unitarian Desolation

Universalists were obviously not Calvinists in any accepted sense of the term. How ought they to identify themselves, then? Were they to be called "liberals"? Here again, it is clear that Universalists were still surer about what they opposed than for what they commonly stood. A widespread concern at midcentury, for instance, was to distinguish the denomination from other liberal groups, particularly Unitarians. For the American public at large, Universalism and Unitarianism had always been identified as branches of a common liberal Christianity; toward midcentury this perception was becoming even stronger than before. It is, therefore, not surprising that Universalist spokesmen grew eager to point out significant differences between the two movements.

Universalists generally applauded the nineteenth-century trend to defend the dignity of human nature against the doctrines of original sin and reprobation, but some denominational thinkers charged Unitarians with going too far in their rejection of Calvinism and filling the mind with a "vain conceit." Ralph Waldo Emerson's remark about the English clergy—that the gospel they preach is "not by *grace* but by *taste* are ye saved"—could well be applied to them, one writer suggested. Universalists, he insisted, did not embrace the high Christian humanism of the Unitarians. The denomination had always been "not as Erasmus, but as Luther," concerned not so much with the dignity of human nature as with the defense of God's glory and honor.[127] The chief difference between Unitarianism and Universalism, according to George Emerson, was that the former saw human destiny in terms of the nature and capabilities of man, while the latter referred all destiny to the deity as the sovereign arbiter.[128]

Alonzo Miner felt compelled to warn Universalists in 1853 that they were drawing too close to the Unitarians, noting that, in zealously opposing "fanaticism," liberal Christians sometimes seemed to forget the necessity of regeneration. Allowing that conversion did not need to be thought of as miraculous in the evangelical sense of the word, he insisted that "divine truth" must operate on the soul, and he condemned talk of the influence of "culture, culture, culture!"[129] Such Universalist thinkers acknowledged that an emphasis on human ability had been an inevitable, understandable result of a growing estrangement from Calvinist forms. But they believed that Unitarianism, the most prominent liberal movement, was guilty of a concurrent abandonment of theology. In 1846, Ballou 2nd deplored the "dissolution of all attachments to systems of faith" and warned that the loss of a settled, definite faith would be attended by "confusion without and desolation within." He made it clear that he was referring particularly to the Unitarians, who exerted "a much greater and wider influence than is commonly supposed."[130]

Calling for a simple and sublime inner piety, Unitarians tended to avoid theological discussion. They were not inclined to criticize Calvinism nor expound on their own Arian teachings.[131] Indeed, the Unitarians' "shrinking from profound speculation" and desire to escape contention with orthodox Calvinists was increasingly in keeping with Victorian anti-intellectualism.[132] But Universalist critics maintained that, by "concealing the changes that it made in doctrine" and implying that "all religious doctrines were indifferent," Unitarianism was undermining true liberal religion. In the eyes of these Universalists, Theodore Parker's *Discourse on Religions*, which seemed to put Christianity on a par with other religions, was a predictable event in Unitarian history.[133]

The popular identification of Unitarianism as "liberal Christianity" was particularly galling to Universalists because, in their eyes, there was no great difference between Unitarians and Arminianized orthodoxy.[134] Until the Unitarians openly avowed universal salvation, Universalist critics insisted, they were not entitled to be termed leaders of the liberal religious movement. Hosea Ballou argued in 1844 that Unitarianism, "the religion which most loudly claims to be rational," actually promoted superstition. It happily charted the progress of human beings all the way to the grave, at which point it let down a veil of "dark mystery" and left people hanging in fear.[135] Universalists commonly assailed the timidity that, in their view, prevented Unitarians from professing a belief in universal salvation.[136]

The Unitarian refusal to embrace this teaching, Universalists suspected, was mainly a way of denying kinship with a group that had little social standing. Always sensitive to what they perceived as the social and intellectual condescension of the Boston-area elite, they charged that Unitarianism suffered from "indecision [and] timidity"; it was "foggy, cold in theological points" and had "a silly fear of losing caste."[137] Midcentury Universalist writers reacted with sarcasm to Unitarian accounts of the spread of liberal religion that completely ignored the Universalist movement. The Universalists, they proudly asserted, had been the first in America to preach "unitarianism."[138] For such critics, Universalism retained its specific identity through a sort of populist disassociation from the supposed leaders of liberal Christianity.

"The Growth and Tendency of the World"

Most denominational leaders took some satisfaction in what they believed was Universalism's enormous influence on the doctrinal changes of the era. Drumming on a consistent theme in Universalist literature, one midcentury columnist announced that the spread of the idea of universal salvation proved that "the Reformation had progressed" and that "Universalist theology alone represents the growth and tendency of the world."[139] The president of Tufts College, A. A. Miner, professed in 1862 to be unbothered by the fact that Methodists greatly outnumbered Universalists, even though the movements had grown up simultaneously. Methodism, he recalled, had been far less courageous than Universalism in the effort to modify a harsh Calvinism. More important, he asked:

> whether the influence of Universalism, outside of its own body, in infusing more Christian elements into the faith of other sects, has not affected a greater revolution of opinions, than the total change occasioned by the rise and growth of the Methodist church.[140]

Naturally, Miner's declaration could be viewed by his contemporaries as nothing more than an easy rationalization of Universalism's failure to keep pace with Methodism. Yet this denominational leader was articulating a sentiment that had been implicit in the movement all along: the success of Universalism could ultimately be measured not by growth in the size and number of Universalist churches but by public acceptance of the idea of universal salvation.

This attitude had deeply ambiguous implications for a denomination that felt it preached a crucial message with unique clarity but that had always struggled in the competition with other churches. It is hardly a surprise that even among leaders who accepted the idea that the spread of the belief in universal salvation and the success of their denomination were ultimately separate, dreams of a great proliferation of Universalist churches were not easily abandoned. During and after the Civil War, several writers expressed the hope that political Reconstruction would be accompanied by a "theological reconstruction," in which the Universalist denomination would reap the harvest it had been so long in sowing.

An image evoked in an 1865 *Universalist Quarterly* article, "Universalism: The Faith of the Future," is revealing. Universalists, the article stated eagerly, looked forward to the opening of the "tombs of our present theological inactivity and non-discussion" where "the warrior of the old creeds lies safely and snugly ensconced." Then, the "reason and thought of the nineteenth century" will "pour their unobstructed light upon his thoroughly oxidized form," and he will "crumble away."[141] In the face of obvious and widespread indifference to theological matters and stagnating growth in their ranks, many Universalists, clergy as well as laity, continued to nourish the hope that eventually a theological reawakening would bring their movement to a greater flowering. Even those adherents who linked their faith directly to moral and social progress commonly looked forward to a broad popular enlightenment that would send believers rushing to Universalist churches.

In fact, as we will see in chapter 6, their own central theological insight was rapidly becoming more an alternative theological position and less a damnable heresy. By the era around and following 1840, American Protestantism was generally becoming more ecclesiological and sacramental and less preoccupied with the salvation of the individual believer.[142] And, as the flames of evangelicalism died, Universalists found fewer and fewer positive bearings for their movement. By midcentury, their hope of maintaining themselves as the upholders of a distinctive popular form of liberal Christianity was fading.

Universal Redemption
and Social Reform

By the 1850s, when their denomination faced serious conflicts over its identity and direction, most Universalists tended to regard Hosea Ballou as a grandfatherly figure, a benign symbol of their heritage. His death in 1851 occasioned a genuine outpouring of grief among his spiritual heirs, who respected him as a great religious reformer; he was honored with a handsome statue in Mount Auburn Cemetery. But for a growing number of adherents, the doctrine of universal salvation was becoming less the crucial core of a saving faith, as it had been for Ballou, than a call to orderly moral reform in light of the brotherhood and perfectibility of humanity. This shift, in many respects a natural consequence of restorationist belief, manifested itself not only in theology but also in the participation of Universalists in various programs of social reform and in the expanding roles of women within the church. There was, nevertheless, no inherent or inevitable connection between Universalism and reform activity. Indeed, a survey of their involvement in social organizations and movements beyond their church will show that nineteenth-century Universalists shared few, if any, common assumptions about the social imperatives of their faith.

Freemasonry

Ballou had always stressed the cultivation of Universalism's central theological doctrine, and he had no definite vision of Christian social activity or involvement.

Significantly, the one nonchurch activity to which he consistently devoted himself was Freemasonry, a social and charitable movement that embodied universal principles. Like many Universalist men in the first decades of the century, he found the broad social ideals of his faith aptly expressed in Freemasonry. With imagined roots in the ancient world and direct antecedents in Enlightenment England, Freemasonry flourished in the young republic in part because growing industry, commerce, and geographic mobility had undermined community cohesion. Quoting a Masonic orator, Paul Goodman writes that Masonry gave men "of the most distant countries and of the most contradictory opinions" an opportunity for fraternal camaraderie and mutual support. In an increasingly transient world, "Masonry accommodated the needs of mobile men."[1]

Post-Revolution Masonry had initially stressed the generally secular, virtue-building aspect of its ideals, but it soon moved from a nonsectarian avowal of "universal love" and toleration toward an explicit identification with Christianity. Masonry, Steven Bullock observes, became "an enlightened middle way" between a "narrow and parochial sectarianism" and "an equally dangerous non-biblical rationalism." Moreover, unlike the increasingly specialized charity groups, Masons deliberately built a "universal organization," attempting "to create an enlightened family." The connection between Masonry and Christianity became more pronounced after 1820, when Masons were called to dedicate a variety of new church buildings by Baptists, Methodists, Episcopalians, and Universalists, among others.[2]

A fraternal, latitudinarian, but clearly Christian order, Freemasonry understandably proved immensely appealing to Universalists, who seem, along with Unitarians, "to have been proportionally over-represented" among religious groups within the order, according to Bullock.[3] Hosea Ballou and Elhanan Winchester were among the clergymen who joined the order early on. From the first decades of the nineteenth century, Universalists were notably active in Connecticut Freemasonry.[4] In Genesee County, New York, Masons assisted in the organization of at least four Universalist churches.[5] There was a strong Universalist association with Masonry in Massachusetts, where Adin Ballou and Hosea Ballou 2nd joined their relative in Masonic brotherhood. Paul Goodman asserts that, in Rhode Island, "the link to Universalism was a link to Freemasonry, for the state's leading preachers were prominent defenders of the Order." In Maine as well, prominent Masons tended to be Universalists.[6]

Those Universalists who joined the order evidently regarded Masonry as completely congruent with their religious faith, indeed, as a logical extension and reinforcement of it. In an address before the Grand Lodge of Rhode Island, Jacob Frieze, Universalist minister and lodge chaplain, asked, "What precept of benevolence can be more sublime than that of Masonry? 'We are the children of one common parent, by whom we are placed here, to aid, support and protect each other.' " Could there be, he wondered, "a more exalted view of charity?"[7] Hosea Ballou, who in 1811 was elected junior grand warden of the Grand Lodge of New Hampshire, also extolled the "brotherly love" of the order.[8] In an 1808 address in Windsor, Vermont, Ballou declared that, in Masonry, "men of different nations, of different colours, of different languages, of different religions and of different politics enter on the same level." There, "the Roman Catholic, the churchmen, with the whole band of various dissenters, meet the Jew and the Mahometan in the inviolable bonds of unaffected friendship." Masonry, he asserted, was "based on Geometry, which is the offspring of God himself" and "the first incontestable evidence of his existence which meets our rational senses."[9] Boston Universalist minister Paul Dean marveled that Masonry "moves us to delight in another's happiness and share in another's woe."[10]

In addition, Masonry's elaborate rituals and ceremonies probably proved an attractive complement to the simplicity of Universalist practice. In any case, a general Universalist affinity for Masonry in early nineteenth-century America was natural; both groups were responsive to the fragmentation of the organic community. As atomistic forces weakened the sense of the covenanted community in the late eighteenth and early nineteenth centuries, Universalism emphasized the divinely wrought bond of universal salvation. In a society with a developing market economy, transient workers, and a hardening class structure, Masonry seemed to give life to the Universalist ideal. It offered a cosmopolitan, nonsectarian, practical fraternalism for mobile young men in pursuit of self-improvement. The attraction of Masonry for Universalists is, therefore, no surprise.

That Masonic fellowship was restricted to men surely contributed to its appeal among early Universalists as well. We have noted the pervasiveness of paternalistic imagery in Universalist preaching and writing. The intellectually active men who found liberation from parochial religious attitudes in this message of God's universal fatherhood were likely to have shared a sense of their own rights and responsibilities as fathers or potential fathers, and among these "rights" was membership in a sort of universal men's club. Periodic escape from the burdens of domestic life — indeed, from the Christian "family" generally — was no doubt part of Masonry's powerful attraction; Ballou himself referred to the lodge as a "celestial retreat."[11] Yet, to some extent, these attitudes also simply reflected prevailing assumptions about gender roles in early nineteenth-century American society; they do not indicate any particularly strong bias among Universalists. In fact, we will see that the implicit egalitarianism of Universalist belief proved a weightier influence than inherited paternalism on the movement's bearing with regard to gender roles.

Despite the attractions Masonry posed, some Universalists came to see the social, political, and even religious ramifications of the lodges as incompatible with their faith. Most notably, Vermont Universalists enlisted in the Antimasonic political crusade that had been ignited by the 1826 disappearance in Batavia, New York, of William Morgan. Antimasons alleged that Morgan, who had broken the Masonic oath and published Masonic secrets, was kidnapped and murdered by Masons, who further conspired to cover up the incident. The affair crystalized suspicions about Masonry's threat to community integrity, republican equality, and revealed religion. Represented by such figures as minister Samuel Loveland, editor of the *Universalist Watchman*, Vermont Universalists viewed Antimasonry as a defense of the community, Christianity, and egalitarianism against the secularism and elitism symbolized by Masonry.[12]

As a frontier state, Vermont had been fertile ground for Universalist growth after the Revolution; here, the movement became a leading denomination, with fifty-seven societies in 1831. Despite continuing serious disagreements over Calvinist theology and evangelicalism, Vermont Universalists found common cause with Congregationalists and Baptists, forming an Antimasonic "odd coalition."[13] As members of an increasingly well-established and influential popular denomination, these Universalists perceived Masonry as socially corrosive and antithetical to their faith. While elsewhere they remained more of a minority and hence more open to Masonry's deliberately transconfessional appeal, in Vermont, where they were relatively numerous and somewhat more socially secure, Universalists were inclined to see competition and danger in such an organization. That Universalists in different regions developed such varying sentiments toward Masonry underlines the flexibility of their movement's social implications.

The Call to a New Labor

By midcentury, Universalists everywhere were increasingly agreed on the need to find definite social programs to express a faith that had long been sustained by little more than theological assertion. The Reverend A. R. Abbott was voicing a common perception among prominent Universalists in the 1850s when he observed that "as a denomination we are not now increasing; we have advanced but little for the last ten years though our distinctive faith never before in all history spread so rapidly." He attributed this slowness of growth partly to the fact that other churches had become aware of the competition for members and had not expelled those with Universalist sympathies. Yet Abbott placed greater blame on the denomination itself for its recent slide. "Hard-shelled" Universalists, who studied the Bible in order to argue with opponents and who found it "easier to fight for their faith than to live it," had set the tone for the denomination. Universalists ignored religious culture, particularly of the young; their efforts to establish Sunday schools lagged behind the work of the evangelicals. And no sect that relied mainly on an "appeal to the intellect" could or should prosper. Abbott complained that the Universalist church, far from being a conduit for Christian charity, had allowed the crucial work of social reform to be taken over by the great benevolent organizations. But Universalists now had a perfect opportunity to renew their denominational life. They were "called to a new labor" and needed to be "as active in this sphere as we have been in the promulgation and defense of our theological opinions."[14]

Taking a different perspective on the matter, a contributor to the *Universalist Quarterly* implied that the general decline of interest in theology was partly responsible for the slackened pace of growth. He argued that this decline had to be recognized and, in effect, accommodated. "The age of dogmatizing is passing away," he warned, and the future of religious discussion would henceforth be "more philosophic and less partizan [sic]." Meanwhile, however, the world rushed on with schemes of money making and pleasure and left the "ecclesiastic to croak to the winds." Universalists should therefore not go "begging for patronage" for their doctrine; indeed, eagerness to gain proselytes was a sign of religious poverty. "We do not suppose that the world is going to gravitate wholly to us, and accept our name and fight under our banner," he admitted, but this did not mean that Universalists had to resign themselves to the margins. They should, he proclaimed with a carefully chosen phrase, strive to be "a city set on a hill," and they could do this by becoming closely identified with humanitarian reform:

> Those great humanitarian enterprises that are the outbirth of this age—such as the anti-slavery and temperance enterprises, and others of a kindred nature . . . are only our faith put into works, confirming the faith and preparing the world for its wider spread.[15]

Such exhortations by denominational leaders give the strong impression of a group quite self-consciously trying to play catch up with better-organized churches in an age when social and religious realities were changing faster than ever before. The realm of education provides a good example of this rush to compete in new projects and programs. The sense that the times demanded more formal and extensive schooling seems to have overtaken Universalist thinkers rapidly as the Second Great Awakening ebbed. "We are the most liberal sect of the age," a *Universalist Quarterly* commentator wrote in 1850, but "we have a want of cultivation and intelligence in our ministry." Good biblical knowledge, he continued, could not replace weakness in the knowledge of history, science, and ancient languages. Many intelligent people, he lamented, "smile at our superficiality and turn away in disgust," join the Unitarians instead, or refuse a church altogether. Universalists needed to throw off their "vain show of learning" and engage in serious study if they hoped to appeal to the "most refined and liberal minds and enlarge the borders of our Zion."[16]

Other observers seconded this sentiment. Around midcentury, it became common for writers to note that piety, to be lasting, must be properly "enlightened" and that zeal must be "in accordance with our knowledge."[17] Acutely aware of the need to give form to their traditional reverence for reason and learning, Universalist leaders moved rapidly in the 1850s, founding Tufts (1852) outside Boston, St. Lawrence University and Divinity School (1856, 1858) in New York state, and Lombard College (1851) in Illinois. Other colleges and academies were founded in the sixties and seventies.[18] The rising educational level of Universalist clergymen in this period is evident from even a casual perusal of denominational publications: the old style of preaching and polemical writing based on Scripture and the common sense of popular Enlightenment rationalism was giving way to a more learned and restrained approach, which involved a far broader range of references and an ever more urbane tone. This broad change in clerical education and outlook reflected and furthered the transformation of a genuinely popular, doctrinally oriented religious movement into an established, reform-minded denomination.[19]

Organizing for Reform

Outside the context of denominational history, there was of course nothing pathbreaking about the founding of colleges in the 1850s; groups such as the Baptists and the Methodists had moved in this direction several decades earlier. Similarly, extensive and organized Universalist involvement in programs of social reform came quite late by the standards of American Protestantism generally. It is true that, by midcentury, one could find Universalists involved virtually wherever there were efforts to reform society. Yet, for the most part, this involvement merely mirrored broad trends among the liberal Protestant groups. In only a few realms, most notably in the expansion of women's roles, does the evidence suggest any truly distinctive Universalist contribution.

Especially for the period before 1850, determining the level of Universalist involvement in most areas of reform is difficult because most of the work was carried out in a decentralized and uncoordinated fashion. Traditionally suspicious of authority and disdainful of the motives of evangelical reformers, Universalists had not been inclined to join national organizations; they also generally believed that secular reform was not the province of an ecclesiastical body. Russell Miller writes that, before midcentury, members carried on such efforts "either with fragmented or uncoordinated organizations, or with no organization at all, and in virtually every instance with a determination to work independently of similar organizations outside of the denomination."[20]

With the creation of their own reform association, however, Universalists lent their efforts somewhat more direction. The New England Universalist General Reform Association, organized in 1846, helped to coordinate what had been highly scattered and sporadic efforts, and it indicated the emergence of support for a broad movement of social regeneration. The association announced a boundlessly ambitious program that looked to social and moral amelioration on almost every conceivable front. The organization came to an end in 1861, not only because of the general tumult of the Civil War but also because a number of its members thought that, by this time, the "spirit of reform" had permeated the denomination as a whole, so that there was no longer any need for a separate association.[21] It seems clear that appeals such as those of Abbott and others had not fallen on deaf ears.

Although the "New England" was dropped from the name of the Universalist General Reform Association in 1847, it is significant that the impetus for organized social efforts came largely from the region where Universalism was strongest, most settled, and most clearly becoming a movement of the educated and comfortable middle class. Amidst the relative social flux of the West, adherents appear to have been somewhat more hesitant to translate their faith into a call for social action. Perhaps partly because of the greater social isolation of Universalist congregations in the West and, especially, the South, the Northeast would supply the denomination with most of its reform leaders. Representative of this group is the Reverend Edwin Hubbell Chapin (1814–1880), who in 1848 became minister of the Church of the Divine Paternity in New York City. Chapin's defense of a moderate reformism, which stressed the inner transformation of the individual as the essential basis of social change, had wide appeal among Universalists after midcentury.[22] This was a general ideal that Universalists were coming increasingly to share with other liberal Christians; it was more famously expressed by both William Ellery Channing and Henry Ward Beecher.

While most of the reforming activity led by figures like Chapin was still informed by the eschatological conviction that all souls would be redeemed through the grace of God, that conviction was increasingly overshadowed by the ideal of the infinite potential for progress and development in each human being. This certainly seems to have been the case for prominent adherents such as Horace Greeley, who became a leading champion of reform in the mid–nineteenth century. Having never been acquainted with a Universalist society or heard a Universalist preacher, Greeley attended a service on the first Sunday after he arrived in New York City in 1831. He soon joined a growing congregation; by midcentury, he and his good friend P. T. Barnum would become probably the denomination's best-known members. Greeley stated in his autobiography that the moral power of the faith had immediately appealed to him. Universalism, he explained, blended "inexorable punishment" for sin with "unfailing pity and ultimate forgiveness" for all. His involvement in reform — particularly his efforts in behalf of the laboring classes — were motivated primarily by his desire to make America a "moral paradise" where, as Glyndon Van Deusen puts it, "Everyman's talents and his understanding of what was good would be developed with painstaking care."[23]

Penal Reform: Escaping Vengeance

Most antebellum reformers began not by aiming directly at a "moral paradise" but by seeking to ameliorate the worst evils they saw in their society. Among the various social evils that attracted Universalist attention, prisons and capital punishment were of notable importance. One scholar thinks it possible to state that "Universalists . . . unquestionably provided more anti-gallows reformers than any other denomination."[24] Hard evidence to support this claim is not easy to come by. It is true that, in the revolutionary era, a number of Universalists, such as Benjamin Rush, had joined Quakers in support of penal reform and in opposition to capital punishment. But through the period of the 1820s and 1830s, when the Auburn Plan for the reform of prisons was becoming widely influential, the record of Universalist involvement is slim. Individual Universalists occasionally issued denunciations of capital punishment, as Thomas Whittemore did in 1828, but throughout this era most proponents of universal salvation seem to have been too busily engaged in theological wranglings with their opponents to become active in the movement to reform the treatment of prisoners.[25]

It was not until the late 1830s and the 1840s that Universalist societies began to issue public resolutions on the matter. Indeed, it was only then that the positive social implications of Universalist belief moved toward the forefront of consciousness for many adherents. Increasingly, writers stressed what they took to be an obvious and immediate application of their faith: the death penalty smacked of vengeance, and since an all-powerful and all-good God was clearly not vengeful, neither should his children be. Those who held this view were certainly not surprised to find that many, if not most, major defenders of the gallows throughout this period were members of the orthodox Calvinist clergy.[26]

Since Universalism had arisen among the humbler social classes and retained a strong egalitarian sense, it may be that some adherents developed a concern to protect the lives of common folk who might be unjustly accused and unfairly tried by a legal system dominated by the socially powerful. In any case, the issue of penal reform was one that hit somewhat closer to home among liberal but still relatively parochial northeastern Universalists than the distant and even abstract problem of slavery or even the temperance crusade. The layman Horace Greeley, for example, gave extensive publicity to the antigallows movement well before he became outspoken on slavery.[27]

Far and away the most active antigallows reformer was minister Charles Spear. A figure of amazing moral intensity as well as high ambition, Spear was a disciple of Hosea Ballou. But, unlike Ballou, he believed that Universalist principles, when applied to society, would "overthrow every existing evil." For him, opposition to capital punishment followed naturally from Universalist precepts. More important, though, he saw himself in the midst of a "great moral revolution" that was transforming human society. Starting in the early 1840s, he threw himself zealously into gallows reform; his major work on the subject, *Essays on the Punishment of Death*, first appeared in 1844, and it had gone through thirteen editions by 1851.[28] This was a work of social science as well as Christian and humanitarian reformism. Spear presented tables of statistics, for example, "to show that crimes diminish with the abolition of the punishment of death."[29]

While Spear could praise his fellow Universalists for their overall contributions to the cause of penal reform, he could also show bitterness at times about their "backwardness" on capital punishment and their reluctance to engage themselves in this and related issues. He was so upset by the failure of Universalist conventions to adopt resolutions openly denouncing the death sentence that he apparently considered withdrawing from the denomination. During the mid-1840s, he felt torn between his commitment to Universalism and the pressing moral concerns that occupied him.[30] This tension reflects on a personal level the major question faced by Universalism at midcentury: was the movement to be focused on the preaching of a central saving truth or were Universalists called, above all, to work for the development of self and society?

Increasingly during the middle decades of the century, Universalists organized to combat the corrupting influence of penal systems in general and of capital punishment in particular; they were gradually gaining a justified claim to leadership in this realm. George Quimby, for example, author of *The Gallows, the Prison, and the Poor-House: A Plea for Humanity* (1856), led a long campaign for penal reform and the end of the death penalty. Quimby edited the *Gospel Banner* in Maine for twenty years after 1864; his frequent appeals certainly played a part in the eventual abolition of the death sentence in that state in 1887.[31] The Universalists were probably more visible than any other group in the heated debate over capital punishment in New York state,[32] and they became prominent in the discussion all over the Northeast. Yet the arguments they put forward were based on broad and ever more widely shared humanistic principles; one searches Quimby's work in vain for arguments that were not also used by Unitarians, Quakers, and even Congregationalists. It is therefore difficult to avoid the conclusion that, on the whole, Universalists became involved relatively late and that, by the time they were working actively for penal reform, there was little difference between their motivations and those of other liberal denominations.

On the Highway to Temperance

The same conclusion seems to apply to Universalist participation in most of the major areas of nineteenth-century reform. Regarding the temperance movement, for example, there is little evidence to suggest a distinctive involvement among the followers of Murray, Winchester, and Ballou. True, Benjamin Rush of Philadelphia is often given credit for pioneering the temperance movement. But Rush's position never came close to John Wesley's call for total abstinence, and few other early spokesmen of the movement concerned themselves with the issue at all. Like a number of other religious groups, Universalists were not averse to holding their meetings in public taverns when they lacked a building of their own.[33]

Throughout the antebellum age, Universalist attitudes seem to have paralleled almost exactly the broad evolution of liberal reformist sentiment on the matter. There was little concern until the 1830s, when individual societies and state conventions began issuing resolutions. Maine Universalists seem to have led the way, but soon denominational leaders in Massachusetts and other parts of the Northeast were calling for temperance, if not total abstinence. Sylvanus Cobb was among the most consistent preachers of total abstinence in the 1830s and 1840s.[34] But during this time, the temperance crusade was already dominated heavily by preachers of the mainline evangelical denominations, and this was probably one reason why some Universalists proved less than enthusiastic.

Like other groups, Universalists could take up the cause without worrying about political consequences, for temperance was generally regarded as a purely moral rather than as a political matter.[35] Inevitably, of course, the crusade had broad political significance. In this connection, it might be plausible to suggest that the Universalist emphasis on the "benign paternity of the heavenly father" was one expression of an "industrial paternalism" that sought to instill a new bourgeois discipline in the laboring classes through temperance, among other means.[36] Yet, whatever we finally make of such arguments, when we consider the level of temperance activity among Universalists relative to that of other groups, we find little reason to credit them with any distinctive role. If, from the forties on, there was anything particularly notable about the Universalist participation in the temperance crusade, it was probably connected with the influx of women into the denomination, a subject to be taken up shortly.

To Preach the Gospel or to Sign Protests?
The Antislavery Question

While it is often assumed that early and mid–nineteenth-century Universalism was closely associated with the burgeoning of reform causes such as antislavery, a more careful assessment requires us to agree with George Williams that "Universalists as a whole . . . were no more in the forefront of the anti-slavery movement than other denominations."[37] Several recent studies of antebellum attitudes toward slavery have shown clearly that Universalists, along with numerous other groups that stood apart from the strident evangelicalism of the age, were generally opposed to abolitionism and were at pains to distance themselves from the position of the Garrisonian agitators. John McKivigan points out that, during the 1830s:

> ritualist, liberal and strict Calvinist churches all objected to one or more aspects of the abolitionists' evangelically inspired claim that slaveholders were inherently sinners and that the churches had a moral obligation to purify their communions by expelling them.[38]

While Universalists such as Elhanan Winchester had joined the voices of revolutionary-era antislavery sentiment, the question faded almost completely between 1800 and the 1830s, the period when the Universalist movement was spreading most rapidly. When the issue began heating up nationally, the denomination's reaction was one of caution. Maine Universalists openly denounced slavery as a sin and a national disgrace as early as 1836, yet the denunciation was couched exclusively in moral, rather than political, terms. When, in the 1840s, adherents in Massachusetts began organizing to oppose the institution, they avoided the major abolitionist associations and formed their own groups. This was also the pattern elsewhere. The result was that Universalists, like the other liberal churches, were virtually excluded from the mainstream of the antislavery movement and had very little influence on it. Of some 600 officers of the four national abolition societies between 1833 and 1864, only two are known to have been Universalists.[39] The aversion, of course, was not limited to one party; the leading evangelical abolitionists, for example, "regarded Universalists as near infidels" and refused all cooperation with them. Abolitionists often criticized the denomination's lack of efforts to hasten emancipation.[40]

During the twenty years before the Civil War, declarations of opposition to slavery became common among individual Universalist conventions and congregations. A united stand by the denomination as a whole, however, was rendered impossible by its decentralized structure. Formal opposition was, in any case, prevented by the refusal of most Universalists to denounce the slaveholders themselves as sinners. When the first Universalist convention was held to debate the issue in the fall of 1842, the proper position of the church was a matter of sharp contest. Ballou himself refused to sign the roll, believing that the discussion of slavery was not a proper denominational question. The General Convention of 1843, meeting in Akron, Ohio, declared slavery inconsistent with Universalist teachings and with Christianity itself, but it took the politically safe route of calling on slaveholders to look "to the gospel, to humanity and to their own consciences."[41]

In 1846, more than 300 Universalist clergymen signed a general "Protest" that condemned slavery as "an insurmountable barrier to the promulgation of the great truth of Universal Brotherhood." Yet this document went no further than earlier declarations issued by local societies and state conventions; it did no more than appeal to the consciences of slaveholders. There were some 700 registered preachers in the church at the time, so even this quite limited and apolitical document did not necessarily represent a majority view.[42] Like Unitarians, Congregationalists, Baptists, and Disciples of Christ, northern Universalists made clear their dislike of the institution but continued to fellowship, or ordain, slaveholders.[43] The attitude of Sylvanus Cobb in 1844 reflected a common view: "[To say that] because one certain item in a man's conduct is inconsistent with Universalism, therefore he cannot be a Universalist, is neither logic nor philosophy." But others felt frustrated by this position, upbraiding fellow adherents for their "slow and equivocal" response to manifest evil.[44] Some of the most pointed expressions of disappointment came from women, who had recently become involved in the life of the denomination. At least one, Frances Gage, openly broke with the church over the slavery issue.[45]

Southern Universalists, who were numerous enough to make themselves heard, reacted with defensiveness to the "unchristian" meddling of their northern brethren. They felt increasingly under siege from both northern colleagues and southern opponents of Universalism. L. F. W. Andrews of Montgomery, Alabama, editor of the Universalist *Southern Evangelist*, was among those who angrily denied that there was any connection at all between Universalism and abolitionism. He and other southern spokesmen for the denomination were openly proslavery; the *Universalist Herald*, published by John C. Burress of Alabama, even carried advertisements for slaves.[46]

Few northern representatives actually defended the "peculiar institution" itself. Yet there was loud opposition to the adoption of any party line on the issue. I. D. Williamson, a Vermonter who had lived in the South, wrote a long and detailed dissent against the "Protest" of 1846, and his position seems to have had the support of many fellow Universalists. Numerous clergymen apparently agreed with the one who refused to sign because he was "not ordained to sign Protests, but to preach the Gospel." The editor of the *Gospel Banner* of Maine complained that the views of the laity as well as the clergy should have been canvassed;[47] here was another reflection of growing tension between traditionally egalitarian lay members and an increasingly educated leadership. There were certainly some Universalists, especially in the period before 1845, who regarded the whole debate over slavery as a potential threat to whatever hard-won respectability their church had gained since the early years of the century. They feared that becoming too closely identified with a controversial movement such as abolitionism would hurt the growth and financial stability of the denomination. This was, of course, a fear they shared with members of other groups that had only recently been viewed as dangerous "sects."[48]

Among Universalist leaders, who looked hopefully to the further spread of their movement into the South and West and who saw their faith as a source of spiritual unity for all of American society, the prospect of offending southern congregations was unwelcome. Otis Skinner accused his more vocal antislavery colleagues of trying to "destroy the church in the madness of their zeal, and overturn all our religious societies and organizations." Like many other Universalists, including Thomas Whittemore, he declared that he was strongly against slavery but opposed to the tactics of radical abolitionists like the Garrisonians.[49] Whittemore refused for many years to allow open discussion of the subject in his popular denominational journal, the *Trumpet*, a policy that earned him disdain among some of his fellow believers.[50] Not surprisingly, many midwestern ministers and congregations showed considerably less willingness than their New England colleagues to denounce slavery, even in principle.[51] Jonathan Kidwell, a prominent Indiana Universalist, saw in the abolitionist agitation a widespread attempt to politicize the gospel, and he even defended slavery as compatible with Christianity.[52]

Thus, while most laymen as well as clergy eventually adopted a broad antislavery platform, the evidence is strong that Universalism as a whole played no notable role in the antebellum slavery debate. Russell Miller demonstrates that there was a wide spectrum of views within the movement and acknowledges that some northern Universalist clergymen "came close to being apologists for slavery."[53] In general, the evidence he presents makes it clear that Universalist opposition to slavery grew vocal only as it did among northern liberals generally; that this response remained limited by theological, organizational, and political concerns; and that it was far from unanimous, even in the North.

Nevertheless, the slavery issue, which focused attention on what most believed was a glaring social evil, contributed to the reshaping of the foundations of American Protestantism in this era, and Universalism could hardly remain unaffected by these changes. In the atmosphere of the slavery debate, Universalist leaders began to distance themselves from the firebrands of social and religious radicalism; at the same time, to many adherents, the old style of preaching and debate over the grounds of salvation appeared more and more out of step with the times. Increasingly avoiding the extremes, Universalism was moving along the road to a moderate, liberal reformism.

"Spiritual Democracy" and Gender Roles

If the plight of the southern slaves was often distant and abstract for northern Universalists, the same could not be said for the lives and actions of the many women who began to make their presence felt in religious life from the 1830s on. Both George Williams and Russell Miller point to the prominence of women in the denomination by midcentury and to the "liberationist forces" within Universalism, that seemed to encourage a broad view of women's roles.[54] It is clear that, for many Universalists and especially for growing numbers of women in the church, the moral implications of their faith called for improving women's status and opportunities and eliminating gender as a barrier to female achievement. The denomination, therefore, did become a leader in the expansion of women's sphere. As I will show, this aspect of Universalist activity should not be viewed as part of the sentimentalizing "feminization" that created a delusional popular culture. Nevertheless, their notable acceptance of the expansion of women's roles offers another important illustration of the way in which midcentury Universalists were shifting their attention from divine power to human potential and were thus becoming ever more typical representatives of the moderate, liberal reformism of the age.

Inclusiveness and spiritual equality had been keynotes of Universalism from its inception, as Judith Sargent Murray (1751–1820), one of its earliest female advocates, so well illustrates. A member of the old and prominent Sargent family from Gloucester, Massachusetts, and one of America's first published female writers, she eventually became the wife of Universalism's "father," John Murray. With her parents and her first husband, she adopted the views of Welsh Universalist James Relly, left the Calvinist church, and helped establish the Independent Church of Christ, with John Murray as minister.

In her brief biography, Sheila Skemp stresses the extent to which Judith Sargent Murray's Universalist faith "enabled her to structure and legitimize her stance on gender relations," since "its very essence derived from a belief in human equality." For Murray, a prolific writer who composed essays, poetry, and two plays that were produced in Boston in the 1790s, Universalism was a liberating force. Murray's beliefs in women's intellectual equality and the possibility of a "genderless meritocracy," Skemp concludes, were "a logical development of her religious and philosophical beliefs."[55]

Despite the pioneering role of Judith Sargent Murray, the Universalist movement in its early decades had been largely a male phenomenon. "When the distinguishing truths of the Universalist Church were first proclaimed in modern times . . . woman—so long repressed—was almost a stranger in our religious gatherings. Men came at once in throngs, but women were 'like angels' visits, few and far between,' " observed E. R. Hanson in her detailed work on Universalist women.[56] The heavy emphasis on theological argument, the generally itinerant nature of the ministry, and strong public disapproval all seem to have contributed to this condition. It is true that, as early as 1810, Maria Cook was preaching from Universalist pulpits to generally approving audiences in Pennsylvania and New York. But she was never formally recognized or "fellowshiped" as a preacher, and the novelty of her actions was what drew most notice.[57] Public religious life in general was mainly a male preserve until the great upheavals of the Second Great Awakening brought what Carroll Smith-Rosenberg has called a "rush of women into the public religious sphere."[58]

We have little or no evidence to suggest that, when women first began crowding to hear sermons and join churches in the 1820s and 1830s, they were drawn to Universalism in disproportionate numbers. Throughout the first decades of the century, the popular impression of Universalism as a disreputable sect undoubtedly continued to limit women's participation. Former Baptist Mary A. Livermore recalled that, as late as 1845, when she married a Universalist clergyman, "Friends forsook me, acquaintances ostracized me, I was disapproved by the church and for a time my father was inconsolable."[59] Yet it is noteworthy that Universalists were early and increasingly inclined to declare that their denomination was the logical home for the advocates of women's full development.[60] There can be little doubt that the long-standing self-perception of the movement as representing "spiritual democracy" played a role here. As E. R. Hanson wrote later in the century:

> When Universalism came to [women] with its God of love and justice, its spiritual democracy, its free and natural reading of the New Testament, without the interposition of an orthodox interpretation, they began to feel that somehow women had a place in Christianity that they had not seen before.[61]

Certainly, as the number and visibility of women in the denomination increased, so did the idea that the Universalist faith was particularly suited to female needs and progress.

Perhaps the clearest evidence that many Universalist leaders, and especially Universalist women, came to believe that the progress of women and the cause of Universalism went hand-in-hand may be found in the pages of the *Ladies' Repository*, a monthly and, later, a quarterly periodical. Started in 1832 by a group of Universalist clergymen, it claimed the largest circulation and longest history of any Universalist periodical. When minister Henry Bacon became its editor in 1836, he proclaimed his overall policy with an addition to the heading: "Devoted to the Defense and Illustration of Universalism and the Rights of Women." During his twenty-year tenure, he consistently advocated a broad extension of women's rights.[62] The reforming zeal exhibited in this journal was a clear outgrowth of Universalism's changing theological perspective. Humanistic convictions about the need for all souls to realize their potential underlay the journal's consistent advocacy of the extension of female liberties. Numerous articles by ministers as well as laypersons underscored the duty to cultivate one's talents and to beware of scriptural interpretations that would "fetter" aspiration.

As publications such as Bacon's sought to make clear the denomination's openness, message of divine forgiveness, and biblical stress on spiritual equality, change came quickly. The 1840s found women entering the denomination in remarkable numbers; a large percentage of Universalist growth in the middle decades of the century must have been fueled by the influx of women. This development was associated with the broadening opportunities for church work. There were two women among the original officers of the General Reform Association at its founding in 1847. By the 1850s, laywomen began to appear as delegates to state conventions. The first woman to be locally fellowshiped as a Universalist preacher was Lydia A. Jenkins of New York state in 1858; this was a highly unusual step in any American church.[63]

The ordination of Olympia Brown (1835–1926) by the St. Lawrence (N.Y.) Association in 1863 was a milestone in American religious history; since the act received approval from the General Convention, Brown became the first woman ordained with full denominational authority.[64] Augusta Chapin, ordained six months later, noted in 1874 that Universalists claimed more ordained women than any other branch of the Christian church. In 1882, Universalists counted thirty female ministers, but many more preached on a part-time basis, and some obtained preaching licenses without being formally ordained.[65] In this respect, more clearly than any other, the denomination departed from mainstream Protestantism; here was the basis for a legitimate claim to uniqueness and leadership. Not all Universalist congregations were prepared to accept the ordination of women, but the traditional decentralization of the movement clearly worked in favor of women who sought to be ministers, and significant opposition never developed in meetings of the General Convention.

By the 1860s and 1870s, women were not only being ordained to the ministry but were regularly receiving degrees from Universalist colleges, becoming recognized for their literary contributions, and participating actively in denominational affairs.[66] At the time of the denomination's centennial in 1870, one commentator could observe that "Universalists are rather proud that they are in the van[guard] of the woman's movement, particularly in its relation to woman's work in the church."[67] In 1874, Augusta Chapin concluded that the "experimental stage" for women in the denomination was long since over and that female ministers could carry on a wide variety of activities with even fewer impediments than their male colleagues.[68] According to one report, in 1875, Pennsylvania Universalists forced the president of the state convention to resign "solely" because of his "non-belief in the ministry of women."[69]

Certainly one reason for the acceptance of women ministers was the acknowledged critical shortage of clergy within the denomination.[70] By the time of the Civil War, the generation of preachers who had joined the movement in its time of fastest growth was aging. While the number of congregations had continued to expand, the recruitment of new clergy had not kept pace, perhaps partly because Universalists shared the general and growing desire for educated leaders, yet had only recently founded their own colleges to train them. Beyond this, Universalists were undoubtedly more prepared than other denominations to take the step of ordaining women since they already favored coeducation. With the significant exception of Tufts, all of the academies, seminaries, colleges, and universities that Universalists established from 1819 to 1870 were coeducational. Lombard College (1851) in Illinois followed Oberlin as the second American institution of higher learning to admit women from the beginning. Significantly, many of the first female graduates of Universalist colleges went on to study for and enter the ministry. This career seemed to them the logical path toward fulfillment of their exciting new freedom and responsibility. The continuing insistence of the Tufts trustees on the exclusion of women (until 1892), despite lively controversy on the matter, surely reflects the continuing dominance—in both numbers and thinking—of an older and more patriarchal generation among New England Universalists.[71]

Christian Women's Liberation

A careful evaluation of the activities of Universalist women in the nineteenth century makes it impossible to agree completely with the well-known thesis of Ann Douglas in *The Feminization of American Culture* (1977) that popular American religion in that age was dominated by a socially regressive escapism and sentimentalism that appealed particularly to women. It is certainly true that in the middle decades of the century, the apparent interests of many liberal clergymen and middle-class women merged in a new and significant way as traditional theological concerns died out.[72] But whether the new popular culture that resulted from this merger was dominated by escapist sentimentalism appears less certain, particularly in light of the evidence we are weighing here. Universalist preachers and writers—both men and women—continued to demonstrate commitment to serious thought and to social issues. While they did often indulge in idealistic flights of exhortation and hope, the program reflected in their writings can hardly be branded as a dreamy sentimentalism out of touch with social realities.

Douglas glosses over important distinguishing characteristics of Universalist literature by and for women. To be sure, by the 1840s and 1850s, many Universalist women had become avid readers as well as producers of cheap, popular fiction.[73]

But this trend was not dominant. Douglas's statement that, by the 1860s, the contents of the Universalist *Ladies' Repository* were "almost purely fiction" and that the magazine had become "more or less indistinguishable from the secular ladies' magazines of the day" is simply incorrect.[74] After Henry Bacon's death in 1856, women had taken over the editorship of the journal. There was, certainly, increasing pressure from the publisher to include more light and secular material.[75] Yet the magazine continued to run many articles devoted to the full development of human potential and, in general, to reflect a high-minded purpose. Typical was an 1869 article on "The Perfectibility of Human Character," in which the Reverend Lydia Jenkins argued that "the measure of all our rightful endeavors" was the "perfection of the Infinite Mind."[76]

This Universalist magazine was by no means the only women's or religious publication to call for the fulfillment of women's potential. By midcentury, declarations of belief in female "advancement" were not unusual and did not imply the necessity of any basic change in the social order. The men and women who edited and wrote for the *Ladies' Repository* were not religious, social, or political radicals; we find little evidence here of spiritualist, communalist, or abolitionist sympathies. Yet the editors had an obvious and insistent agenda, which combined the encouragement of female endeavor with a call for the removal of all barriers to achievement. By the 1860s, the reader's sympathy for women's suffrage was all but assumed. Contributors declared often and in ringing terms that there was nothing peculiar to women that necessarily made them domestic creatures.[77] Social arrangements, labor conditions, and professional opportunities needed to be changed to allow for the personal needs and capabilities both of poor women who needed to support families and of educated ones who wished to pursue a chosen occupation. Henrietta Bingham, editor from 1869 to 1874, looked to the "millennial day" when women would consider only their needs and best abilities when choosing a path in life.[78] Nancy Thorning Monroe, a regular contributor to the journal from 1837 to 1874, decried as "sentimental" any distinction between what was proper men's or women's work. A lifelong Universalist, Monroe predicted that, in the future, women's traditional tasks would be handled by professionals, so that women could pursue the occupations for which they were most suited.[79] These Universalist editors and writers wanted to encourage "The Highest Form of Manhood" for women as well as for men.[80]

Further evidence of a genuine push among Universalists for the liberation of women is abundant. George Weaver, a representative Universalist author of advice literature from the fifties to the seventies, issued several frontal assaults on the condescending relegation of women to the domestic sphere. Despite what the title might lead us to expect, for example, *The Christian Household* (1854, 1878) gave no place to conventional visions of the wife as a pious guardian of hearth and home. The work forcefully and categorically denied that women's aspirations should be limited in any way or that they should in any sense be dependent on men.

> I seek to elevate woman. I look to her elevation as to the elevation of the race. I
> see in her, powers capable of great actions and a sublime life. But I see no way
> in which these powers can be developed and that life lived but in active and
> useful employment. Women ought to stand by man's side in all that is great and

good in thought and action. The history of every country should have as much to record of woman as of man. But this can never be till woman's field of employment is extended. She must go out and work. She must do her own business, execute her own intentions, act nobly her part in life wherever she can be the best rewarded for her industry and judgment.[81]

Weaver expanded on this theme so frequently that his sincerity cannot be doubted. In *Aims and Aids for Girls and Young Women* (1856), for instance, he wrote, "Woman may overcome all the obstacles in her way if she will educate herself to *think*, and think soundly and forcibly. She must be her own deliverer from these barbaric customs and laws, and her own *thought* must be the instrument of delivery." He went on to complain of the "superficial, trifling, babyish" education to which women were now consigned, and exhorted them to make their "life-education . . . deep, useful, and practical."[82]

Obviously, Universalist women and clerics were not parties to an alliance born of insecurity and sentimentality. On the other hand, it is clear that Universalist women were not generally among those who "sought intellectual and spiritual purity in an increasingly antistructural religious and reform posture."[83] They were certainly not anarchist radicals by the standards of the day, not women who chose to "cling to disorder and war against form."[84] During the 1850s, when sweeping programs for social change were everywhere, Universalist women were taking a markedly moderate stance simply by virtue of their association with an organized church. We have already noted that hard-line abolitionism was generally foreign to the denomination; in chapter 5, we will see that, in this period, Universalist leaders moved to divorce their movement from other forms of political or social radicalism. The women who received degrees from Universalist colleges or joined the denominational clergy starting in the fifties were thus not likely to be rebels against all structure.

Throughout America in these years, the most extreme feminists tended to look upon church-oriented activity with suspicion, if not disdain. To many of them, the clergy formed a pillar of the reactionary establishment. In 1850, Lucy Stone, later president of the American Woman's Suffrage Association, tried to dissuade Antoinette Brown from her plan to become a minister and to encourage her to think instead as a "free spirit." "Our strongest enemies," said a young Elizabeth Cady Stanton, "entrench themselves in the Church." Only a nonchurch, with a total lack of structure, was acceptable in the eyes of leading political suffragists. As Stanton and Susan B. Anthony wrote in the 1880s, "The only religious sect in the world . . . that has recognized the equality of women is the Spiritualists."[85] Yet, as we will see, during this very period, when Universalists were most eager to disentangle themselves from spiritualist associations, women became highly active and visible in the denominational organization of the church. Those who became so involved were looking for something other than political empowerment or social revolution.

Who were these women who entered the life of the Universalist church in such numbers in the mid–nineteenth century? They cannot be clearly distinguished from the larger group of women who became active in reformist causes during this period.[86] For the most part, they came from relatively comfortable middle-class or upper-middle-class backgrounds. Most of them were relatively well-educated, or at least had aspirations to genuine education. By the postbellum era, if not earlier, they were mainly middle-class liberals, looking for an institutional outlet for their energies that was not excessively restrictive but that offered some structure in place of literary isolation or spiritualist anarchy. Universalism offered a kind of balance, for many educated middle-class women at midcentury, between structure and disorder, between the extremes of the happily homebound orthodox housewife and the antichurch feminist radical. Universalism fit these needs so well because it had always preached what many educated women now sought: a balance between competitive individualism and the Christian ideal of society as a communitarian whole.[87]

The most widely known Universalist women were not necessarily typical, but we should note that some were among the leading social reformers and pioneering professionals of the nineteenth century. Olympia Brown and Phebe Hanaford are often recognized today more for their leadership in the suffrage cause than for their clerical careers, but they saw themselves first and foremost as ministers of the gospel. Brown served as a vice president of the National Woman's Suffrage Association. Hanaford was active in the American Woman's Suffrage Association and was asked to preach at the funeral services of Elizabeth Cady Stanton and Susan B. Anthony. Harriott K. Hunt (1805–1875), one of the first female physicians in the United States, was born into a Universalist family and was dedicated by the acknowledged founder of the movement, John Murray. Not only did she have a significant medical career, she also became a missionary preacher. Clara Barton, the Civil War nurse known for her work to establish the American Red Cross, similarly came from a Universalist family, and although not officially a member of the denomination, she remained sympathetic to its beliefs.[88]

The preeminent Universalist woman of the nineteenth century was Mary A. Livermore (1820–1905), leader of and participant in a staggering number of reform movements and activities. Livermore served as president of the Massachusetts Women's Christian Temperance Union and founded the *Agitator*, a suffrage periodical that later merged with the *Women's Journal*. As the agent for the U.S. Sanitary Commission in the Northwest during the Civil War, she traveled widely to raise money; she was also a popular lyceum lecturer. Within the Universalist church, Livermore founded the Women's Centenary Aid Association and served frequently as a pulpit speaker.[89] Far more of a gradualist than many of the famous proponents of women's rights, Livermore was a highly influential model among middle-class women of the late nineteenth century.

To be sure, there had been and continued to be some strong countercurrents working against women's expanded role in the denomination. A desire to preserve the traditional family structure, reinforced by the consistent paternal imagery of the movement, was clearly in evidence throughout the middle and latter decades of the century and worked to limit support for reform in this realm. Many members continued to refer fondly to "Father" Ballou, and names like Church of the Divine Paternity reflect the continuance of the inherited cast of mind. It was largely the older guard that was cool toward women's involvement. In 1859, Thomas Sawyer was still opposed even to allowing women to speak at religious meetings. Thomas Whittemore believed that women's special role should keep them from getting involved in the public sphere, especially politics; only toward the very end of his life (1861) did his views about women in the pulpit begin to change.[90]

Even as women became regular members of the Universalist clergy, the denomination as a whole refrained from endorsing the women's rights movement in politics, and its spokesmen were notably reticent on the issue in general.[91] Through the end of the century, Universalists exhibited no clear consensus on the rights of women beyond the issues of ordination and coeducation. Despite the efforts of many prominent men and women of the denomination, the General Convention refused to pass a resolution endorsing female suffrage until 1905—and this statement was rescinded two years later. At least among most active Universalist leaders, spiritual equality did not imply full political and social equality; the idea remained powerful that most women had a high—but still separate—role to fulfill.

Such attitudes probably contributed to the growth of the feeling among many reforming women of the late nineteenth century that somehow the stage of specifically religious liberation was passing, that the times now called for a less idealistic, more systematic, and more pragmatically political approach to reform. Gail Parker has nicely described the growing sense in the postbellum period that "they just didn't make women like they used to" or perhaps that the heroic ideals that had motivated women at midcentury were no longer there to inspire.[92] The suffragists of the last decades of the century increasingly settled down to the less-than-exciting but necessary tasks of organization and administration.

Universalist women saw what was happening in a typically optimistic light. For example, when the *Ladies' Repository* came to an end in December 1874, the editors did not reflect a sense of defeat. The parting editorial by Henrietta Bingham is telling. She observed that the Universalists, like the Transcendentalists, had needed an organ for their religious sentiment; Bingham and other women had shaped the *Ladies' Repository* in much the same way that Margaret Fuller had directed the *Dial*. Now, she concluded, the journal had perhaps outlived its major purpose. With the growing acceptance of universal salvation and the publication of formerly "heretical" ideas in "orthodox" journals like *Scribner's*, "liberal-minded" Christians no longer needed special publications. She could see a parallel with the *Liberator* and the abolitionist movement.[93] The *Ladies' Repository* had helped both to spread belief in universal salvation and to enlighten readers about the "larger liberty" that Universalist women now enjoyed "in comparison with those of other communions and in comparison with their own past."[94] Bingham hinted that it was time for women such as herself to turn their attention to other tasks.

If, in the antebellum era, many women had been attracted specifically to Universalism because of its antihierarchic message of universal forgiveness, the words and actions of women after the war suggest that the teachings of a specific religious group were regarded as less and less crucial. Livermore, for example, increasingly played down her denominational identity; she often aroused resentment among her Universalist colleagues for this reason. "In truth," said Russell Miller, "her thinking went beyond denominational boundaries, and she never stressed Universalism *per se*."[95] Impatient with the pace of women's progress within the Universalist fold and within society generally, Livermore was outspoken; in one lecture she even praised

Buddhism for its concern for women. Whether the Universalist church could survive under that name or not, she announced in 1872, "I do not know—I do not care. I do know, just as surely as I know the sun is to rise tomorrow, that the blessed faith of the Universalist church is to be the faith of the church of the future."[96] Here was a late but extreme expression of the traditional Universalist ambivalence about the very need for an institutionalized church structure.

The Universalist women who continued to be active through the late nineteenth century and after 1900 shared the increasingly practical and even social-scientific approach of reformers generally. Livermore became less and less known as a religious figure calling for moral regeneration and became increasingly associated with the institutional approaches to reform represented by the modern professional social worker. To be sure, she continued to see herself as a Christian doing the Lord's work. But for her and for many women who shared similar ideals, the work of reform had become virtually identical with religion.

Our look at Universalism and women makes it easy to agree with a forceful rejoinder to Ann Douglas, that "the identification of piety with femininity could aid in the expansion of women's options and contribute to the potency of a comprehensive moral idealism."[97] Moreover, Universalism definitely had a leading role in the expansion of female activity beyond conventional cultural limits. It is true that Unitarians, Congregationalists and others were beginning to move toward a similar acceptance of female ministers in the second half of the nineteenth century, but no other group could match the Universalist record in this regard.

Earlier, as we saw, large numbers of Universalist men had found a form of sanctuary in the secure fraternalism of Freemasonry. Universalist women, with few if any outlets of this sort, came by midcentury to regard their faith as the one open door to a world of infinite promise. Many Universalist women were eloquent in their testimony to the inspiring power of belief in the universal redemption of humanity. They were attracted to Universalism at least partly because of the traditional openness and spiritual egalitarianism of the movement, which had been based on that central eschatological teaching.[98] But their lives had become devoted less to the propagation of an ostensibly rational and unifying belief in divine providence than to social projects that built on the ideal of the limitless potential of every human being. In a general way, they could afford simply to take for granted the spreading acceptance of the notion of universal salvation. Increasingly, however, they came to express a concept of salvation very different from that which prevailed among their forebears. Thus, while the influx of women into its life and work gave the denomination a renewed claim to liberal leadership, on a deeper level it reflected and gave further impetus to the shift from eschatological faith to the ideal of humanist reform.[99] Few Universalists recognized that this shift was undermining what was most truly distinctive in the movement.

Universalism and Spiritual Science

As we have seen, a major part of Universalism's appeal through the first half of the nineteenth century was its proponents' reputation for contentiousness. The movement had always attracted more than its share of self-taught religious critics, and this was never more the case than during the Second Great Awakening, when the opportunities for denouncing irrationality and superstition seemed endless. As the revivals subsided, however, the targets for popular rationalism became less obvious. Universalist energies were forced to seek new outlets; we have discussed the sudden rush into social reform by the 1840s. Indeed, without their traditional enemies, many Universalists began to waver in their sense of direction, and the denomination became subject to powerful centrifugal tendencies. Among the major new preoccupations of Universalists in this period were the popular "spiritual sciences" of phrenology, mesmerism, and spiritualism. The heirs of John Murray and Hosea Ballou were remarkably receptive to these and related teachings, which flowered in the period from the 1830s to the 1870s.

A Motley Brood

In the shifting currents of mid–nineteenth-century religion, these spiritual sciences could be accepted on a variety of levels by a variety of people. Phrenology and mesmerism, in particular, attracted audiences with a broad range of religious convictions. Americans of disparate religious persuasions could embrace phrenology as a

wonderful new insight into human character and potential, mesmerism as a similarly exciting new practice that might improve the physical as well as the mental
state of humanity. Even spiritualism could be accepted, despite its challenges to conventional Christian doctrine. But Universalists, more than any other group, chose to
read the most profound significance into the new sciences: the promise of an objective foundation for piety. Phrenology and mesmerism provided mainstream Universalists with welcome confirmation of their interpretation of scriptural truth, as
well as with new insights into God's government. Spiritualism tended to draw the
attention and allegiance of those Universalists who felt more restless in their traditional faith, those in search of a belief system based on new, "scientific" foundations.

Although Universalist participation in these spiritual sciences has long been
noted, few scholars have offered more than a cursory analysis of the popularity of
such movements among members of the denomination.[1] As early as 1852, a *Universalist Quarterly* editor exclaimed, "Taking them together, what a brood of Mes-
merists, Rationalists, Fourierists and Necromantists we have hatched!" He believed
that a lack of both ecclesiastical and theological discipline had caused the Universalists' attraction in "disproportionate numbers" to these popular currents of thought.
His suggested remedies were a "more wholesome ecclesiastical order" and a "far
more thorough course of mental discipline."[2] He seemed hesitant to recognize that,
as early as the 1830s, the popular rationalism that was so essential to Universalism's
broad appeal was beginning to undermine, rather than support, the unity of the
movement.

Ballou and the other early preachers of Universalism had sought to revive piety
by replacing a traditional Calvinist eschatology with carefully reasoned assurances
of divine power and goodness. Piety, they held, rested at least in part on rational
conviction about God's loving intention; it could not be nourished in an environment of uncertainty or fear about salvation. Universalists saw their teaching as providing a necessary balance between reason and faith; a reasoned belief in universal
salvation would strengthen and sustain faith in divinity. Yet the rationalism that had
initially formed a large part of the movement's appeal ultimately led adherents far
beyond biblical teachings. Universalism had shifted attention away from God's judgment to his benevolent sovereignty. Exploring the nature of divine power and its
operation in the material world would thus pose a natural attraction for some Universalists.

The strong rationalist bent of the movement, so prominent in its efforts against
both traditional Calvinism and revivalism, had long contributed to the widespread
tendency to associate Universalism with free thought. Although denominational
leaders repeatedly condemned the freethinkers' outright rejection of revelation, both
free thought and Universalism drew many followers from the self-educated among
the lower economic classes. Freethinkers were "intellectual heirs of the Enlightenment"; Ballou was likewise indebted, as we have seen, to earlier rationalists like
Ethan Allen.[3] Perhaps more significant is that a number of freethinkers had come
from Universalist ranks. Along with the notorious Abner Kneeland, well-known freethinkers like Russell Canfield, Orestes Brownson, and Orson S. Murray had been
Universalists.[4] Such radicals were admittedly exceptional among those who saw
themselves as heirs of Ballou. Yet rationalism remained a volatile undercurrent in

the denomination and manifested itself in a more broadly acceptable way through widespread Universalist involvement in phrenology, mesmerism, and spiritualism.

In a sense, these spiritual sciences were extreme manifestations of the antebellum effort to ground religion in natural reason. Until the 1850s and, more particularly, before the appearance of Darwin's *On the Origin of Species* (1859), leading Christian writers accepted and praised the natural sciences as confirming and illustrating biblical truth. Combined professorships in geology and Old Testament studies testified to the assumed union of religion and science; in natural theology, "Christian philosophy and empirical science merged."[5] While natural theology also admirably served the purposes of more orthodox Christians, who believed they could see the workings of the divine economy, it was an endeavor of particular import to certain Universalists. Evangelicals still struggled with the problem of salvation. Meanwhile, Unitarian liberals were occupied with expounding the moral nature of man, while freethinkers had no uniform convictions about the existence or rule of divinity. But Universalists, eager to see God's purposes at work everywhere, were driven to investigate divine operations in the world. Convinced of the benevolence, order, and rationality of God's plan of redemption, they tried to confirm this belief by uncovering the links between nature and the supernatural. There was thus a basic affinity between the prevailing Universalist outlook and the goals of the spiritual sciences.

Initially attracted by the rationalism of phrenology, Universalists remained prominently involved in the spiritual sciences as these currents grew progressively more radical. Eventually, a faction devoted to the spread of spiritualism abandoned the Universalist church. The interest of many Universalists in the spiritual sciences ultimately prompted the denomination to define the sort of rationalism it could tolerate. Having advanced their cause by exposing contemporary Calvinism to popular reason, Universalist leaders began to fear the growth of a thoroughgoing rationalism that dispensed with traditional faith. When spiritual scientists began to expound an openly materialistic pantheism, many Universalists sensed for the first time the need to rein in the popular rationalism that had always characterized their movement.

Discovering Universal Law: Phrenology

Universalism's intellectual leaders acknowledged that the new science of phrenology held great appeal for both ministers and lay members of the denomination, but rarely did they inquire into the reasons for this appeal. In retrospect, we can recognize that the rationalism of phrenology offered a perfect extension, in the context of that era, of Universalism's reasonable piety. Phrenology's location of the religious "organs," its confidence that these organs could be strengthened, and its forward-looking hope that everyone could reach phrenological balance, complemented Universalism's necessitarian faith in the salvation of all.

When the fad of phrenology swept the United States during the 1830s, 1840s, and 1850s, it was not because the public understood much about the scientific methods and theories of Johann Gaspar Spurzheim and Franz Josef Gall. What had been a scientific and medical discipline in Europe quickly became a popular obsession in America, much to the consternation of those in both places who were interested in the serious study of phrenology. Instead of a controlled and precise study of the brain, phrenology became simply "character reading" or, more crudely, "bump tracing"; it could thus appeal to all orders of society. The enterprising Fowler brothers, Orson and Lorenzo, helped turn phrenology into a mass phenomenon through their New York museum, the Phrenological Cabinet, which displayed thousands of casts and skeletons. For a moderate fee, the Fowlers "read" and interpreted skulls; one could go to their offices in person or send a daguerreotype. To feed the demand for phrenological knowledge that they had helped to create, the Fowlers also trained lecturers.[6] Thus, it was mostly as a commercial venture and popular science that phrenology gained widespread attention in America.

Essentially, phrenologists attempted to identify the controlling traits or the most powerful characteristics of individuals. Not surprisingly in view of the religious ferment of the age, a leading concern was to establish how these traits were reflected in differing religious orientations. In an 1840 address before the New York Phrenological Society, the Reverend T. J. Sawyer, a prominent Universalist minister and writer, discussed the influence of cerebral organization on religious opinions and beliefs. Clearly viewing phrenology as a fortuitous complement to recent advances in liberal religion, Sawyer outlined the contributions of the science to spiritual progress. Many people had long believed humans to be religious by nature, Sawyer observed, but it was left to phrenology to prove it. Man worshiped a higher authority not on account of revelation but "because the Creator endowed him with the faculties necessary to constitute him a religious and social being." The chief organ of religious sentiment—"veneration"—existed in all people and was primarily responsible for their spiritual inclinations. But "veneration" worked in conjunction with other faculties, including "causality" (the seat of rationality), "marvellousness" ("which brings within our grasp all that is supernatural"), and "conscientiousness" (which "tends to invest the recipients of our homage with equity and justice").[7]

Most phrenologists did not presume to understand completely the genesis of religious sentiment. Yet phrenological writers and practitioners characteristically portrayed their science as a comprehensive method of both physiological and spiritual healing; indeed, their science was a peculiar combination of supposed medical knowledge and spiritual concern. They tended to conflate religious and medical terms and described clergymen as "physicians." Despite the medical profession's disdain for it, popular phrenology addressed its audience from a position of assumed medical expertise. Phrenologists also adopted many of the methods of evangelism, including missionaries and tract distribution; they invested their teachings with a clearly religious significance.[8]

Likening ministers to physicians, one advocate of the science asserted that, if clergymen did not understand the necessary treatment for the mental and physical organs, they would be "incompetent to prescribe moral remedies adapted to the diseases of the soul." The practice of phrenology adjusted the disproportions in the mental and physical constitutions; the new science identified—and thus allowed treatment of—defective outlooks as well as organs. Using traditional Christian language, the writer maintained that the science served "to prepare degenerate man for the renovating and sanctifying influences of the Holy Spirit."[9] A major reason for the limited acceptance of Christianity was that people did not know how to apply Christianity to moral disease. One needed to know what his own constitution required: "phrenology offers to give us this knowledge."[10] For many who accepted the science, the idea of phrenological balance, a natural harmony among the mental organs, was virtually equivalent to spiritual health.

Not surprisingly, such new theories were not equally attractive to all religious sensibilities. In the eyes of many evangelical leaders, phrenology offered no religious insight. They could not even accept it as a harmless fad. Neither an innocent pastime nor a form of scientific knowledge for the masses, it was a positively dangerous teaching. Phrenology seemed to deny the orthodox nineteenth-century Christian notion of God as moral governor and, according to its critics, it appeared to assert materialism, determinism, and even atheism. They believed the new science directly threatened the critical concepts of human responsibility and free will. Not only did phrenology make human beings into machines and imply an antichristian fatalism, some evangelicals charged, it also dispensed with original sin and human corruption, making people Godlike.[11]

By contrast, among people convinced of divine sovereignty but unconcerned about salvation in traditional terms, new discoveries about the physical dimensions of mind and soul could generate considerable appeal. When the Scottish phrenological lecturer George Combe toured upstate New York in 1837, he encountered strong evangelical opposition, but he received warm support in the Universalist press of the area. The ardent Universalist Horace Greeley also gave "aid and comfort" to the new science in the columns of the *New Yorker* and the *New York Tribune*.[12] In 1852, the *Universalist Quarterly* could reflect back on the popularity of the science within the denomination by remembering that

> when Phrenology became prevalent in our country, one could hardly enter a Universalist minister's study, but there hung the chart, or stood the bust, like the guardian angel of the place, with the "organs" all marked out and numbered on the cranium.[13]

Indeed, phrenology, which purported to explain human intelligence, emotions, and behavior at least partially in terms of the development of "mental organs," offered confirmation of Universalism's central conviction of the divine determination of humankind. The science located evidence that one could literally touch, tangible evidence of God's hand.

Both movements constantly fought charges that their systems led to fatalism, even atheism. Answering that contention in an 1839 article titled "Phrenology in Relation to Fatalism, Necessity and Human Responsibility," a phrenologist declared his belief that the nature of every created thing was "fixed, determinate, unalterable," the product of an infinitely wise and benevolent intelligence. In words reminiscent of countless Universalist tracts, he asserted that any other view would put in question God's wisdom, power, or goodness. Yet phrenology did not teach that man was unaccountable for his actions. Quite the contrary, phrenology proved, anatomically, that man was both free and accountable. Insisting that he differed from the atheistic determinism of Enlightenment thinkers such as Diderot, this writer stressed the phrenological principle that humans possessed faculties enabling them to examine the motives for their actions and foresee the consequences. Phrenology sought to provide physical proof for the idea that, even as he remained subject to the superintending will of God, man retained a degree of free will. Universalism had taught the same thing as a matter of self-evident truth.[14]

It is easy to see why, in an age that still regarded science as a vital buttress to religion, many Universalists could come to view phrenology as a rationalized or scientific extension of their religious outlook. Phrenology, according to the *American Phrenological Journal*, linked "unbounded confidence in the Creator" with "an eager desire to discover his laws and obey them." It envisioned science and philosophy becoming "pioneers of religion" and religion constituting the "vivifying and presiding spirit of human undertakings."[15] Looking as always for signs of God's superintendence, Universalists found phrenology compelling especially because it promised to inaugurate a new era of insight into God's ordering of all nature, including human character. They were less interested in the control over human activity that the new science seemed to promise than in the wonderful confirmation of the divine order that it would bring. As the well-known Universalist writer, educator, and phrenology enthusiast George Weaver maintained, "Human powers are all of God; human agency is all of God; the results of human life and action are of God; human destiny is of God."[16]

Weaver's *Lectures on Mental Science according to the Philosophy of Phrenology* expounded at length on the notion "that matter is in subjection to spirit" as the "bottom principle of phrenology." The principal of the Western Liberal Institute in Marietta, Ohio, Weaver argued that phrenology had proven that the human spirit could be seen and studied through matter. Past metaphysicians, Weaver maintained, had neglected to acquaint themselves "with the material connections of mind." But only the study of the physical opened "the mysterious pathway to the court of the soul." Weaver preached the standard phrenological line that use and exercise of certain organs could increase their size and thus their power; man, therefore, had a definite role in the development of his character. But his emphasis was clearly not on phrenology's disclosure of new human capacities. Rather, he stressed the valuable scientific sanction phrenology gave to Universalism's central teachings of the equality of all souls and God's plan for every soul to overcome sin. He predicted:

> When all the organs [of mankind] are of equal strength and activity, then with us the millennium has come, the day when the gate of joy and usefulness will be thrown wide open, for us to enter the kingdom of righteousness and peace.

So did Weaver describe—phrenologically—the final salvation of all.[17]

Similarly, Universalist minister T. J. Sawyer believed that phrenological discoveries, by offering a material explanation for religious differences, held out great hope for the future understanding and acceptance of the Universalist faith. Only in Jesus, Sawyer pointed out, could we behold phrenological perfection. All other men suffered from imperfections, which were reflected either in their flawed religious systems or their lack of faith. Differing cerebral organizations inclined people to particular sorts of religious belief: those with large "destructiveness" concentrated on the threatening passages of the gospel, while those with large "benevolence" saw its promises. As human constitutions changed, so would religious beliefs. The editor of the *American Phrenological Journal* agreed with Sawyer's implied conviction that the dominant evangelical religion reflected phrenological imbalance among believers. An 1841 piece, "On the Abuse or Perversion of Certain Faculties in Religion," charged that the prevailing religious sensibility was the outgrowth of "selfishness" and appealed primarily to "self-esteem," "cautiousness," and "destructiveness." Current religious interest centered primarily on soul saving, and the result was an underdevelopment of the faculties of "conscientiousness," "benevolence," and "veneration."[18] Sawyer also believed that the science provided persuasive arguments for religious toleration, even of bizarre and seemingly cruel practices. It may be, he pointed out, that people who engage in religious sacrifices or who harshly punish dissenters are "less criminal than we suppose." Instead of springing from a perverse or wicked disposition, their problems more likely resulted from a bad cerebral organization.

Sawyer clearly implied that the world as a whole had not yet advanced to the point at which it could appreciate or adopt a demanding Christian Universalism. But he believed that gradual changes in human cerebral organization and the passing away of old systems of thought and religion ensured continued progress until "that distant period when humanity shall have arrived at its perfection." Phrenology thus anchored a great hope of Universalists—that the world would gradually progress toward acceptance of their vision of Christianity—in the manifest physical process of phrenological development.[19]

It is noteworthy that the editors of Universalism's scholarly journal did not seem especially worried by the new phenomenon sweeping the ranks nor did they find any great danger in the attraction of members to it. During the years of greatest popularity for the new science, the *Universalist Quarterly* had virtually nothing to say on the subject. Although most leading Universalist theologians did not embrace phrenology, neither did they feel compelled to denounce it. The editors and writers of the denomination's scholarly journal appeared to view phrenology as no more than a superficial popular craze that was, at worst, irrelevant to their brand of faith. While some could complain that its adherents betrayed a certain "shallowness," they surely recognized the natural appeal of the science for the Universalist religious sensibility.[20] Most other religious groups of the era were not nearly as receptive to phrenology's demonstration that all men possessed the religious impulse. Many evangelical leaders, in particular, concerned with the transcendent and ultimately mysterious experience of individual salvation, had little use for this sort of "evidence." Reluctant to predict a truly universal redemption, they concentrated on warning people about the state of their souls. But evidence of God's all-encompassing plan was precisely what Universalists sought; the science provided a new channel for the strong rationalist currents that remained within their movement after the battles against Calvinism and revivalism had begun to subside.

Proof of a Higher World: Mesmerism

Like phrenology, animal magnetism, or mesmerism, had reached the height of its popularity in Europe long before it attracted much attention in America. In the

1770s, Viennese physician Franz Anton Mesmer had identified an "etheric medium," which was supposed to function as a curative agent. By the following decade, Mesmer's discovery had made a striking impact on European medical and social thinking, since it implied that "physical health, moral improvement, and social progress could all be lawfully engineered." Mesmer's disciple, the marquis de Puysegur, actually documented the manner in which "magnetized" patients fell into trances or sleeplike states of consciousness. His work downplayed the attempt to identify a physical magnetic fluid and emphasized instead the psychological link between the magnetizer and the patient. Mesmerism thus became a forerunner of dynamic psychiatry by providing a peek at the unconscious self, but it continued to locate the connection between the conscious mind and a deeper psychic reality in an invisible substance; it maintained Mesmer's physically based magnetism.[21]

When animal magnetism gained fame in America during Frenchman Charles Poyen's 1836 New England tour, it was, like its sister import phrenology, quickly transformed from an ostensibly scientific upper-class diversion into a popular phenomenon. And, like phrenology, it had a manifold popular appeal. It could be regarded as little more than entertainment, but more often it was pursued as a mysterious and breathtakingly promising form of medical healing. It could and did tantalize Americans, finally, as a key to human understanding and spiritual potential. Although Poyen had regarded the hypnotic and clairvoyant states induced by magnetism as simply discoveries about the natural order, many of his listeners soon found in the science revelations of the supernatural, proof of the power of mind over matter, and renewed assurance of spiritual life. Indeed, mesmerism's role in medical healing often faded behind its promise of insight into and contact with "more sublime levels of reality."[22]

The popular promoters of mesmerism operated along the same circuit, particularly in the burned-over district of New York, as some of the most prominent revivalists of the Second Great Awakening, such as Charles G. Finney. In an atmosphere charged with religious excitement, medical healing took a back seat to mesmerism's power to deliver people from spiritual emptiness and doubt. Robert Fuller argues that, for those "infected by the Arminian spirit," mesmerism became a substitute for "the messy business of contrition and self-flagellation formerly thought indispensable to the process of regeneration." Yet his broad contention that mesmerism was "but one more permutation of the nation's revivalist heritage"—an extension of the "progressivist religious outlook" of Finney—takes no account of mesmerism's particular popularity among Universalists.[23]

Sharing the same rationalist assumptions that lay behind phrenology, popular mesmerism went well beyond the attempt of its sister science to uncover the physical root of religious feeling. It sought proof of a higher world through scientific examination of human extrasensory powers. The new science appealed to Universalists "infected" by rationalism, not Arminianism, and more anxious to gain knowledge of the laws that underlay the phenomenal world than to find a secular replacement for the intense New Birth experience. To be sure, the process of mesmeric transference seemed to hold certain keys to individual and social transformation. But the primary attraction for a movement that had consistently opposed revivalism lay in the science's exciting offer of an understanding that was at once rational and spiritual.

Although historians have observed strong Universalist interest in mesmerism, evidence showing the extent of Universalist involvement is extremely difficult to obtain. Popular mesmerism was unorganized, involving more practice than theory; the science was spread primarily through public lectures and demonstrations. Attempts to publish journals proved abortive and converts never instituted a fellowship.[24] Thus it proves virtually impossible to establish in any satisfactory way the religious affiliations of mesmerism's followers. Yet there is good reason to believe that the science was a bridge on which many Universalists dallied before plunging headlong into the murky waters of spiritualism. The voluminous works of the Universalist minister John Bovee Dods, one of the nation's most prominent mesmerist theorists, offer good insight into the way mesmerism could appeal to the Universalist mentality. For Dods, the study of mesmerism lent rational support to religious belief, and to Universalist teachings in particular.

Long before he became a prominent lecturer on animal magnetism, Dods, pastor of a Universalist church in Provincetown, Massachusetts, indicated his intense interest in religion as a process of rational learning. He complained in the late 1830s that religion had become "a species of reverential homage paid to God," or merely belief in certain creeds or confessions of faith or the experience of "mysterious changes." Religion, Dods maintained, ought to "reconcile the mind to the administration of God's government." Stressing the Universalist teaching of God's ultimate control over all events, he insisted that happiness and permanent satisfaction depended upon "the contemplation that God governs the world" and the practice of "pure and rational piety." Rationality was the firm foundation of religious conviction, he concluded, and the key to our contentment in a divinely-directed world.[25] Articulating powerfully the antebellum conjunction of science and religion, Dods declared that the "chariot of science" would "roll through the eternal world, discovering great, immutable truths."[26]

When he published his first lectures on the philosophy of mesmerism in 1848, Dods had been a minister for twenty years and had also lectured on natural science. He had, he admitted, been a skeptic on the subject of mesmerism for five of the seven years he had studied it; he now knew it was no more a humbug than "the brilliant science of Phrenology!"[27] Indeed, he believed his own study of mesmeric force, which he termed "electrical psychology," had helped him understand the physical basis of divine governance. Dods maintained that the discovery of the mesmeric or magnetic power served to illustrate how the "all-powerful, self-existent spirit" created and ruled the world by and through electricity, "the inexhaustible foundation of primal matter."[28]

Along with many professional scientists and most of mid–nineteenth-century society, Dods was fascinated by electrical force, "the God principle at work," as one spiritualist called it.[29] But far more than any trained scientist, he was certain of what it was and how it operated. Electricity, galvanism, and magnetism were the effects of the same "fluid," an "emanation from the Eternal Mind." Electricity was the tangible link between God and his creation, the evidence of the actual control of creation by the Creator. Through electricity, God moved the world; knowledge of electricity proved that God was "connected with his universe," that he oversaw "all its multifarious operations."[30] The study of electricity allowed man to apprehend not only that infinite mind ruled the universe but also something of how this rule was exercised. If divinity made use of electricity as its agent, he pointed out, then it had to possess the positive and negative forces of electricity. These corresponded to the "*voluntary* power," which created the universe, and the "*involuntary* power," which sustained it.[31]

In lectures delivered to a congressional audience in Washington in 1850, Dods elaborated on what he obviously believed was a profound spiritual as well as scientific insight. He explained "scientifically" the enduring paradox of misery and suffering in the creation of a good God: the rule of the deity was to some extent determined by the laws of electrical force. After the earth was created and the "first link" of all animal and vegetable life was moved into existence by the voluntary power (positive electrical force) of the Creator, then, out of "philosophical necessity," control of physical events passed to the involuntary powers (negative electrical force) of the infinite mind, and thus was the physical world "governed through the established laws of nature." Dods reasoned that, if God could govern the universe through his voluntary powers only, then the world would be perfect. Yet natural accidents, freaks, and tragedies abounded. Dods confidently laid these at the door of the deity's involuntary powers, for "here casualties may naturally arise, but nowhere else under the government of the Supreme."[32] A bolder use of natural theology to explain the mysteries of creation would be difficult to find.

It was not until the publication in 1852 of *Immortality Triumphant*, however, that Dods set forth his full-blown defense of a rationalist, scientific Christianity. Subtitled *A Short and Easy Way with Atheists and Deists*, the book was intended to fight public skepticism about a future life and about the existence of God. Dods argued for greater rationality in religion, asserting that current atheistic tendencies arose from the mistaken emphases on the immateriality of spirit, the idea that spirit created all things out of nothing, and the notion that only human life was immortal. All life, he wrote, was a species of the universal electrical mind, part of a vast chain of being and therefore immortal; recent discoveries about electricity (he probably meant those of Michael Faraday) had given humans tremendous insight into that chain. Theologians needed joyfully to embrace new scientific revelations instead of persisting in such "unphilosophical and absurd" notions as God's creation of the world ex nihilo.[33] Yet Dods finally cautioned that the scientific wonders to be discovered through human rationality would only serve to illustrate and confirm the ultimate truths of revelation. Despite his infatuation with science, he remained at heart a Universalist preacher whose respect for reason could never entirely displace his faith in scriptural truth.

"Electrical psychology" not only provided powerful weapons against creeping atheism for Dods, it also gave support to his specifically Universalist convictions. He seems to have believed that his identification of an electrical connection between infinite mind and its creation gave definition to the often vague Universalist conception of a divinity of love and reconciliation. Mesmerist teaching also appears to have complemented his faith in the final advent of cosmic harmony. All of life, he rhapsodized, "will rise in one unbroken beauty, and stand complete in perfect and immortal harmony," for all that possessed life had been shown to be inextricably linked.[34]

For Dods, electrical force was the key element in scientific understanding of the process of universal restitution, specifically of the role that human beings could play in that process. He suggested that electrical imbalance contributed to a person's spiritual disharmony; the practice of mesmerism allowed that balance to be readjusted. Humans were able to magnetize each other by an exchange of "nervo-vital fluid," which was manufactured in the lungs through inspired electricity, he asserted. All human beings could produce nervo-vital fluid but in varying amounts; through mesmeric transference, those with greater quantities supplied those in need, putting them in the magnetic, "or more properly, the spiritual state." Although even the most zealous practitioners had maintained that only one in nine could be mesmerized, Dods contended that all humanity was receptive to additional nervo-vital fluid. Underscoring a central teaching of Universalism, he asserted that not only would all share in ultimate harmony, but all were open to spiritual regeneration even in this life. Practice of the new science, he thought, allowed people to take the first step toward the goal of spiritual concord.[35]

In Dods's vision, then, the minister should also become mesmerizer or physician. Exploration of the "very subtle" connection between mind and body might lead to explanations of how the mind caused bodily illness, he hoped. Even his discussion of Jesus healing the sick centered on the passage of nervo-vital fluid into afflicted persons.[36] Ultimately a means of imitating Christ, mesmerism gave humans a way of participating in the universal order by reestablishing the equilibrium of the lost and weak.

Through his mesmerist tracts, Dods tried to illuminate Universalist teachings with exciting new scientific findings; he did not openly challenge or attempt to supersede Universalism with his discoveries in animal magnetism. Nevertheless, in 1848, the year after the publication of his *Six Lectures on the Philosophy of Mesmerism*, he was disfellowshiped by the Massachusetts Convention of Universalists and read out of the denomination. Russell Miller, the most thorough historian of the Universalist movement, cannot discover the reason for this action, a highly unusual one for the self-consciously tolerant Universalist denomination. But there is a later report that Dods was among a number of "Universalist ministers persecuted or excommunicated" for propounding heretical ideas, and it seems reasonable to conclude that his mesmerist teachings had something to do with the action of the Massachusetts convention.[37] For while many Universalist leaders had earlier tended to view phrenology and mesmerism as more or less harmless fads, in the teachings of men like Dods they were now coming to see a more dangerous form of rationalism. Universalist theologians, after all, had maintained only that a healthy piety must not contradict reason; they did not envision human rationality as capable of seeing into the inner workings of divinity. In particular, Universalists were not likely to approve of Dods's rather crudely materialistic interpretation of divine rule, especially his theory that God himself was limited or defined by the laws of electrical force.

Scientific Religion: Spiritualism

John Bovee Dods apparently did not follow a common path from interest in mesmerism to concern with spiritualism.[38] Whereas Dods viewed scientific study as a key weapon in the battle against unbelief and atheism and sought to buttress religious belief, particularly Universalism, with scientific evidence, he ultimately claimed that science was only the handmaiden of revelation. Those Universalists who, in the early 1850s, ventured into spiritualism, on the other hand, elevated the study of natural theology to new heights and looked to a purely scientific religion. Many of them saw spiritualism as a positively necessary scientific extension and fulfillment of Universalist theology. Truths that Universalists had grasped emotionally in larger outline would now be fully and rationally evident to humanity. While the evidence of pervasive Universalist involvement in the spiritualist excitement of the age remains impressionistic, it is nevertheless compelling.[39] E. Douglas Branch observed the continued presence of many Universalists and former Universalists in positions of influence in spiritualist circles,[40] and Frank Podmore's detailed study, *Modern Spiritualism*, asserts that "No religious body gave a larger contingent to the new faith than the Universalists."[41]

Many Universalists felt naturally attracted to spiritualism, which was, as R. Laurence Moore remarks, an extreme attempt to "make religion rational." Although spiritualism had links with occultism, as with Madame Blavatsky or the religious mysticism of Emanuel Swedenborg, in general it stressed not the mystical but rather "the observable and verifiable objects of empirical science." Indeed, the spiritualists' tenacious attachment to the scientific method was bound to exercise a strong appeal during a period in which many envisioned the universe as a well-regulated machine.[42] Dedicated to examining the physical aspects of creation and even deity, spiritualists took natural theology to radical conclusions: study pushed aside worship. Science did not simply validate revealed religion; science itself, they believed, could instill a religious sensibility or a concern for matters beyond immediate existence.

Various instances of supposed spirit communication, such as the existence of mediums in the Shaker communities of the 1830s, had arisen among Americans earlier in the antebellum era. But the spirit rappings reported by Margaret and Kate Fox in Hydesville, New York, in the late 1840s marked the real beginning of mid-century popular spiritualism. The Foxes did not gain immediate fame; it was not until 1849, two years after the rappings began, that they achieved much publicity. After their initial venture into "commercial" spiritualism, their November 1849 public seances in Rochester, the Fox sisters moved on to a more profitable market in Albany in early 1850; admission increased from 25 cents to a dollar. *New York Tribune* publisher and Universalist Horace Greeley, bereft after the sudden death of his five-year-old son, "Pickie," and worried about his wife's mental state, invited the Foxes to conduct a seance, and both Greeleys continued to have spiritual conversations with their dead son.

Chaperoned and encouraged by their older sister, Leah, the Fox girls had also acquired two noteworthy friends and sponsors in Universalist ministers R. P. Ambler and Calvin Brown.[43] To Ambler, the rappings represented not merely a great spiritual gift but the onset of a new age of religious enlightenment. Crude as the rappings might seem, he explained, they betokened the opening of dramatic new vistas to mankind. Ambler was eager to explain the larger significance of the exciting developments in New York. By 1851, he was publishing The *Spirit Messenger* at Springfield, Massachusetts, and asserting that faith was not a "voluntary act of the mind" but depended instead upon "evidence."[44] Only suitable investigation could prepare the mind to form a "rational and truthful belief." Phenomena such as the communications of the Fox sisters now presented the perfect opportunity for doubt-ers to be convinced of the existence of the spiritual realm. But Ambler became much more than a publicity agent for the Foxes; he had, by the early 1850s, iden-tified himself as a medium and begun publishing messages received from the spirit world.

In *Elements of Spiritual Philosophy*, for which Ambler served as medium to "spirits of the sixth circle," Universalism was clearly, if implicitly, credited with preparing the ground for the spiritualist era. The world had long suffered, Ambler explained, under "gross and earthly theories of religion"; Christianity had consisted of superstitious beliefs adhered to in order to escape the punishments of hell. For years, spirits had been repelled from earth, but finally religious thought had reached a point at which spiritual communication was possible. Simple demonstrations (rap-pings) by a lower circle of spirits were merely the beginnings of a whole new period of intercourse.

The knowledge imparted by the spirits had already confirmed a basic Universalist tenet: that no being could infinitely or eternally oppose God, that no positive prin-ciple of evil existed in the universe. Messages from the beyond indicated that the ranks of spirits contained no evil or everlastingly condemned souls, and they cau-tioned people to remember that divinity would bring goodness out of apparent evil. Above all, Ambler pointed out, communication with various levels of spirits agreed with human reason, which rejected the static concepts of heaven and hell. Spiritual growth did not occur in the "twinkling of an eye" but by progression through various stages. This view had clear links to restorationism, the position adopted by a large number of midcentury Universalists that some sort of spiritual education through limited punishment followed death.[45]

Ambler again served as medium for the "spirits of the sixth circle" in *The Spir-itual Teacher*, an 1852 work that stressed even more strongly the connection between spiritualism and human reason. Uncritical reliance on biblical authority served to contract the reason and constrain the powers of the soul, according to Ambler's sources. Presenting a novel scriptural interpretation, the work maintained that the biblical prophets had not been directly inspired by divinity but were actually only mediums, subject to errors and bias. Since the channels of communication had now been reopened, and spirits again made their appeals directly to human con-sciousness, the attitude of "blind and childish reverence" toward ancient Scripture should end.

Spiritualism, the medium Ambler predicted, would deal a final blow to the old church weapon of terror. Already, Universalism had done much to reduce ignorance and fear. But now, "an intercourse which cannot be destroyed or overthrown by worldly bigotry" was established.[46] As the age of "superstitious" belief in hell drew to a close, a new era of spirit communication was dawning; Ambler felt privileged to be a witness. Thus, a Universalist minister became the most prominent associate of the leading figures in nineteenth-century spiritualism because he saw them as heralds of a new religious consciousness.

Other spiritualists who shared a Universalist heritage also saw the new movement as giving added depth and meaning to a theology that adumbrated fundamental truths. Adin Ballou, best known for his Hopedale community, had been a Universalist since 1822, a minister at Milford, Massachusetts, and a leader of the restorationist defectors from the denomination. His restorationist beliefs have been linked to the development of his moral progressivism, which amounted to perfectionism. Like a number of disaffected restorationists, Ballou eventually became a Unitarian. Yet he continued to defend the Universalist Winchester Profession of faith, and Universalists still claimed him as an adherent.[47] Ballou asserted that a "just and discriminating" faith in spirit manifestations would promote individual and social regeneration.

This did not mean that spirits would reveal any new religious or moral philosophy essentially different from Christianity, but rather that they would reaffirm fundamental truths, purify them of error, and powerfully commend them to humanity, especially atheists and deists. Those truths were essentially the teachings of Ballou's own restorationist brand of Universalism. A basic spiritualist teaching was that at death one ascended to a level appropriate to one's spiritual development. Spiritualism also demonstrated that death did not alter one's ability to progress spiritually and that "*all*, however sluggish, will be attracted upward" by an impartial, all-loving deity.[48] Although Ballou did not explicitly invoke the doctrinal formulas of restorationist Universalism, he was certainly trying to confirm and deepen its main insights.

For Woodbury Fernald, too, spiritualism seemed to fill the gaps in Universalist theology and make its teachings more palatable. As a minister in Cabotville, Massachusetts, Fernald, one of the most active religious seekers spawned by mid–nineteenth-century Universalism, had issued forceful defenses of Universalist belief in the late 1830s and early 1840s.[49] Venturing beyond the denomination, he became first a follower of the medical clairvoyant and spiritualist philosopher Andrew Jackson Davis; according to the *Universalist Quarterly*, he was "the only expositor of the seer's revelations who approached intelligibility." For a time he became a rationalist who denounced biblical authority.[50]

By the 1850s, Fernald had settled on a version of Swedenborgianism, and he issued a popular compendium of Swedenborg's works. Swedenborg's views of the spirit world, drawn from his experiences in clairvoyance and communication with spirits, had been adopted in large measure by American spiritualists. But these popularizers emphasized that the ability to communicate with the beyond was not limited to a select few.[51] Because Swedenborg denied the traditional notions of hell, at times suggested a belief in universal restoration, and argued that all souls are capable of salvation, some Universalists could regard his theology as a "great advance" that complemented their own rejection of traditional theological doctrines. While they tended to reject the idea of spiritual flights to other worlds, Universalists could envision Swedenborgianism as part of the movement toward "the great church of the future."[52] For Fernald and perhaps for other Universalists who feared that strict Universalism could "quiet the conscience with an unwarranted sense of security," one appeal of Swedenborgianism was its greater allowance for the exercise of man's moral freedom and its offer of insight into the range of spiritual movement a soul might exercise.[53]

As Fernald continued to work out his own religious ideas, though, he came to reemphasize his Universalist faith that human freedom was subject to divine governance, and he praised this inheritance from Calvinism.[54] He believed that spiritualism helped to soften the edges of an inexorable providence without yielding to the notion of free will. If we see nothing but the "iron working of mechanical law, then woe be to our faith," he warned. But if we realize how subtly yet powerfully we are changed and touched "by the unseen beings who hover over us with their benignant powers," our faith will be enriched. There was, to be sure, a growing popular recognition of spiritual agency, Fernald admitted. But instead of addressing the regeneration and salvation of humanity, those who publicized such matters were concerned with materiality and aimless communication with "promiscuous spirits." What was needed was a deeper sense of "these spiritual beings in the care and governance of the world."

In the end, Fernald seems to have sought a reconciliation between Swedenborgianism and his original Universalism. He quoted Swedenborg to underscore a strongly Universalist sentiment: that in the midst of evil and disorder, humanity could take consolation in a vast and complicated divine plan. And he asserted an obviously Universalist type of spiritualism. God would not forsake any, he stated, although no one could predict how high anyone would be able to ascend in the spiritual realm.[55] Woodbury Fernald was thus among those who came to regard spiritualism as an extension of, rather than a departure from, Universalist teachings.

A Prophet of Universal Harmony

Despite the harmony that some saw between spiritualism and the basic elements of Universalist theology, the leading prophet of a scientifically oriented spiritualism moved in an orbit that departed sharply from the combination of piety and rationalism that had characterized Universalism since Hosea Ballou. The teachings of Andrew Jackson Davis shared enough of the central ideas of Universalism to exercise a considerable attraction among members of the denomination, yet his teachings ultimately left no room at all for the piety that was essential to the religious movement. More than any other proponent of the spiritual sciences, Davis forced Universalists to draw a clear line between the forms of popular rationalism that were acceptable to a Christian denomination and those that were not.

Born in Orange County, New York, in 1826 to an improvident father and an illiterate mother, Davis suffered failures at school and at several apprenticeships before succeeding at fourteen as a pupil and later as an instructor at a Lancastrian school in Poughkeepsie, New York. Following a two-year apprenticeship as a shoe clerk, he discovered at seventeen his talent for medical clairvoyance. On a tour in 1843, the prominent magnetizer and phrenologist J. Stanley Grimes had whipped Poughkeepsie into a frenzy of "magnetic" activity, prompting citizens to "operate" on each other. Davis displayed a curious talent when under magnetic influence: the ability to "see" and diagnose the causes of disease.[56] One of his first patients, Universalist minister Gibson Smith, faithfully recounted his amazing diagnostic feats, noting his ability to travel mentally over great distances in order to give examinations.[57]

Unlike the Fox sisters, Davis resisted commercial sensationalism. Following his reported encounters with the spirit of the Greek physician Galen, who offered him medical instruction, and with the spirit of Emanuel Swedenborg, who certified him as a transmitter of divine truth, he established a medical practice extending into Connecticut and, eventually, to New York City. He was also moved to record more general "revelations" for the benefit of humanity. After choosing "botanic doctor" S. S. Lyon as his magnetizer and Universalist minister William Fishbough of New Haven as his scribe, he proceeded to dictate his first massive tome, *The Principles of Nature, Her Divine Revelations and a Voice to Mankind,* which was published in 1847. Fishbough, a self-educated pastor who had earlier served the Universalist church in Taunton, Massachusetts, regarded Davis's request as a divine command. Although he may have held reservations about some of the seer's ideas, he became a disciple of Davis.[58] In his solemn and effusive introduction to *The Principles of Nature,* Fishbough described Davis as "exalted to a position which gave access to a knowledge of the structure and laws of the whole material and spiritual universe."[59] He would soon be joined by other Universalists who shared a fascination for the thoughts of Davis, even if they were not always in total agreement with them.

Many contemporaries recognized Davis as a prodigy. Dr. George Bush, a professor of Hebrew language and literature at New York University with a keen interest in Swedenborgianism, expressed astonishment at Davis's knowledge of ancient languages and culture. Brook Farm founder George Ripley and Fourierist Parke Godwin conveyed their amazement at his grasp of literary history and powers of integration. Naturally, he also had his critics: Edgar Allan Poe, for example, thought he was an outrageous dreamer. But his acquaintance and even familiarity with fields of knowledge ranging from ancient history to modern science seem to mark him as an eccentric genius, and the way he came by his learning remains something of a mystery. While he probably borrowed geological ideas from Robert Chambers's *Vestiges of Creation* (1844) and was obviously immersed in Swedenborg's writings, there is little evidence that he spent much time reading scholarly books or conferring with highly educated people.[60]

Davis did not share the obsession of other spiritualists and mediums with physical phenomena, such as table lifting or materialized forms, and he frowned on an overemphasis on some ideal "other side."[61] Perhaps for this very reason, a group of his faithful followers, led by Universalists and former Universalists, saw Davis as the herald of a new age of scientific religion. William Fishbough exulted that "the sublime results of science" would expand the mind "beyond the narrow circle of which *self* is *centre*" and "unite the soul with those things which it beholds, contemplates, admires."[62] For Davis and his followers, spiritualism offered insight into the universe and the divinity that controlled it, and it promised man a new religious sense by giving him scientific evidence instead of miracles.

Davis was apparently not raised with any particular denominational affiliation. Yet, like so many eventual Universalists, he had early questioned received beliefs. In his autobiography, *The Magic Staff*, Davis described his childhood disillusionment with the teaching that an omniscient and omnipotent God allowed people to go to hell.[63] It is likely that he refined many of his notions with the help of the Universalists and former Universalists who became his followers, including Fishbough, the scribe to whom he dictated his major works. His autobiography quoted a critic who charged that his "theology is inclined toward Universalism" and who noted his association with Fishbough and "others of like faith."[64]

His first published work, *The Principles of Nature*, presented ideas that certainly seem to have owed something to Universalist preaching and writings. Davis's major goal in *The Principles of Nature* was to demonstrate the reign of universal goodness and harmony. He acknowledged that, to the naked eye, disorder and confusion seemed to mark the world. But this was because people viewed their surroundings from a severely limited perspective. Speaking from the "second sphere" above the earth, he assured his audience that the universe was structured to produce "unity, harmony, reciprocation and no inequity among parts." All people would eventually experience harmony through spiritual growth in life or thereafter. Ultimately, there would be one body "whose organs will promote each other's good," since all things were "but parts of one stupendous whole."

One could have confidence, the seer argued, only in that which was beyond the influence of all contingencies and circumstances; the Creator's laws manifested a "universal security and divine benevolence." Thus, Davis proclaimed it impossible that a "positive opposite" could exist in nature. He also asserted that, although people exercised a degree of earthly freedom, ultimate moral freedom could not exist, for if it did the universe would be "disunited"; confusion and chaos would reign because ignorant and imperfect humanity would control the universe. It was precisely such emphases on human will and power that had resulted in a theological system built upon twisted notions of original sin and atonement, a system that unfairly portrayed God's wisdom and love.[65] Davis believed that it was the role of departed spirits to instigate the spiritual growth that would raise the earthbound above such views.[66]

Davis vigorously condemned the idea that fear should play any role in religious sentiment and argued that it produced a selfish and anxious concern about one's future state. The idea that the judgment of sin was postponed—the traditional Christian eschatology—upset Davis; sin brought its own punishment in this life. His conception of a perfectly balanced universe, in which humanity as a whole necessarily suffered for the sins committed by individuals, showed a conviction of the organic wholeness of the human race. "Man must die to egoism and be born again into the spirit of universal life," he advised.[67] For Davis, salvation necessarily involved a profound realization of the interdependence of all life.

Yet, even if Davis's ideas may have been shaped partly by traditional Universalist teachings, in basic ways he departed radically from those teachings. That he was no Universalist was made clear in his multivolume work *The Great Harmonia*, which he began publishing in 1850. With an overwhelming flood of verbiage, Davis sought to explain his supposedly scientific understanding of universal harmony. Blaming most religious misunderstandings on the divorce between spirit and matter, he argued that truth was a unit, that spirit was simply the flower of matter, that both were actual substances.[68] He insisted that human beings were fully integrated entities, that diseases of the body and sins of the soul could not be treated as isolated conditions. Davis attacked the "superficial" materialism that treated spirit as outside the realm of scientific investigation and that relegated spiritual matters to the uninformed speculations of metaphysicians and ministers.[69] "Spirit" was only substanceless and formless to those who were in a natural state of perception. Transcending that state required a kind of scientific proof; biblical faith and sectarian doctrine, he asserted, could no longer sustain belief in immortality.[70] Davis elaborated endlessly on the belief that, if people could move beyond the restrictive dualities of nature and the supernatural, matter and spirit, they could actually begin to see the present, eternal harmony.

We may be in danger of finding a coherence in Davis's work that was not there; his writings often read like interminable hallucinations. But the main tendencies of his conception seem clear enough. Whereas, to Universalists, the pain and disorder of the world had to be accepted and faced through faith in a benevolent divinity, for Davis, "faith" had become as outmoded a concept as original sin. Sinfulness became an imbalance to be corrected not an integral aspect of the human condition. Davis also rejected any notion of Christ as redeemer; miracles were by definition, impossible. Unlike earlier spiritual scientists, who had retained some sense of transcendent divinity, Davis was a thoroughgoing pantheist and rationalist who believed that man must—and eventually would—cease to revere a divine "idol" in order to appreciate the marvelous functioning of the harmonious cosmos.

Beyond Supernaturalism: The Spiritualists' New Age

James Turner has observed that by the 1850s—the period when Andrew Jackson Davis was writing—divinity had been awkwardly divided in the minds of many American Christians. God operated both personally, on a spiritual and often sentimentalized level, and also impersonally through natural law. In this latter mode, his rule was regular and predictable but more distant and less meaningful for individuals. Theoretically, God's omnipotence was not reduced by this division. Nevertheless, the "intimacy, security and immediacy of God's presence was compromised psychologically" by the growing tendency to associate divine rule with natural law.[71] Among Universalists, there had always been a strong desire to hold together the personal and impersonal aspects of divine rule; God was a loving and benevolent father but an all-powerful creator and impartial governor as well. Ultimately, the almost desperate need to maintain a unified conception of divinity led some Universalists to embrace spiritualist visions, such as those of Davis, who rejected any separation of nature and spirit.

Shortly after the appearance of *The Principles of Nature*, a journal dedicated to the study and spread of Davis's teachings and of spiritualism in general, the *Univercoelum and Spiritual Philosopher*, began publication. Edited by former Universalist minister S. B. Brittan and including articles by many Universalist or former Universalist ministers, the magazine announced that, in order to "preserve faith" and "increase piety," a new and higher revelation was needed. "We need a truer idea of Nature in order that what is called supernaturalism, with all its blinding and obstructing influence, may be banished from among men." Rational, objective confirmation of the soul's immortality was called for, declared the first issue. People had relied for too long on a blind belief in Christ's resurrection, and such faith was no longer sufficient.[72]

The world was awakening, though, and human reason was now stirring against "the chains of theological authority." Davis's revelations provided a key for hope. Disbelief had reigned for years, according to one contributor, because people sought evidence of immortality in the nature of things but were unable to see the connection between material and spiritual existence; skepticism and creeping materialism were the result.[73] The religious belief of most people, another writer asserted, was a kind of supernaturalism, which they did not expect to understand, and "which is esteemed in proportion to its distance from the sphere of human comprehension."[74] William Fishbough explained the appeal of Davis's system to human reason by noting that it presented a unified conception of the whole universe. In the present age, the old superstitions were vanishing, he concluded, and people had to have rational bases for belief.[75]

Again and again, the *Univercoelum* attacked what it regarded as a superstitious and crippling supernaturalism. It was now necessary to satisfy men regarding "how God exists" and to convince them that, in the attempt to visualize a being apart from nature, they were only "perplexing their mind to no profit." People had to understand the "mode" of God's existence; faith required knowledge about the "structure of the immortal, spiritual body."[76] One writer, echoing Davis, maintained that religious sentiment would ultimately settle at two poles: rationalism and Catholicism. There was no middle ground for consistent belief between the two, he asserted; one had to settle for reason or authority. Protestantism, certainly, had eliminated many of the Catholic "abominations," but in rejecting the ideal of unity and in maintaining the old emphasis on faith as a mystery, it had opened itself to blind and destructive squabbling. A healthy rationalism was now extending itself into Protestant thought, as demonstrated by the increasing German skepticism about miracles. Eventually, he predicted, Protestants would have to become rationalists or re-accept Catholic authority.[77]

For its editor and contributors, the *Univercoelum* heralded the next logical step beyond Universalist theology. Woodbury Fernald, whose general attraction to spiritualism we have already noted, lamented that God was "set apart to bewilder the imagination and divide the mind."[78] The journal's objective was to overcome this division through the demonstration of a "universal and harmonious unity."[79] Before the advent of the spiritual revelations, a contributor observed, people had only vague notions about the spirit world and conscious existence in the hereafter. Spiritualist teachings remedied this problem by showing the universe to be one great body, of which deity was the soul. Exclusiveness of feeling among humans could now be overcome, as they looked beyond "mere evanescent gratification of the outer sense" to "stupendous views of future existence."[80] In comparison with the promise of such visions, traditional Universalist faith in a final restoration must have seemed feeble indeed.

In his *Macrocosm and Microcosm; or, The Universe Without and the Universe Within* (1852), Fishbough implied that theology (and, presumably, Universalist theology in particular) needed to be replaced by a scientific spiritualism. Fishbough emphasized that his writings represented a "rational deduction of philosophy" and not the "teachings of Scripture." But his was not any traditional sort of philosophy. Newtonianism, he believed, had engendered materialism and skepticism, especially among scientific minds, because it was only a "mechanical" form of philosophizing, which ignored the spiritual. Our minds thus conceived of the spiritual as some "unsubstantial figment," an unsatisfying and unconvincing belief. But the concepts advanced by the spiritual scientists, which indicated that there was a simple universal reality, a "divinely-constituted fabric," were, he asserted, more compatible with the notion of immediate divine superintendence.[81] Fishbough was convinced that spiritual science would help people recapture the needed sense of omnipotent divinity directing all events for good.

Similarly, in his book *Man and His Relations* (1864), Davis's disciple S. B. Brittan pointed out the objective grounds that the spiritual sciences provided for religious belief. Formerly minister of the First Universalist Church in Albany, Brittan described the electromagnetic aura surrounding all beings. He lauded recent scientific discoveries that illustrated the lack of human freedom and the mutual dependencies in the "complex web of existence." He noted, too, that scientific investigation had helped to indicate how psychological and physical factors directly influenced behavior. People would be more charitable, he hoped, once they realized how much in life was beyond their control. And in a typical Universalist refrain, he observed that they would be likely to accept forms of criminal punishment that were "benevolent in nature."[82] Like Fishbough and other spiritualists, Brittan regarded the rational study of spiritual science as a means of moving beyond a Universalist theology that had stopped short of full religious truth.

Indeed, in the eyes of many who had come to spiritualism through Universalist ranks, the shortcomings of their old faith were only too evident. Many contributions to the *Univercoelum* included polemical assaults on the denomination for its attitude toward members who were attracted to spiritual sciences. The first issues of the journal complained of the "uncharitable spirit" shown by Universalists and loftily proclaimed that many had "stepped beyond that sect."[83] When the prominent Universalist minister and journalist Thomas Whittemore charged Davis and his followers with "infidelity, pantheism, materialism, virtual atheism and mercenary motives," he brought down a hail of sharp responses from defenders of the new ideas.

One contributor concluded that Whittemore and others were angry because many spiritualists had not withdrawn from Universalist fellowship. With dripping irony, he pointed out that "when we joined, we were not required to take a thought test, or to incarcerate our reason"; indeed, Universalists had asserted the "largest liberty." And, he contended, we "still believe in the true relationship of men established by the universal father." Universalism was "petrifying," since its leading voices found it necessary to use terms like "infidel" and "pantheist."[84] John Murray Spear, namesake of the father of American Universalism, brother of prison reformer

Charles Spear, and now a spiritual medium, made similar points. In 1852, he reported observations on the current state of affairs transmitted to him by the deceased John Murray himself. Priests had always been deadly enemies of Christian freedom, Murray warned from the beyond. Now, some who profess entire freedom have "stopped in their onward course," but the advance of truth could not be stopped, he stated, assuring those who were receptive that ever greater insights were to be expected.[85] Rather than continuing to trust in human rationality and upholding freedom from creedal forms, spiritualists charged, the denomination itself had become hardened by dogma.

The Boston Universalist Association, the *Univercoelum* pointed out in January 1848, now insisted that one had to believe in miracles and the resurrection of Jesus in order to be considered a Christian.[86] In Pennsylvania as well, there had been a "retrograde movement" among Universalists to institute a biblical creed.[87] Universalist minister and early spiritualist convert R. P. Ambler noted that the New York Universalist Association had proposed a resolution to allow only the ordained to administer communion, betraying a superstitiousness highly uncharacteristic of the denomination.[88] Perhaps most upsetting, according to S. B. Brittan, was that mainly clergy had been encouraged to attend a recent meeting of the U.S. Convention of Universalists, a major departure from earlier lay involvement. Liberal, progressive clergy, he maintained, had stayed away.[89] Over the years, another writer asserted, Universalists had justly protested against misrepresentation and abuse; they had been champions of reason. But denominational leaders like Whittemore, Thomas Sawyer, and others now simply denounced Davis and his cohorts instead of treating them with respect and engaging them in rational discussion, as they did other opponents.[90]

In the eyes of the *Univercoelum*'s staff, then, Universalism was becoming another closed-minded sect. The journal's editors were delighted to print a letter from a former Universalist who insisted that the denomination's supposed openness and encouragement of freedom of thought was a "fraud."[91] And they happily reported that the Reverend Z. Baker had withdrawn from his pastorate of the Fourth Universalist Church in New York City because he could not avow that the Bible contained a "special, sufficient revelation from God"; he had become a contributor to the *Univercoelum*.[92]

In a slightly more charitable vein, former Universalist minister and *Univercoelum* contributor Thomas Lake Harris argued that, as the spiritual nature "developed in wisdom," one passed from the orthodox to the "pseudo-liberal" churches — Unitarian, Universalist, Christian, or Quaker — and eventually to knowledge of the grand spiritual universe. The "noblest spirits in Universalism" had already begun that journey.[93] When the young clairvoyant Semantha Mettler of Connecticut left Presbyterianism for Universalism in 1843, she had not yet reached, as she then believed she had, the "highest ideal of the Christian faith," according to her spiritualist biographer.[94] Universalist minister–turned–spiritualist J. M. Peebles sat with an entranced medium in his library in 1863 and saw Hosea Ballou, then dead twelve years, appear; Ballou took a Bible off a shelf and read to him kindly. Peebles remarked, "We believe in Universalism still, as a *faith*; and, in becoming a Spiritualist, have only obeyed the apostolic injunction, 'Add to your faith . . . *knowledge.*'"[95]

Critical of Universalism as an incomplete faith and sometimes bitter over their treatment by Universalist notables, spiritualists nonetheless offered insightful obser-vations about the state of mid–nineteenth-century Universalism. Referring particu-larly to ultra-Universalism, which taught that all punishment for sin ended at death, Brittan concluded that this view had "little or no vitality," that as a reaction of the mind against the "ultra-orthodoxy of the past" it had largely achieved its mission and was now withering.[96] The spiritual scientists also appear to have recognized that, as the idea of universal salvation became less controversial, the denomination had begun to lose its rationale as a distinctive liberal Christian movement.

These critics believed Universalism's spiritual retardation was particularly evident in its reluctance to implement programs of practical reform. While the original pious Universalists had projected a universe that operated under a benevolent God, who aimed toward a unity of all life, current members, spiritualists charged, were doing nothing to build on that base. Reporting on a meeting of the Universalist General Reform Association in Boston, the *Univercoelum* observed that the denom-ination seemed concerned only with its own perpetuation and, while ignoring the needs of "suffering humanity," continued its "usual cant about partialists and endless woe."[97] Instead of promoting true brotherhood, Thomas Lake Harris charged, Uni-versalists encouraged a divisive, sectarian spirit.[98]

Other spiritualists attacked Universalism for failing to sponsor communal living arrangements, thus falling short in its supposed commitment to universal brother-hood. Andrew Jackson Davis believed his own revelations sanctioned and confirmed what Charles Fourier had proven by "mathematical induction"; Davis's Universalist followers also applauded the "harmony and brotherhood" of associationism as a practical expression of the Universalist eschatological ideal.[99] The *Spirit of the Age*, which absorbed the short-lived *Univercoelum* in 1849 and also included a number of writers with Universalist associations, announced its dedication to Christian so-cialism in its prospectus. The journal sought the "reconciliation of conflicting clas-ses" and respect for the "laws of universal unity."[100] Fourier's ideas found favor in the periodical because he "viewed man collectively as one historical or social being, made up of many parts or organs."[101] Denominational Universalism, by contrast, appeared obstinate and backward, preaching universal salvation to those already converted and refusing to embrace the higher knowledge that its own teaching foreshadowed.

Universalists had, in fact, been prominent in the six Fourierist phalanxes that sprang up in the mid-forties around Rochester and Watertown, New York. And the well-known Universalist layman Horace Greeley, who had exhibited a strong per-sonal interest in spiritualism, had been an active promoter of Fourierism at Brook Farm and the Sylvania and North American phalanxes.[102] Universalist minister and later spiritualist Adin Ballou had started a socialistic community in Hopedale, Mas-sachusetts. But the denomination as a whole, in the eyes of its spiritualist critics, had neglected or refused to take advantage of its liberation from the weight of traditional eschatology, and thus it had done little to realize its vaunted goal of human brotherhood.

The Universalists who were drawn to extreme spiritualist ideals thus viewed the denomination as strangely indifferent, if not hostile, to the marvelous possibilities opened up by the new scientific revelations. The dead were now taking a central role in the reformation of the living; it was necessary to heed their messages. John Murray Spear, functioning as a medium for spirits, offered the most elaborate picture of spiritual intervention in mortal affairs. In April 1853, he was moved to write about an Association of Beneficents, which had been formed in the spirit world to accomplish certain benevolent ends on earth. The Beneficents represented only one of seven bodies, including the Healthfulizers, the Governmentalizers, and the Electricizers, which were all subordinate to a General Assembly, or Council, of the Spirit World; Daniel Webster directed the supreme body. The spirit world sought to advise the living on the construction of a new government, a new church, and a new code of moral principles to ameliorate the human condition.

Spear also received instruction from Benjamin Franklin, head of the Electricizers, on the construction of an electrical machine, a "New Motive Power." With supporters including former Universalist minister and spiritualist editor Simon Crosby Hewitt, Spear asserted that the machine would derive power not from "frictional or galvanic evolution" but from the *"electric life-currents of the universe."* This mechanism, Spear avowed, would be a " 'thing of life,' — having motion *in itself."* The machine, built at High Rock, outside of Lynn, Massachusetts, in 1854, was a "combination of mineral substances impregnated by magnetisms — the whole arranged and charged in accordance with precise directions from invisible instructors."

Appointed as the "Mary of the new Dispensation" was Semantha Mettler, a former Universalist, who went into a trance and essentially gave "birth." Filled with life force, the machine produced a *"pulsatory* motion," according to observers, that suggested the action of a "heart, beating, possibly, in sympathy with the Grand Central Magnetic Heart of the Universe, by whose pulsations all things live." "Unto your Earth a child is born," Spear announced, "Its name shall be called the Electrical Motor. It is the offspring of *mind,* — of the union of mind with matter impregnated by invisible elements."

His excitement notwithstanding, Spear's machine made a miserable debut — it was "unable to turn even a coffee mill," according to one critic — and was partially destroyed by a mob in Randolph, New York, in 1854. Yet Spear remained serene about the project and its promise for the future spirit-directed technological advancement of humanity. Toward the doubters and scoffers, his perspective was "Father, forgive them, for they know not what they did." Indeed, Spear clearly saw himself as a herald of a teaching that would supersede "Christianism." A faith that did not present God as "tangible, material Existence," "Christianism" failed to see the present life as but a "rudimental state, the commencement of a vast series of unfolding and progressive lives."[103]

Spear and other Universalist popularizers of Davis, especially Fishbough and Brittan, certainly represented the most flamboyant involvement of Universalists and former Universalists with mid–nineteenth-century spiritualism. Yet it would be wrong to imagine that they were fully exceptional Universalist figures, caught up in a foreign set of ideas. In the early 1870s, the Reverend Olympia Brown could still assert that "half of Universalist ministers are Spiritualists and make no secret of it."[104] There is evidence that well into the 1860s many Universalist ministers could participate in spiritualist activity and expression without risking denominational discipline. The biographer of James M. Peebles noted that he left his Universalist pastorate in Baltimore in 1856 free of any formal denominational discipline. In 1871, Peebles visited with the Reverend H. Bain, a Universalist minister in Goldsborough, North Carolina, who was also a "firm, out-spoken Spiritualist" and whose daughter was a medium.[105] In the same year, the Vermont State Convention of Universalists considered, but did not pass, a resolution to close Universalist churches to spiritualist teachings that did not grant the primacy of Christian Scripture. Spiritualist ideas were essentially prohibited in most other churches at this time; in failing to agree even to set any conditions for these teachings, Universalists underscored both the denomination's historic devotion to toleration and the strength of spiritualism within its ranks.[106] Spiritualists appear to have used Universalist facilities frequently for their meetings; in one or two cases, Universalist congregations even abandoned the denomination to become spiritualists.[107]

These strong connections should hardly surprise us. Since Universalists were often engaged in an intense quest for religious understanding, their views had always held the potential to produce various forms of radicalism. There seems to be little room for doubt that midcentury spiritualism took considerable impetus from a group of Hosea Ballou's more radical heirs. Recent scholarship has confirmed, moreover, that there were close ties not only between midcentury spiritualism and idealistic communal reform movements, such as Fourierism, but also between the spiritualists and the most radical forms of feminism and even abolitionism.[108] There were, in short, clear links among religious, social, and political radicalism at the time. As followers of Davis and other spiritualists criticized Universalism for stopping short in progress toward both spiritual maturity and social progress, the movement's leaders had to respond to a variety of unsettling trends, which were all the more threatening because they seemed to have such close links with their own movement.

In Defense of Revelation

After a number of Universalists had become prominent disciples of Andrew Jackson Davis in the late 1840s, Thomas Whittemore, a stalwart defender of traditional Universalism, plaintively hoped that "the time would come when the Universalist denomination will not be the receptacle of every strange thing under heaven."[109] While Whittemore could record some favorable remarks about a work such as Fishbough's *Macrocosm and Microcosm*, noting that it tried to blend spiritual faith and natural science, Swedenborg and Comte, he vigorously rejected both spiritualist communications and the notion that they could supersede biblical revelation.[110] By the 1860s, Whittemore's wish had essentially come true: Universalism was no longer serving as a breeding ground for the spiritual sciences. Increasingly, Universalists were forced to draw the line between the sort of rationalism that complemented piety and the sort that they believed destroyed it.

Many Universalists found in the spiritual sciences evidence to support the grand symbol of the denomination: the human race as one body or organism perfected in the restoration.[111] Phrenology, mesmerism, and spiritualism aimed to reveal not only the inner mechanisms of human actions but also the heretofore unperceived relationships among human beings, who were part of a divine family. The spiritual sciences, moreover, appealed to Universalists as new approaches to the human condition that seemed to promise a replacement for the traditional eschatology that Universalism had rejected. This scientific interest in the physical makeup of humanity and the environmental influences on it, in effect a concern with individual and social psychology, amounted to an early form of modern liberal behaviorism. Again, it is not surprising that Universalism, a movement that emphasized the fulfillment of God's will and the lack of human freedom, was one of the important spawning places of this outlook.

The new currents of phrenology and mesmerism could be reconciled with Universalism to the extent that they continued to recognize divine transcendence. Apparently offering marvelous new insights into humanity and its relation to the divine, phrenology and mesmerism could be considered highly promising fields of natural theology. Spiritualism, on the other hand, had pantheistic overtones; it usually dismissed the whole notion of a pious regard for a superintending deity and the necessity of revelation. Spiritualists tried to use their discoveries to herald a new revelation, which they saw as superior to the Bible and in which the natural swallowed the divine. A Universalist reaction against such notions was probably inevitable, especially in light of the broader midcentury breakdown of natural theology.

Among many rationalistic Universalists, the confident natural theology of the antebellum era encouraged ever-greater expectations that science could confirm and illustrate religious truths; the advent of "spiritual science" was particularly exciting. But, by 1849, with the publication of Horace Bushnell's *God in Christ*, natural theology was starting to show signs of weakness, and American Protestant thought began to move in a very different direction. Even traditional, hard-line Calvinists, who fought against Bushnell's attempts to discredit scientific natural theology, continued to retreat under the force of new philosophical currents and scientific learning. Apologetics — "extended analogies, complex disquisitions on causation, incessant criticism and interpretation of new scientific theories and discoveries" — did not, in Bushnell's mind, provide the basis for faith; his writings helped remove religious belief from the realm of rational proof.[112]

By the 1860s, natural theology was fading in the face of positivism's insistence that only what could be perceived could be known and with the spreading acceptance of Kantian principles among American intellectuals. Natural theologians "began to conclude that their discipline could not produce a great deal of information about God." Especially after the publication of Darwin's *On the Origin of Species*, theology became more of a historical and cultural discipline, less closely tied to natural science, for Universalists and other liberal denominations. Conservative evangelicals as well, faced with geological and biological evidence that seemed to cast doubt on, rather than to confirm, divine providence, eliminated natural theology from the curricula of their seminaries. Among most American Protestants, science was no longer viewed as a means of validating religious belief.[113]

For spiritualists, this move away from a scientific approach to religion had dangerous implications. Davis commented on the trend in *The Approaching Crisis* (1869), a review of Bushnell's thinking. Davis believed that the great problems of the age—growing skepticism and religious infidelity—were rooted in the existing gulf between rationalism and supernaturalism. He contended that only a "rationalistic Christianity" could resolve human anxieties and doubts. But Bushnell insisted on keeping the rational and the supernatural separate, making the supernatural miraculous, mysterious, beyond comprehension. In place of the "dying dogmas" of the "supernatural, oriental scheme," Davis argued, man needed the understanding provided by phrenology and the corrective measures of Fourier's organization.[114] These and other enlightened programs had no room for spiritually retarded notions of sin and repentance.

While Universalists, as we have seen, could agree with Davis on many key points, through the 1850s and later, they more and more openly opposed the relentless "rationalism" of views such as his. The 1854 break between Davis and his long-time associate, former Universalist minister William Fishbough, was significant in this connection. In a long letter, which Davis reproduced in his autobiography, Fishbough asserted his belief in Christ as savior; he could no longer associate, he wrote, with Davis's admirers, who found the idea of humbling themselves and taking up the cross "extremely distasteful." Fishbough declared his belief in the Bible as the highest and truest revelation and predicted a coming struggle between "religionism and anti-religionism, Bibleism and anti-Bibleism." In response, Davis rejected any "scheme of salvation" as recorded in any book, proclaimed his belief in the progressive growth and harmony of all humanity, and labeled Fishbough an "orthodox" believer.[115]

Not surprisingly, the *Universalist Quarterly* made sarcastic comments on Davis's state of mind and the distressing fact that he had attracted so many Universalists to his notions.[116] In 1859, the *Quarterly* lauded Bushnell's *Nature and the Supernatural* as "the most philosophical attempt to resist rationalism yet given to the public" and condemned the tendency to resolve the supernatural truth of Christianity into a "nature-religion." Especially disturbing were materialistic efforts to enslave man to his bodily organization.[117] Universalists could not blithely describe sin as merely incidental to human growth, as Davis did. Although most rejected any traditional notion of the fall, they believed human beings were spiritually weak, heedlessly pursued their own pleasures, and were prone to sinful behavior. Humanity required redemption by, and reconciliation to, God, not simply greater knowledge and growth. The recent spread of pantheism, a *Quarterly* contributor asserted in 1857, robbed God of sovereignty and freedom, eliminated human accountability to law, and denied the need for worship.[118]

Throughout the 1850s and 1860s, the *Quarterly* presented an increasing number of articles that warned of the spread of a rationalism dangerous to piety. To be sure, many of these were in reaction to such currents as the new biblical criticism that was emerging from Germany. But Universalists were also responding to the dangerous tendency among their kindred, including those who had ventured deeply into the spiritual sciences, to insist on rational explanations instead of transcendental faith. A commentator in April 1858 was compelled to emphasize how much about life was simply beyond human comprehension. Christianity, he insisted, was "not wholly a matter of intellectual conviction."[119]

In a long discussion of "rationalistic theology" in 1860, a *Quarterly* writer attempted to explain the difference between a rationalist and a Universalist. A rationalist, he pointed out, gives the soul "unlimited positive authority; we give it certain negative authority." The rationalist "says the soul—unaided—discovers every necessary truth; we say many truths could not be discovered but, which being revealed, we can identify and confirm." Rationalism, he believed, had served a good purpose; it had arisen in response to the "arbitrary attempt" of Calvinism and Arminianism to "tyrannize over the human soul." But having helped the cause of religious faith by showing the weaknesses of both systems, rationalism now attacked that faith by raising doubts about revelation.[120] Adin Ballou, an active spiritualist who had transcribed his dead son's communications, reflected by 1871 the *Quarterly*'s continuing criticism of spiritualism. Although he did not disavow a belief in spirit communication, Ballou had become disenchanted with spiritualism because it placed scientific knowledge above faith and, in denying Christ's divinity, had become antichristian.[121] Ballou's disillusionment would not have surprised the Reverend A. St. John Chambre, who predicted in 1866 that rationalism would eventually lead to an unsatisfying "bald naturalism." But such a teaching could never prevail: "We feel, we know, that somewhere are the realms of the supernatural," he concluded.[122]

Nor did the answer to individual and social needs lie in "community schemes" that looked to the right organization of society for progress and redemption.[123] In a long piece titled "Fourierism and Similar Schemes," Hosea Ballou 2nd strongly attacked the idea that the removal of the "outward occasions of evil" by a restructuring of external social conditions was the answer to individual reformation. Such thinking, he believed, reflected the attitude prevalent in France at the end of the eighteenth century. Ballou cited approvingly the observations of French historian Guizot on the state of the French public mind at that time. While there was little faith in God or a future life, there was much love for man and an immoderate search for his immediate happiness. Blame for human misery was assigned to correctible social arrangements, but the result was chaos brought on by the rule of ideologues.[124] These thoughts suggest that, in their efforts to repudiate the excesses of spiritualism, Universalist thinkers were also seeking to divorce their movement from any form of political or social radicalism.

It seems less than accidental that, in the 1860s, as these intellectual limits for Universalist teachings were being ever more widely propounded, the first serious efforts to establish an overall system of church organization were carried through, and basic standards of worship and discipline for the entire denomination were established. Church committees began to debate whether it was possible to adopt "some form of organization that shall give us system, unity and harmony as a Christian body."[125] In part, such moves were an inevitable reaction to the near-anarchy that had marked the movement from its beginning. But the push for uniform rules had more immediate causes as well. A threatening "radicalism" emerged as a central concern of denominational leaders in the years following the Civil War.

In 1867, the first and most famous meeting of the Free Religious Association was held in Boston, and the ideas expressed there seemed to confirm common suspicions, shared by many Universalist leaders, that proponents of spiritualism, scientific rationalism, pantheism, and atheism were working together to destroy all Christian belief. It was an outwardly bewildering assembly; among the speakers was Ralph Waldo Emerson, whose expansive remarks could have supported the most extreme forms of spiritualism: he asserted that "the perfect law of duty corresponds with the laws of chemistry, of vegetation, of astronomy."[126] Prominent among the other speakers was Henry Blanchard, a self-described "radical" and "liberal Christian," who had recently left the Universalist clergy "because I was not willing to owe allegiance to denominational authority."[127]

Blanchard saw two tendencies among Universalists: a "growing liberality" among the laity, which he applauded, and a mostly clerical desire "to have ritualistic services and a ministry quite distinctly separated from the people; and something of a desire to have a church government, like the Episcopalians." The latter tendency was dangerously powerful, and it prevented Universalists from working with other liberal groups. "No one," concluded Blanchard, "desirous of securing a free religious association, can hope for any assistance from an organization so compact, sectarian, [and] intolerant as this."[128] Unitarian Thomas Wentworth Higginson lamented the fate of "young Universalism," which had paralleled that of other liberal churches; ministers who had been progressive twenty years earlier "now control the body, and keep it immovable."[129] Clearly, many who had once thought the movement in the vanguard of true liberalism were now becoming deeply alienated.

That critical changes were taking place in the denomination is beyond question; Russell Miller shows that, by the time of the centennial convention in 1870, a "real organizational transformation" had been effected.[130] The changes involved not only outward forms but the very meaning of what it was to be a Universalist. In 1867, a Committee on the State of the Church had reported to the General Convention a growing and dangerous religious skepticism within the denomination; the General Convention had responded with a "Declaration and Interpretation" of the Winchester Profession of 1803, citing the "evident intention of the authors . . . to affirm the divine authority of the Scriptures and the Lordship of Jesus Christ." At the centennial convention in 1870, a revised denominational constitution for the first time made consent to the Winchester Profession "a specific condition of fellowship"; even more notable is that the long-cherished liberty clause was dropped.[131] The effects of such changes were broadly evident. The Reverend J. O. Barrett, biographer of James M. Peebles, complained in 1872 that he had been excommunicated by the Illinois State Committee of Universalists in 1869 "solely for teaching the gospel of angel ministry." He also listed almost twenty Universalist ministers who had suffered similar fates, including an N. Connor, who was dismissed for "disbelief in the plenary inspiration of the Bible, the resurrection of the physical body of Christ, and other minor opinions."[132]

The dramatic high point of this effort to define and limit Universalism was the heresy trial of Herman Bisbee in 1872. Bisbee, a Vermont native who had become a Universalist minister in St. Anthony (now St. Paul), Minnesota, was openly denounced in the denominational press for a series of "radical lectures" that he had given in Minneapolis. Though Bisbee considered himself an ardent Universalist, his lectures explicitly denounced the traditional understanding of biblical authority, all belief in miracles, and any faith but "natural religion." According to the *Uni-*

versalist (Boston), he had utterly disparaged the Bible and Christianity and had shown "an entire disregard of the obligations of fellowship by preaching and publishing sentiments subversive of the very foundations on which he ostensibly stands."[133] Local enemies of Bisbee pushed to bring a case against him before the Minnesota Convention, which proceeded to withdraw Bisbee's fellowship. Despite a unanimous vote of confidence from his own congregation, Bisbee resigned. He would study at the Harvard Divinity School and in Heidelberg; later, he became a Unitarian minister in South Boston. The whole affair became a subject of heated controversy in Universalist publications, but the judgment stood.[134] No longer could Universalism be associated in any way with rationalistic materialism, spiritualism, or pantheism.

We saw in chapter 4 that even as the denomination as a whole came to sanction moderate reform efforts, it increasingly held at arm's length the most radical forms of abolitionism and feminism. The evidence of this chapter's look at Universalism and the spiritual sciences adds a further dimension to our picture. It becomes clear that, after midcentury, denominational leaders made a conscious decision to dissociate their church from any vision or program that seemed to threaten either basic Christian doctrines or fundamental social structures. Thus, as Universalism gained social respectability, as the denomination founded colleges and universities and moved into the mainstream of American Protestant culture, it also discouraged many of the more adventurous lines of popular thought. Not surprisingly, it appears that, in the 1870s, more than a few Universalists were drawn away to Christian Science, a movement that sought the realization of spiritual power now, rather than the assurance of a sovereign God and future redemption.[135]

Winthrop Hudson has asserted that the denomination never completely recovered from its encounter with spiritualism, but he does not explain exactly what he means.[136] The evidence of this chapter suggests that Universalist leaders, recoiling from trends to which the popular rationalism of their own movement had given rise, encouraged a newly restrained view of the role of reason in the cultivation of popular liberal religion. Since before the time of Hosea Ballou, Universalists had tried to balance a searching, questioning rationalism, in the tradition of the Enlightenment, with a pietistic faith in the supernatural rule of God. But the forms taken by the unbridled religious rationalism of the antebellum era were unpalatable to the majority of a group that was only now achieving a settled and comfortable status, at least in the Northeast. Thus, even as the movement sought to define and structure itself more clearly, its original character as a spontaneous blend of popular piety and rationalism was fading.

Winning the Battle, Losing the War

W hen Hosea Ballou died in 1852, belief in the supernatural rule of God apparently held sway among most American Protestants, but the idea of universal salvation remained highly suspect. Twenty years later, supernatural rule had fallen under serious question, but except among outspoken theologians and conservative evangelicals, few appear to have considered universal salvation a particularly threatening or controversial issue.[1] Such major shifts in outlook naturally had deep and complex cultural roots that resist generalization. Yet one general point seems inescapable: the traditional focus of religious attention on the hope of eternal redemption was becoming culturally irrelevant.[2]

Protestantism and Moral Progress

In the mid- and late-nineteenth century, evangelicals and liberals alike increasingly came to regard God as a reasonable and just father; sentimentalism bestowed on him a benign countenance. The Romantic movement extolled the aspiration and development of the individual; sin and the salvation of the soul were shunted to the fringes of religious consciousness. Even more basic challenges to traditional Christian assumptions appeared rapidly after midcentury. Darwinism and new geological discoveries gave impetus to scientific materialism and delivered a powerful blow against natural theology. The positivism of Auguste Comte, denying the possibility of any knowledge of God, helped further the spread of evolutionary theory and the Higher Criticism.[3] With the physical and scriptural arguments for God's rule under attack, agnosticism emerged as a culturally acceptable alternative to belief.[4] A "diminished intellectual clarity and uncertain emotional commitment" came to characterize Victorian religion.[5]

Protestants were becoming more occupied with instructing the child than with worrying about the state and destiny of the adult's soul.[6] Horace Bushnell's immensely significant *Christian Nurture* (1847) encouraged the virtuous to think more about moral education and progress than about ultimate salvation. This preoccupation had manifestations in every aspect of the culture. Even P. T. Barnum appealed to the pervasive search for moral improvement; he advertised his circus as a "Great Moral Show" and gave free admission passes to the clergy as well as to journalists.[7] A growing emphasis on the moral training of children through the ministry of the mother highlighted the increasingly subjective and individualistic nature of Protestant piety. The influential Catharine Beecher advised mothers to become aware of the peculiar personality traits of their children and to modify their religious instruction accordingly.[8] It was implicit that ministers, whose influence came from outside the home, were less able than mothers to mold young souls. And it was the potential of the child, not the ultimate judgment of the soul, that increasingly commanded attention.

Discomfort with the idea of eternal punishment was a logical outcome of the nineteenth century's acknowledgment of the individual's capacity to develop and improve. In the postbellum era, fewer and fewer ministers insisted on conformity to specific theological views.[9] Convictions about a heaven or hell following the present life were coming to be regarded as private and personal, really beyond the direct concern of the local minister. Perhaps more important, the whole question of salvation as traditionally conceived was rapidly losing meaning, as religious discussions of life and death reflected a deep shift in cultural values. Following these currents, Universalists also moved away from an eschatological belief in divinely effected universal salvation toward a typically liberal acceptance of faith in human free will and moral perfectibility.

Some leading Protestant theologians tried almost desperately to shore up belief in endless punishment. These thinkers believed such a teaching was necessary to guard the now widely cherished conviction of the freedom of the will. Yet these theologians were so far from reflecting common attitudes that, by 1870, many Universalists were rejoicing in the imminent triumph of their own central belief. Maine governor Sidney Perham, president of the Universalist General Convention, declared to a huge Universalist centennial celebration in Gloucester, Massachusetts, that "no religious idea has ever taken such firm possession of our public mind in this century as the idea on which our denomination is based."[10]

By this time, however, Universalists themselves were adapting to the "public mind," as they downplayed their central eschatological concept of universal restoration and emphasized instead the unlimited potential of the individual. We have already seen that the denomination's rapidly deepening involvement in programs of social reform, as well as its pronounced support for the expansion of women's rights and sphere, were closely associated with its embrace of a humanistic faith in individual capacity, which had become widespread in American Protestantism. At midcentury, Universalists were expressing this faith through an increasingly explicit theological concern for human liberty. By the 1870s, most denominational thinkers were coming to define salvation in terms of the infinite development of character; in this respect, they mirrored more and more clearly the broad evolutionary optimism of American religious culture. There was, as we will see, continuing and strident opposition in some quarters to the abandonment of Universalism's historic vision of divine transcendence and purpose. While the denomination as a whole paid them little heed, these dissenters nevertheless provided an acute commentary on the state of liberal Protestantism in the late nineteenth century. These Universalist critics also foreshadowed an important theological reconstruction, which would take on fuller dimensions in the twentieth century.

Toward a New Heaven

By the last decades of the nineteenth century, the true fear of an endless hell had all but disappeared from the consciousness of many American Protestants, especially members of the mainline churches of the Northeast. Following the fate of other strict Calvinist tenets earlier in the century, the notion of eternal punishment now had only a tenuous grip on the popular mentality. Traditional teachings built around a final judgment and endless hell fit awkwardly into the mindset of postbellum America. Amid the later nineteenth century's material and social changes, its acceptance of evolutionary ideas, and its overriding faith in human progress, orthodox eschatology appeared to be a relic of a stunted, discouraging, even regressive religious mentality. As William McLoughlin has observed, the mid-Victorians "yearned to believe that God and his love directed the universe, and there was no room in it for the Devil or for Hell."[11] McLoughlin overstated the case but only slightly. Far from the terrible reality it was for the Puritans, hell had become a vague, abstract notion, defended, if at all, on moral grounds as a necessary counterpoint to a glorious heaven.

More particularly, midcentury American Protestants evinced a growing distaste for the sort of "mechanical" eschatology in which a life of virtue brought a definitive, static heavenly reward. Idealistic philosophy and the individualism of the Romantic movement helped to foster an understanding of Christianity in which salvation became an ongoing process, peculiar to each person. Virtually no limits were placed upon the potential of the individual soul. Adopting an attitude that had been evident in germ among Unitarians much earlier, many Protestants had come, by the last decades of the nineteenth century, to envision immortality as self-realization, and they emphasized the growth and rehabilitation of the soul while they greatly downplayed the orthodox doctrine of salvation by God.[12] Richard Rabinowitz recognizes that, among New Englanders by midcentury, "divinity came to be a more inward experience, as the human mind came increasingly to center on its volitional faculty, its most godlike powers." "Personality" supplanted "soul" and "character" as the best term to describe the "self," for it captured the "perfect individuality" of that idea.[13]

A hopeful belief in the inevitability of progress also marked the latter third of the nineteenth century, encouraging the separation of salvation from its traditional eschatological associations. Different from the optimism of the early national period in America, this idea of progress resulted at least partly from the mixture of the Christian doctrine of providence with the scientific idea of evolution.[14] In the second half of the century, divine providence was increasingly understood in general rather than specific terms. God's providence remained "universal" but was conceived more as a vague divine superintendence than as direct involvement in the course of events. An evolutionary vocabulary, reflecting the idea that the social order was "in the process of becoming," superseded a providential theodicy based on the belief that human society remained always subject to the same basic forces and conditions.[15]

While evolutionism and scientific determinism posed serious religious questions, in the 1870s, "most Protestants still believed that the world was getting better and better."[16] It is no accident that Henry Ward Beecher became a spokesman for so many of these mid-Victorian Protestants. He employed the Romantic and evolutionary conception of human redemption through the "law of development and growth."[17] As Rabinowitz observes, for Beecher "life had an internal thrust to its own right end."[18] He thus became the outstanding exponent of a religious sensibility that had virtually discarded traditional notions not only of hell but of heaven as well.

Beecher's outlook reflected the results of a broader shift away from a theocentric vision of heaven to an anthropocentric one. The grave had been a terrifying and morbid preoccupation for the Puritan, death the occasion when God executed his awful judgment. Salvation came on God's terms, and deliverance was to a transcendent and ineffable abode. By the second half of the eighteenth century, heaven was becoming less foreign, a moral reward generously dispensed by a governor God. Death meant removal to a place of rest designed by God with his human creatures in mind and properly respectful of their individuality. Boneyards evolved into cemeteries, grim death's head markers into comforting symbols of peaceful eternity. With the rural cemetery movement of the 1830s, graveyards became gardens of moral uplift, places that beckoned the living to commune with the departed.[19]

No longer a static and incomprehensibly blissful realm ruled by God for his own pleasure, heaven became fertile ground for the sentimental imagination in the second half of the nineteenth century. Consolation literature, epitomized by Elizabeth Stuart Phelps's *The Gates Ajar* (1868), portrayed the beyond as remarkably earthlike.[20] One was transported to a familiar heaven to continue moral activity rather than to be saved once and for all eternity. A popular and diverting genre, consolation literature invited people to imagine a heaven that suited their needs.

Ironically, however, even as heaven became less distant, death itself became more complicated. The moment when natural life ended took on an aura of tremendous drama and mystery. Harriet Beecher Stowe created the ideal of a triumphant death with Little Eva's shining passage "from death to life." "Ah, what said those eyes, that spoke so much of heaven?" Stowe asked, along with so many others.[21] It was a question of acute importance to the Victorian mind. In all the popular media of the era, we can find a preoccupation with human mortality.[22] Unlike the Puritan, who meditated on death because he knew the terrible judgment that awaited him, the Victorian dwelled on death because of the anxious uncertainty of it all. Ann Rose's study of seventy-five Victorians—those who came to maturity at midcentury—finds that they exhibited more anxiety about their religious condition than had their parents. Even for those of the earlier generation with little personal faith, religion was firmly planted as "a matter of institutional structure and metaphysical definition." Many of their children, on the other hand, "dimly sensed the marginality of religion in the modern world."[23]

In this atmosphere, death and the rituals surrounding it received ever more attention. Bodily remains reposed in increasingly decorative and expensive "caskets" rather than matter-of-fact coffins. Professional funeral directors assumed the duties previously performed by family and friends, adding numerous embellishments in the process. Elaborate mourning, including special dress and withdrawal from society, marked the lives of the bereaved.[24] Deep grief was respected; indeed, it was expected. Even Mark Twain, who found in the Romantic, morbid fascination with death a target for his cynical wit, could regard grief with indulgence and tenderness. In one of his novels, the friends of the departed support his widow in her recurrent illusion that her husband will return, sensitive to her inability to accept his death.[25]

The passage of death was undoubtedly difficult to take in stride for those whose sense of what lay beyond the grave was increasingly indefinite and subjective. Margaret Deland's popular *John Ward, Preacher* (1888) illustrated the tendency of the age to take refuge from troubling eschatological questions in the marvel of the human personality and the possibilities for spiritual growth. Regarding belief in hell as the relic of a bygone era, Deland declared, "We look into the mysteries of God when we see how divine a human soul can be."[26] This sort of writing reflected the preaching of ministers such as Henry Ward Beecher, Phillips Brooks, and other liberal New Theologians of the 1880s.[27] These thinkers dwelled on the wonder of the human personality and the unlimited potential for human progress; their preaching reflected the broad waning of eschatological dualism. By this time, it was increasingly difficult to admit a religious view that split human experience into the natural and the supernatural, the here and the hereafter, the secular and the sacred.[28] Heaven itself, no longer really God's domain, had become a vague extension of the human moral sphere.[29] More and more people were ready simply to live in the present and to put aside whenever possible the "religious" issues that had traditionally accompanied death.

Hell as a Necessary Evil

Along with traditional eschatological concerns, support for older ideas of human depravity and responsibility for sin had diminished dramatically by the last third of the nineteenth century. God's judgment of the individual soul appeared problematic especially to proponents of the New Theology or Progressive Orthodoxy, who had begun to focus on social explanations for behavior. Shaped by social relations and by inheritance, human beings hardly seemed legitimate objects of "judgment," as customarily conceived. Looking to modify eschatological categories and ideas to make them more compatible with their current experience, theologians needed especially to reexamine the whole notion of future punishment.

Ironically, for some Protestant thinkers, a conception of hell became necessary to the whole conception of personality. The denial of hell, no less than the materialistic determinism of natural science, threatened their paramount idea of individual moral freedom.[30] As we shall see, they taught that hell existed in spite of God's loving desires. According to this view, God had to "allow" hell, although he looked on sadly whenever humans willed their own moral destruction. Hell had to exist to glorify man. A more thorough repudiation of Calvinist theocentrism is difficult to imagine. At the same time, the hell many of these theologians described was not very hellish. The last third of the nineteenth century was the era of the alleviation of hell, as notions of a second "probation" beyond death, a variety of degrees of punishment in the hereafter, and annihilationism gained attention.[31]

In the early 1880s, Universalist historian John G. Adams observed that, while all major Protestant bodies had been shaken by growing uncertainty on the question of future punishment, the Congregationalists had shown the greatest agitation.[32] Indeed, at its 1880 meeting in Boston, the National Council of Congregational Churches opened the door to the idea of a second probation by not denying the chance for repentance after death. Professors at Andover Theological Seminary led the development of this idea, which was expressed in an 1885 book of essays, *Progressive Orthodoxy*.[33] Progressive Orthodoxy, or New Theology, regarded a belief in future probation as a key article of faith and a natural development from New Divinity theology.[34] An editorialist in the *Andover Review* of 1888 argued:

> the dogma of the universal decisiveness of this life . . . is irreconcilable with the doctrine conspicuous in [contemporary] New England Theology, and in the history of modern missions, of the universality of the atonement, and the implied relation of Christ to human salvation.[35]

Other denominational leaders worried, nevertheless, about the tendency to forget about hell altogether. Writing in the *Congregational Quarterly* in 1873, Daniel Merriman argued that the increasingly popular belief in universal salvation deprived love "of its moral character" and degraded it "to a mere natural attribute," so that the kingdom of God became merely a "kingdom of physical dynamics." For Merriman and other Congregationalists, the denial of endless hell spelled the denial of human freedom, which was "the citadel of Christian theism, on the maintenance of which depends the whole question of God's personality and man's superiority to matter." He lamented that sentimentalism, in league with science, had obscured the reality of human freedom.[36] In 1878, President Noah Porter of Yale stressed the need to "maintain . . . ethical views of the relation of character to salvation." Yet, at the same time, he acknowledged the possibility that in some cases the education of character could be "resumed in another life."[37]

The popular "mediating" theologian Lyman Abbott, successor to Henry Ward Beecher at the Plymouth Church in Brooklyn and in the editorship of the *Christian Union*, best exemplified the shifting direction of thought. Explaining to a convention of Universalists in Boston why he did not embrace their belief, he observed,

"If I were a Calvinist I should be a Universalist . . . If I believed that God could make all men righteous I should be sure that he would." God's grace, he acknowledged, was available to all, even beyond the grave. But individuals had to decide to accept it.[38]

The New Theology permitted, and even welcomed, revision and softening of the doctrine of future punishment as long as "character" and "will" were understood as the ultimate determinants of human destiny. But Congregationalists by no means universally accepted the new notion of limited future probation, as Newman Smyth learned in 1881.[39] A likely candidate to succeed E. A. Park at Andover Seminary, he failed to secure appointment because of his belief in a future probation for those who had not yet heard the gospel.[40] Despite calls for changes, many Congregationalists remained hesitant to tamper with a dogma of "great restraining power."[41] The leaders of nominally Calvinist denominations were certainly in no hurry to change their official doctrine. Writing on the subject of endless punishment in 1883, Unitarian Samuel Barrows observed, "Orthodoxy is not ready to revise its belief," but "its beliefs are constantly suffering revision without its consent."[42]

Willful neglect of hell seemed a growing danger to Austin Phelps, professor emeritus at Andover, who in 1886 emphasized anew his belief in the necessity of future punishment. Phelps declared, "We need to tone up our faith in the absolute sovereignty of the human will. . . . God can not save a sinner if he will not be saved." Phelps elaborated on the power of the human will:

> Moral freedom is a prerogative of godlike nobility. It is the chief thing in which man is God's image. The stellar universe is not equal in imperial dignity to one thinking, sentient, self-determining mind. Man's supreme endowment is not immortality: it is the ability to be what he wills to be, to do what he chooses to do, to become what he elects to become in the growth of ages.

Although he insisted that a hell existed for those who chose to remain in sin, Phelps did not paint a picture of suffering and torment. In fact, the sinner had a moral affinity for hell and would be miserable existing in the presence of a holy God. Souls thus gravitated to a natural "moral segregation," which made everyone happy.[43]

Unitarian Edward Cornelius Towne had already noted in his 1873 work *The Question of Hell* that "free will has become the 'dogmatic last ditch' in support of endless punishment."[44] But it would have been closer to the mark to say that, among leading theologians, endless punishment had become the dogmatic last ditch in support of free will. William G. T. Shedd of Union Seminary reminded his readers that lost spirits were not "forced" into a sphere that was unsuited to them: "There is no other abode in the universe which they would prefer."[45] Robert Memminger, an Episcopalian from South Carolina, contended that, while God ruled providentially, man could prevent "any good done him personally in spirit." God, in short, "can not bring the will to voluntary subjection under Him"; he had created mankind as a "God upon earth." Lamenting the steady progress of Universalism, which he saw as a form of supralapsarian Calvinism, Memminger condemned the pantheism that was the "logical result of a Monoistic principle" behind both. Such a principle magnified God's power at the expense of human individuality and responsibility. The idea of endless punishment was thus a "moral and psychical necessity."[46]

A hell for intractable sinners — even a shrunken, vaguely defined arena of unending moral rebellion — was thus comforting as well as essential. Horace Bushnell's *Vicarious Sacrifice* (1865) had foreshadowed the view that hell consisted of the flailings of the resolutely sinful against God's goodness:

> Strong enough to suffer, and wicked enough to sin, the tendrils of adhesion to God are dead, and [the soul] can not fasten itself practically to his friendship . . . All its struggles are but the heavings of lower nature — the pains of defeat that are only proving by experiment their own perpetuity.[47]

Liberal religious thinkers, following Bushnell, reduced hell to the barest essentials while insisting that a soul must be allowed to decide its own course. The distinguished Unitarian Frederic Hedge concluded that a sinner's evil tendency resulted in "a process of mortification" that ultimately brought a loss of consciousness and voluntary power, "for consciousness supposes a capacity for distinguishing good and evil and voluntary power also involves a moral element." The sinful soul was thus finished as a "moral agent and a conscious individuality." It survived no longer as a person but as a thing, a "monad; its condition is thenceforth not a question of psychology but of ontology."[48] The sinner sinned himself to moral death.

Hedge stopped short of true annihilationism, or the idea that the souls of the unsaved were simply obliterated. Set forth in the works *Debt and Grace* by American Charles Frederick Hudson and *Life in Christ* by Briton Edward White, annihilationism argued that immortality was not an innate quality of the soul but rather conditional. As William Huntingdon, rector of All Saints Church in Worcester, Massachusetts, pointed out in 1878, conditional immortality was far superior to a belief in endless torment, since it allowed for the benefits of the doctrine without the "blemishes" of that "harsh view." The chief benefit was, of course, free will. Indeed, Huntingdon objected to the term "annihilationism" since it implied an arbitrary divine decree rather than a freely determined state.[49] In harmony with evolutionary theory, annihilationism merely allowed that the persistently unredeemable — the morally unfit — would become extinct, presumably painlessly.[50]

While many Protestant leaders in the second half of the nineteenth century were not fully comfortable with the idea of hell and put forth a great many alterations of traditional eschatology, most still feared the growth of a full-fledged, explicit universalism. They believed that universal salvation, like the scientific orthodoxy of the age, denied the preeminence of the human will. At a time when, as Harriet Beecher Stowe remarked in 1869, nature seemed to reveal itself as "a more tremendous and inexorable Calvinist than the Cambridge Platform," these thinkers argued for the ultimate significance of individual moral choice.[51]

Approaching Triumph or Danger?

The attempts of other Protestants to prop up the collapsing dogma of endless punishment both amused and encouraged late nineteenth-century Universalists.[52]

Chronicling the efforts of the self-styled orthodox to change the doctrine of hell, some predicted confidently that the idea was staggering on its last legs, and they expressed glee as well as amazement at the willingness of theologians to modify it practically out of existence. Among Universalist thinkers, there were also those who saw deeper danger in the softened concepts of hell, but these observers were largely out of step with their cohorts, who sensed victory in the air. The majority did not perceive that, even as they celebrated, their own historic conception of universal salvation was losing meaning. For the fading popular conviction of the reality of hell was to a large extent the reflection of sentimental religion's lack of concern over the whole matter of salvation.

In 1862, the Reverend M. J. Steere had predicted that "orthodoxy" would reach Universalism within thirty years if it stayed on the same course it had followed during the previous years.[53] By the 1870s, with their movement a century old, Universalists were often content simply to bear witness to the apparently triumphant progress of their belief. As the Reverend A. J. Patterson pointed out in 1874, if the preachers who actually avowed universal salvation in their "so-called orthodox pulpits" would "come out and join our church," Universalism "could be augmented four-fold."[54] Citing the general uneasiness increasingly evident over the "heathen doctrine [of hell]," a contributor to the *Universalist Quarterly* declared in 1876 that orthodoxy had "already come half-way to us on this" and would eventually come the other half.[55] Protestants were now revolted by the idea of hell, another Universalist writer confidently asserted, but needed to move away from it "by several lesser steps, taking only one at a time."[56] The process and even the speed with which the belief in endless hell declined did not seem especially important to these Universalists. What mattered was that an exodus was taking place. Using the image of the Jews' flight from Egypt, one writer hailed the movement "from the bondage of creeds" to the "liberty of individual judgment," and he marveled at the present "irreverence" toward ancient doctrine.[57]

Anticipating the imminent end of belief in hell, some Universalists were inclined to savor what they supposed were the last moments of their great struggle. An 1882 editorial writer found it "amusing" to see the evangelical press turn out increasingly labored defenses of endless punishment; he observed a common attempt to show both that most souls would be saved and that hell existed.[58] Those with a keen recollection of their movement's outcast status in the earlier part of the century found particular satisfaction in watching the continuing efforts to qualify the doctrine of hell. Increasingly, however, with victory over endless punishment apparently in sight, most commentators seemed greatly relieved that the debate was coming to an end. A contributor to the *Universalist Quarterly* in 1886 believed that progressive orthodoxy, with its extension of probation beyond death, spelled the final blow to belief in hell. The "force of logic" would now move theologians "inevitably toward Universalism."[59]

Universalist minister George Emerson observed in an 1883 study that theologians such as the prominent Newman Smyth could not consistently posit a moral probation, which implied a time limitation, and then assert the "indestructible power of moral choice." Triumphantly, Emerson declared that it was precisely the "New Orthodox" emphasis on the power of moral choice that ensured the ultimate acceptance of belief in universal salvation.[60] Given enough opportunity, in other words, all souls would choose the right moral course.

A few prominent Universalists were neither amused nor encouraged by what Emerson called the New Orthodox modifications of hell. Thomas Sawyer of New York, for example, was seriously disturbed by the new twists to the old idea of eternal punishment, particularly the notion that an endlessly sinning soul was subject to infinite moral decay. He argued that Horace Bushnell had utterly failed in his *Vicarious Sacrifice* to present a religiously meaningful conception of the moral death of some souls. Indeed, he exclaimed, Bushnell virtually admitted that his idea "utterly fails to glorify God!" Similarly, Sawyer asked, what joy or glory could God obtain from the unconscious "monads" in Unitarian Frederic Hedge's vision of the damned? The recent efforts to mitigate the horrors of hell only complicated the problem of endless punishment. On this point, said Sawyer flatly, "Orthodoxy can not be improved or modified."[61]

A *Universalist Quarterly* editor agreed that recent attempts to transform hell were futile. Theologians, he noted, had turned to the ideas of the endless punishment of conscience, the torture of remorse, and the gradual extinction of the moral nature. But, he asked, if the sinner's moral nature were reduced, how much could a spiritual punishment of conscience affect him? Logically, this meant the worst sinner received the least punishment.[62] Numerous contributors to the journal in the 1870s and 1880s concurred that those who tried to revise traditional ideas about hell while resisting a declaration of belief in universal salvation only ended up with notions antithetical to the whole spirit of Universalism. The Reverend. A. C. Berry called the New Orthodoxy the "Gospel of Uncertainty." Ministers like Henry Ward Beecher (before his explicit avowal of universal salvation), who comfortingly extended chances for repentance into the hereafter, only succeeded in picturing God as "indifferent and neglectful."[63]

"Great moral danger" existed in the religious tendencies of the present age, the Reverend. S. S. Hebbard warned in 1885. Far from improving upon the old orthodoxy, the New Orthodoxy was a "retrograde movement," a merely emotional attempt, arising out of ethical feelings, to improve upon Calvinism. Unable to accept the admittedly terrible divine sovereignty taught by Calvinism—but still opposed to Universalism—the New Orthodoxy was caught in a hopeless quagmire. The theologians could see "no outlook for the future save that of 'endless sinning,'" and consequently of endless rebellion against the sovereignty of God." In this sort of thinking, God's greatness was utterly eclipsed.

Indeed, warned Hebbard, popular religious belief seemed to be drifting toward paganism as an "increasing multitude seem to have lost all conception of God save as a mere name for the aggregate of physical forces." Implicitly pointing to the enormous influence of Henry Ward Beecher, he charged that God had become "Nature personified and made poetic." Sentimentalism and atheism, in other words, were two sides of the same coin. This was no surprise. The world would revert to pagan naturalism, Hebbard predicted, if modern theologians continued to picture God as struggling eternally and ineffectually against some who were determined to sin. Physical nature was actually a worthier object of worship than this morally impotent ruler. Hebbard maintained that Universalism, with its traditional understanding of the irresistibility of divine love and goodness, needed to stand its ground against the threat of modern paganism.[64]

Yet such views were not to prevail among Universalists. As the religious sensibility of Ballou and his followers continued to fade within the denomination, members joined the chants about individual perfection and progress. Olympia Brown, the first woman to be ordained by the denomination, preached that the opportunities for spiritual growth were endless. She was struck by the greatness of human potential, echoing the lofty words of Hamlet: "How noble is man! How noble in reason! How infinite in faculties! How admirable in action! How like an angel in apprehension. . . . How like a god!"[65] Phebe Hanaford, the second woman to be ordained a Universalist minister, expressed similar sentiments in the mid-1860s, exulting about "what delights of mind! What varied pursuits of the intellect. . . . What uses of reason and exercises of the imagination" would accompany eternal and universal progress.[66] Countless articles in popular Universalist periodicals, such as *Manford's Monthly*, echoed these sentiments, arguing that the deity had placed no finite limits on the expansion of even the most degraded soul. Typical was the 1866 assertion of an anonymous author that Universalists believed in "the eternal progression of the soul" and "the acquisition of heavenly knowledge and divine wisdom, such as we can form no adequate idea of."[67]

In such descriptions of the astounding potential of all souls for fulfillment, Universalists, like the wide variety of other Protestants who drew similar pictures, scrupulously noted that the spiritual growth of persons occurred at different rates and depended upon individual initiative. Universalist writer George Quimby was careful to allow in his contribution to consolation literature that all were made "equally pure as to the substance . . . of their being."[68] The primary object of his work was not to convey the message of such universal redemption, however, but rather to portray heaven as a place of bustling business and the perfect atmosphere for the cultivation of mind and soul. "Heaven is not a place of idleness," Quimby cautioned, "we must *do* something in the future." Indeed, one's degree of celestial happiness depended on one's advancement in "knowledge and spirituality."[69] A contributor to a Universalist journal in 1867 similarly praised the "venerable Dr. Henry Ward Beecher for his preaching that heaven will be a place of ceaseless activity." How dull, he exclaimed, to think of "great minds only engaged in psalm-singing."[70]

As Universalists came to depict heaven as a grand celestial university from which one never really graduated, they implicitly pushed the doctrine of universal salvation into the background. There was, to be sure, open admission to heaven, but student performance could be expected to vary widely. God the savior became God the instructor or, rather, God the personal tutor, as the vision of individual, infinite human progress superseded the older stress on the ultimate unity of mankind accomplished by divine restoration. Perhaps no one expressed this turn of Universalist belief in the second half of the nineteenth century more clearly than the highly active Universalist layman P. T. Barnum. The moderator and a trustee of the First Universalist Church of Bridgeport, Connecticut, and a generous contributor to Tufts College and other Universalist causes, Barnum proclaimed that the present life was only the first step in a "moral order whose progressive stages are to be endless."

Such immortal life was not given so that man could "sit on a flower-bed and sing and play harps, but for the endless development of immortal souls."[71]

Not only in the attitudes of laymen like Barnum but also in the writings of most denominational theologians, there was little awareness that the universal salvation toward which Protestantism was tending was far different from what Universalists had historically taught. In the era after the Civil War, the term "salvation" was quickly acquiring for many if not most Protestants the oddly quaint ring it has now among educated Americans generally. God no longer really saved or damned. The universal salvation that was now increasingly accepted was, in fact, a belief that every soul had the power for infinite moral growth. This idea bore little resemblance to the piety that envisioned a sovereign God who was saving a fallen humanity.

A New Departure

To the liberal thinkers of the postbellum era, traditional Universalism could appear intellectually petrified in its single-minded, relentless insistence on the salvation of all. This dynamic age, full of the both exhilarating and disturbing sense that humanity and the world were not finished products but constantly changing and growing, seemed to have outgrown a faith centered around the ancient abstractions of the Last Things.

Universalist thinkers sought to adapt their teachings to the spirit of the era through an increasingly explicit emphasis on the freedom of the will. The problem of individual moral responsibility—and the theological issues of free will versus divine power—had long disturbed the movement. Hosea Ballou had clearly denied free will in the *Treatise on Atonement*, but growing numbers of Universalists had become uneasy with what, to Ballou, was merely a logical deduction from the concepts of divine omniscience and omnipotence. The adoption of the restorationist doctrine of limited future punishment had served essentially to correct what adherents saw as the faith's inattention to human moral accountability. Yet, in later decades, as traditional eschatological thought waned in American Protestant culture, Universalists tended to move beyond restorationism to a more inclusive idea of human free will and the development of moral character.

The leading Universalist proponents of free will were largely members of a rising generation of denominational leaders who had received much more formal education than most earlier Universalists. We have noted that the denomination was moving into a new phase with the founding of Tufts and other institutions of higher learning. The changing educational background of Universalist writers and publicists is reflected in a shift from dependence on the Bible and popular rationalism to the use of more sophisticated concepts drawn from European philosophy. Following the lead of American Protestant theology in general, Universalists who wanted to reinforce the already prevalent theological moralism in the denomination turned above all to early Scottish Common Sense philosophy to support their position.

Asserting that the will was a distinct faculty of the mind, separate from reason and emotion, the psychology of Common Sense cleared the path to free agency for antebellum Protestant thinkers. Moral judgments, or the dictates of conscience, became, like other Common Sense dictates, "self-evident intuitions."[72] Aided by revelation, the conscience could "bridge the epistemological distance between man's mind and moral law" and thus influence the will. No longer simply sinners, human beings became independent moral agents, with the power to choose right or wrong.[73]

Universalist scholars, in common with other Protestant thinkers, increasingly adopted the language of Common Sense and argued for moral freedom as a basic fact of consciousness. A contributor to the *Universalist Quarterly* in April 1854, for example, declared that the denial of free will "contradicts the insuppressible dictates of our moral judgment."[74] This view appears to have reflected the sentiments of most midcentury Universalists. Arguing that, within its domain, the human will is as potent as the divine, another author noted that the simple philosophical alternatives were "freedom or Pantheism." Reflecting the larger Protestant culture's exaltation of the will as the highest faculty of the soul, he insisted that humans were invested with a "noble freedom"; salvation could not be accomplished without a change of will.[75] The Reverend George Emerson took a somewhat different tack, dismissing all speculative arguments for necessity and free will; it was impossible to demonstrate by logic that which came before logic. "Consciousness," he exclaimed with the voice of Common Sense, "is the great instrument of truth." The implication was clear: Emerson's "consciousness" told him his will was free.[76]

Demonstrating a similar immersion in Common Sense teaching, Hosea Ballou 2nd sought in 1858 to remove Universalism once and for all from the outdated theological conceptions that he believed had haunted and retarded it. The president of Tufts and one of Universalism's most acclaimed scholars, Ballou 2nd argued that "common sense" and "intuition" established the reality of merit, demerit, duty, and responsibility. He openly deplored the influence of British Enlightenment thinkers David Hartley and Joseph Priestley in Universalist thought. The necessitarian teaching associated with Jonathan Edwards and with certain Universalists had had pernicious effects; this sort of philosophical fatalism invalidated any notion of moral sense and thus moral choice. The absurdity of the argument that we remain under divine direction, even though we are completely unaware of it, is "at once manifest from our own consciousness, which tells us we act freely."[77] Responding in a later work to leading Universalist advocates of the doctrine of "universal necessity," Ballou 2nd argued that their teaching left no room for the moral "fact" of responsibility and duty; without these, Universalism could have no moral force.[78]

The prominent Universalist minister Thomas Sawyer concurred that efforts to rehabilitate the pietistic necessitarianism of Hosea Ballou were badly misconceived. The great majority of early Universalists, he acknowledged, had been brought up in "high Calvinism" and were content simply to make election universal. But ideas of foreordination and necessity had gradually lost ground, he explained; the few advocates of them in the denomination were older laymen and ministers, of whom some were, indeed, "venerable." Sawyer believed and certainly hoped that most Universalists had long since turned away from the deterministic views of Hartley and Priestley, who had peered at the mind as if it were a fantastic mechanism and had ignored the "moral phenomena" of the universe. Sawyer's detailed argument for the reality of human moral freedom illustrates the extent to which he had dropped the movement's earlier emphasis on God's eternal and unchangeable plan.[79]

Reflecting even more explicitly the turn away from the traditional and distinctive teachings of the movement, Elbridge Gerry Brooks, pastor of the Church of the Messiah in Philadelphia, proposed in 1874 a "new departure" for Universalism. The heart of his lengthy book involved a plea for Universalists to get out of the "ruts of the Ballouian period," ruts that "have been exceedingly mischievous elements of our denominational life." Essentially, Brooks credited Ballou with being a path-breaking reformer whose central insight was critically in need of modification for a new era. Even though most Universalists were now restorationists, he argued, the denomination was unfortunately associated with the belief in "certain, immediate salvation at death, without regard to conduct or character." This notion functioned as an "opiate," lulling the religious conscience and sense of responsibility and leading to the decay of Universalism.

He contended that Universalism must make a "new departure" by preaching that "salvation is *offered*, not *secured*," except as each soul met the conditions that God established. Universalism could remain a viable movement only if it called people to activity, to change, and to growth. Salvation, Brooks declared, should be understood as the achievement of a renovated character. We must ask, he said, "What must we do to be saved?" Universalists were still to chant "the sublime anthem of a complete salvation." But it was necessary that "we pitch it to another key-note" as Universalism entered a new phase.[80]

Of course, Brooks was not just changing the key; he was singing a different song. Yet, as a rule, Universalists seemed to concur implicitly that the denomination should not be bound by its traditional emphasis, it could now simply reap the harvest of religious change. Maintaining that "vaticanism," "evangelicalism," and "rationalism" were all in decline, Henry I. Cushman predicted the victory of a "Catholic Universalism"; he argued that, in the early church, before the growth of vaticanism, Universalism was no heresy. Referring to Brooks's *Our New Departure*, "the greatest work which the Universalist Church has produced," Cushman declared that Universalists had to "free themselves from the tyranny of their one distinguishing truth." With attention less exclusively directed to the idea of universal salvation, he implied, Universalists could become leaders of a great, ecumenical, "Catholic" church.[81] The main tendencies of liberal religion, with its dying belief in hell and lessened concern for doctrine, seemed to Brooks and his followers to presage Universalism's future influence and glory.

Necessitarians and Neo-Calvinists

By no means did all of Universalism's intellectual leaders agree with Brooks's rosy hopes for the future of the denomination. In the decades after midcentury, small but vocal groups of Universalists continued to worry about a general waning of Christian piety both without and within their own church. Rejecting the growing belief in free will as antithetical to Universalism's traditional stress on the absolute certainty of universal salvation, Universalist conservatives threw themselves into a newly philosophical effort to buttress what they saw as a fading piety. Later, by the 1870s and the 1880s, a handful of emphatically Christian Universalists, disillusioned with all such theological reasoning and particularly with the rationalism of liberal religion, called for a return to a simple and even unreasoned piety that included a renewed emphasis on original sin. A look at these dissenting voices throws the evolution of the denomination as a whole into sharper relief.

The sense that the Universalist movement itself was being swept away by the dangerous currents of the age lay behind the effort, led mostly by older conservative thinkers after midcentury, to retain and revive what was left of the original pietistic thrust of the movement by giving it a firm philosophical foundation. This attempt to ground the teachings of the denomination in philosophical necessitarianism was clearly a rearguard action; we have seen how fully Universalists in general had adopted prevailing assumptions about moral freedom. But even if these arguments had little or no influence on the direction of the church as a whole, they illustrate the broad ways in which Universalist attitudes were changing.

Although Scottish Common Sense thought supported the antebellum shift toward Arminianism, the growing use of philosophical terms also added to the overall confusion of the theological picture. By the second half of the century academic theologians were coming to assert quite openly what revivalists like Charles Finney had been saying for years: all men were free to choose the grace of God.[82] As Sydney Ahlstrom observes, Common Sense led Protestants into a "neo-rationalism which rendered the central Christian paradoxes into stark, logical contradictions."[83] For those Universalists still strongly influenced by Enlightenment ideals, a theology involving logical contradictions was anathema. More important, neorationalism in defense of human moral agency ran directly counter to the traditional Ballouian use of reason to uphold an attitude of trust in divine providence.

Obadiah Tillotson's *The Divine Efficiency and Moral Harmony of the Universe* (1854) was among the first defenses of a necessitarian school of thought that continued into the 1870s. Arguing against the "Arminians" in a striking echo of Jonathan Edwards, Tillotson refused to give up the principle of universal causation, fearing that this would surrender the proof of God's existence.[84] "It is naturally impossible for God to create any Being and not totally control it," Tillotson declared, noting that every effect required a cause. It was crucial for people to understand that God was really the author of all things, the cause of all human volitions, including the sinful; indeed, sin was "an instrumentality which God uses to promote his purposes." Deeply opposed to the prevailing idea of God's "moral government," Tillotson proudly identified himself as an "ultra-Universalist" and "Necessitarian."[85]

Tillotson was soon joined by a small but strongly committed group of thinkers who saw themselves as the philosophical upholders of Ballou's legacy. They carried on much of the debate with their opponents in the pages of the *Universalist Quarterly*. It made no sense for Universalists to be in sympathy with the doctrine of a free, self-determining will, a distressed commentator insisted in 1855.[86] Another writer observed that it was a vain effort to invoke "consciousness" as proof of free will: "we are not conscious of ever having formed a motive."[87] The Reverend I. D.

Williamson repeatedly argued against the tendency to treat intuitions of the conscience as empirical evidence. Responding to opponents such as Hosea Ballou 2nd, Williamson vented frustration with what, to him, seemed a mystifying Universalist concern for "liberty." He could reduce his position to the simple statement, "God reigns." The doctrine of necessity, like Universalism itself, was at bottom an affirmation.[88]

In his 1870 book *Rudiments of Theological and Moral Science*, Williamson insisted that the only true basis for moral conduct was faith in a sovereign divine will. "To say that [God] may not work, even by that which we call evil" was to presume to understand the methods of a transcendent and unfathomable deity. Williamson used Kantian teachings to argue that human beings, bound by time and space, inevitably lived by faith. Yet faith was nourished by the intellectual conviction that God was in complete control of his creation, by the belief that "*nothing* is free in any absolute sense."[89] Man could not trust himself to the hands of a good God, minister and *Universalist Quarterly* contributor O. D. Miller maintained, "unless he knows, rationally and logically knows, that God controls events, controls human actions, shapes the course of history and individual human experience."[90]

Universalists such as Tillotson, Williamson, and Miller condemned the elevation of the morally free conscience as the ultimate ground of duty and responsibility because they believed this teaching diminished the comforting and unifying appreciation of God's control.[91] We affirm, declared Williamson, "that there is in man no natural, intuitive consciouness" of moral duty, and "hence he who builds on that foundation builds upon the sand."[92] True morality, they held, was not inspired by a feeling of freedom but by a sense of participation in God's good purpose. Their doctrine of necessitarianism was an extreme effort to provide an objective, reasonable defense of such piety. Certainly Thomas Sawyer was accurate in his exasperated rejoinder that necessitarianism was contrary to the whole "spirit of the age."[93] But for these conservative Universalist thinkers, that was precisely the point.

In the late 1870s and into the 1880s, divisions in the denomination became even more evident as strident dissenters against prevailing trends expressed their discontent. Especially in the pages of the *Universalist Quarterly*, Universalists now witnessed intense, if not widespread, reaction in their ranks not only against popular trends in American Protestantism but also against the very basis of nineteenth-century Universalism: Hosea Ballou's effort to combine reason and piety in the *Treatise on Atonement*. Anticipating in some respects the neo-orthodox movement of the next century, a group of Universalist critics insisted that their denomination needed to revise both its beliefs and its mission. Disturbed by the general disintegration of theology and fearful that Universalism would be swallowed by an increasingly tolerant liberal evangelicalism, these thinkers sought to reconstruct the movement on Calvinist foundations and to reinfuse it with an explicitly Christian piety.

In the eyes of these Universalist critics, the new departure of E. G. Brooks represented the scuttling of historic Universalist thought in an effort to lead the bandwagon of a moralistic, nondoctrinal Christianity. Even antebellum Universalists of the most intensely restorationist stripe, they pointed out, would not have thought of asking what they needed to do in order to be saved. To ask such a question was to cancel the whole thrust of the original movement, which had vehemently opposed the growing strain of Arminian moralism in early nineteenth-century American Protestantism.

Universalism needed a new departure, the Reverend R. O. Williams admitted in a review of Brooks's book, but it certainly should not deny its traditional and essential theological foundation, as Brooks seemed to suggest. Williams plainly perceived that Universalists were struggling to obtain a meaningful denominational existence in the final quarter of the century. Perched awkwardly between increasingly liberal evangelical Protestants, who were less and less upset by the idea of universal salvation, and Unitarians, whose ecumenicism seemed to know no bounds, Universalists were more uncertain than ever of their own direction. Williams and several theologians who followed him argued that one of the central problems was Ballou's theological legacy. Ballou's rationalistic perspective and rejection of key Christian doctrines, they feared, had left the denomination vulnerable both to moralism and to those who would abandon Christianity, even theism, altogether. They asserted that universal salvation had to be preached as the crucial element of Christian faith, illuminating and giving force to other doctrines. Universalists, in short, had to stand up and be counted as true Christian believers.[94]

Addressing the Divinity School of Tufts College in 1877, the Reverend A. D. Mayo, minister of an Independent Liberal church and a former Universalist minister, described "an abyss yawning between the different classes of Liberals": those centered on Jesus Christ and those, known by a number of names, who allowed each person to design a new religion for himself. The liberal Christian denomination that held to the clear gospel of Jesus Christ and offered a home for the weary sinner and skeptic would capture the future, not the one that was a "roosting place for birds of every feather." The liberal Christian church could not be a "spiritual restaurant" with an "endless clatter of thronging guests and convivial cheer"; a church that was merely a forum for continual religious debate could not have a meaningful life or community roots. The denomination that would successfully lead liberal Christianity, he warned, would not attempt to please those who had rejected the Christian label. Yet, if no liberal Christian church was "strong enough to face that urgent call of the Master, then the advancing host of Liberal Evangelicalism will lap up what is left of us."[95]

Like-minded critics asserted that the denomination could no longer afford to be vague and utterly without consensus about the person and mission of Christ; Universalists needed to develop a higher, clearer Christology. Liberal Christians had been overzealously rationalistic, according to one Universalist writer, and had reduced Christianity to a "few great ideas" surrounded by mythology. But faith in abstract ideas had no power to regenerate humanity.[96] Charles W. Biddle, emphasizing the need for faith in a "personal Christ," believed current liberal, or "abstract," religion had been drained of all life and power.[97]

Through the 1880s, such vocal critics within the denomination called upon Universalist leaders to address the historic questions of Christian theology. If the Christian work of the future involved only "emotional and ethical instruction," S. S. Hebbard advised, then Universalists should merge with the larger, better-equipped Christian bodies. Yet the world already had sufficient reverence for the "ethics and spirit of Jesus." The chief peril of the age, he insisted, lay in a growing sense of helplessness about the possibility of attaining religious truth. The "supreme need of the human heart is truth," and Universalism embodied the one central truth. In its ability to preach universal salvation as the crowning doctrine of a larger Christian theology lay the "hope of the Universalist Church as a distinct organization."[98] Chicagoan W. H. Ryder, a leading denominational benefactor, warned that Universalists had better recognize the perilous direction in which the denomination was headed. While they rejected rationalism's denial of the supernatural element in religion, he pointed out, Universalists had nevertheless adopted its theory of personal salvation, "which has no place for either the death of Christ, the grace of God or the Holy Spirit." There were few mistakes in the practical religion of the age, he maintained, that were more serious than confounding "salvation in Christ with character" and representing it as "growth."[99]

Instead of preaching that "we shall be changed," Universalists now ignored the doctrine of the resurrection and taught that the self-formed character determined its own destiny, lamented L. W. Ballou.[100] In the eyes of the Reverend E. C. Sweetser, even the philosophical necessitarianism that marked Hosea Ballou's *Treatise* had had the practical effect over the years of reducing sin "at the worst to a human mistake, which God intended that men should make," thus weakening our sense of "the exceeding sinfulness of sin" and diminishing "our conception of the atonement Jesus Christ produces."[101] But if Universalists did not develop their own broader Christian theology, warned W. C. Stiles, they would soon find themselves with no reason for a separate ecclesiastical existence, since many large Christian bodies now tolerated Universalism's main tenet. As he saw it, Universalists had a clear choice: they could turn away completely from evangelical faith, or they could become reformers of dogma and practice on "advanced and ultra-Christian ground." Advising the latter course, he proposed, in effect, an overhaul of Ballou's *Treatise* that would underscore both Universalism's Christian, Calvinistic foundation and its divergence from liberal religion as popularly understood.

Stiles charged that Ballou had insufficiently appreciated sin as a deep-seated and radical alienation from God; the denomination had thus drifted toward "naturalism," the idea that sin was curable by "moral solicitation." Now, however, there was a movement among Universalists to "look beyond the level of will and conduct for what is really radical in the fact of sin." Critical of traditional Universalist opposition to the "irrational" notion of original sin, Stiles asserted that the whole body of humanity was linked in sin by the ties of blood. Indeed, Stiles declared, "the doctrine of natural depravity gives force to our [uniquely Universalist] idea of human brotherhood. . . . Levelling all the barriers of caste in the momentous conclusion that we are all sinners before God." No power of will could change this humbling condition. Such essential depravity demanded more than Christ's "solicitation" or "example" but required the "divine force of God, entering the world through Christ."[102]

Religion had to address itself, S. S. Hebbard warned, not to particular transgressions but to "the deeper, more pervasive guiltiness . . . of a common humanity." Specifically, Universalists had to move beyond the glib assertion of liberal religion that there could be "no individual guilt without the free act of the individual" and appreciate the deeper truth symbolized by the theological doctrine of original sin. Universalist ministers, he argued, should speak out against a rationalism that termed human feelings of guilt and the desire for divine deliverance "mere superstition" and that held Christ to be only a wise teacher.

Hebbard acknowledged that his ideas were at variance with the opinions that prevailed in the denomination. But he cautioned that the continued existence of Universalism as a Christian church depended on the ability of its adherents to cultivate its central insight in solidly Christian soil.[103] To this end, he and his fellow Universalist critics like A. St. John Chambré called upon the denomination to reassert its connection with "the historic Church of Jesus Christ" by imposing some kind of uniformity in doctrine, government, discipline, and ritual; otherwise, it would become nothing but "Christianity mutilated and nerveless." It must proclaim that its mission was to save souls, and "there must not be a fear of such words," however strange they sounded to Universalist ears.[104]

Until it ceased publication in 1891, the *Universalist Quarterly* supplied a forum for these thinkers who, like the neo-orthodox theologians several decades later, objected to the increasingly pervasive theme of continuity between the present world and the divine, "the major positive principle of the liberal mind." Essentially calling Universalists back to their Calvinist heritage, they rejected the idea of the immanence of God, which was the basic theological implication of continuity and "the most characteristic doctrine of the nineteenth century."[105] It was not far from the arguments of Stiles and Hebbard to Reinhold Niebuhr's stinging criticism, decades later, of the modern church for its neglect of, even embarrassment over, its eschatological heritage. Religious leaders, he cautioned, needed to look beyond the "mundane interests of religious idealism" to nourish belief in the transcendent, in hope outside human history and power.[106] Indeed, Niebuhr's criticism of the secular idea of the "autonomous self" reflected much of traditional Universalist belief.[107]

In the eyes of critics like Hebbard and Stiles, Hosea Ballou's modified Calvinism, his belief that the reasoned assurance of universal salvation fostered a communal piety, was too much the product of an enlightened optimism. They chose to stress instead a universal sense of sin, a universal separation from God, and a universal need for divine redemption. Such dissenters maintained that the denomination could either nourish new sprouts of a definitely Christian piety and thus maintain a clear identity or resign itself to slow extinction through absorption into a sprawling, amorphous liberalism.[108] At a time when, in Henry Commager's well-known words, "religion prospered but theology slowly went bankrupt," this group of Universalists tried to reconstruct their theology by paying less attention to the idea of humanity united by enlightened hope and more to the common need for God's saving grace.[109]

The Great Liberal Alliance

Unmoved by these mostly older critics within their ranks, the majority of Universalists shared with Elbridge Gerry Brooks a notable lack of concern about their denomination's distinctiveness and ability to survive as it entered its second century.

A large proportion probably continued to take for granted a pathbreaking role, agreeing with Richmond Fisk of Watertown, New York, that "however near other branches of the church are coming to us, or we approaching them, it is clear enough that they are many steps removed from our positive attitude relative to the nature of the divine government."[110] They continued to see the Universalist church as a beacon of light, leading the liberal Christian church into the future.[111]

In reality, as Universalists looked away from their traditional providential doctrine and stressed more and more the pursuit of individual fulfillment and social progress, the denomination could no longer lay claim to a distinctive liberal theology. In many respects, adherents seemed only too happy that their denomination was shedding its old identity; as we saw in chapter 5, the midcentury saw a widespread desire to throw off the old association of the movement with social radicalism. The long-standing concern to make clear the differences between Universalism and Unitarianism was fading. In 1867, a Universalist writer argued against the primary importance of any belief save "love to God and Man" and spoke of a "Liberal Faith, both Universalist and Unitarian."[112]

By this time, the convergences between the beliefs of most Unitarians and those of most Universalists were becoming ever more apparent, as Universalists typically professed to believe that, from the beginning, "human nature has been improving."[113] Exuberantly declaring his belief that God directed "the entire course of human affairs . . . ever onward and upward," Horace Greeley expressed in his 1868 autobiography a general liberal faith in human progress, an outlook by now quite characteristic of liberal evangelicals and Universalists, as well as Unitarians.[114]

Those Universalists who questioned the popular emphasis on individual spiritual growth feared the trend within their own denomination and within Protestantism generally that made morality, in the words of James Turner, "the living core of belief." With their call for renewed attention to human sin and the need for redemption, they were reacting to a waning sense of the divine.[115] Markedly reduced concern about hell was part of the general change in the perception of God, who had become, said Sidney Mead, "like Alice's Cheshire Cat," sometimes threatening "gradually to disappear altogether or, at most, remain only as a disembodied and sentimental smile."[116]

As eschatological tensions eased and the traditional defenses of belief collapsed, Victorian Protestants tended to find less and less comfort and inspiration in inherited religious forms. The increasingly rich and accessible material world lured thoughts away from salvation to more immediate earthly gratifications.[117] Karen Lystra has shown how a new emphasis on romantic love in the mid–nineteenth century made the lover, not God, the symbol of ultimate significance among middle-class Americans. Romantic love helped give form to the overpowering individualism of the age and offered an ideal of personal spiritual fulfillment that could rival or even take the place of the Christian concept of salvation.[118]

To be sure, church affiliation still went hand-in-hand with respectability. The representative American churchgoer in postbellum America "wore his religion much as he did his Prince Albert Coat; it was a thing of pride, a symbol of status, pointing to his dignity as a man."[119] Church membership increased dramatically over the last half of the century: in 1850, 16 percent of the population was affiliated with a church; by 1900, the percentage had swelled to 36. Once largely simple and functional, church buildings were becoming imposing structures, home to robed choirs, massive organs, even professional singers.[120]

But the vital spiritual center in the bustling society of the latter half of the century was increasingly the home, not the church. Buffeted by pluralism and seculariza-tion, Protestants and Catholics alike elevated the home as a "private, sanctified religious community." Victorian Catholics and Protestants shared a domestic ma-terial culture, replete with parlor organs and pictures of madonna and child, which emphasized a good home's abiding quality.[121] Jon Butler points out that "Mother became the Evangelical Mary, lifted to an intercessory role for the American house-hold." The dead mother in heaven worked to bring her family to salvation.[122]

With the growing acceptance of the soul's "probation" and moral progress after death, Protestant and Catholic sensibilities became increasingly compatible. A strong latitudinarian strain, long evident in American religion and noted in the 1780s by Michel de Crèvecoeur, had become more clearly developed.[123] Particular theo-logical beliefs mattered less and less to American Protestants, even if they continued to care, sometimes deeply, about what label of religious affiliation they wore.

Protestants attended far less to divine salvation; the grave provided both further opportunity as well as reward for individual exertion. For some evangelical Protes-tants, in fact, reward was the operative word. Revivalists like Dwight Moody and R. A. Torrey of Chicago's Moody Bible Institute taught that a person's position in heaven corresponded to his good works; his "crown" would be studded with stars according to the number of souls he had helped to save.[124] Most Protestants probably did not adopt such an overtly hierarchical, moral vision of heaven. But many cer-tainly did share the belief that they were the captains of their personal destinies and that, as Lyman Abbott put it, "character-building" was the "object of Christianity."[125]

Most Universalists accepted and celebrated the way in which the notion of end-less hell had been put to rest. Few seemed concerned about how far Universalism had strayed from its original path. Thus, an eschatological faith in universal salva-tion, which had supported the ideal of a unifying, objective, reasonable piety, yielded to a concern for the more immediate cooperative work of God and humanity in the progress of the individual and society.[126]

As their movement had flowered in the first decades of the nineteenth century, Universalists had proudly asserted their unique claim to the "liberal Christian" label. Those early Universalists would have been surprised and saddened to learn that, little over a century later, most Americans recognized Universalism as related to Unitarianism, if they recognized it at all. Toward the end of the century, most Universalists had come to see themselves in a grand liberal alliance with the "Chris-tian" Unitarians—as distinguished from free-thought Unitarians—and with the En-glish Unitarians led by James Martineau. Many still harbored vague notions that their denomination would play a crucial role in the enlightenment and transfor-mation of Christendom, indeed, of the world. But the "great organizing mind" they awaited to give them direction and energy in their next century, as Ballou had in their first, never appeared.[127]

Conclusion

As a denomination, Universalism proved less and less viable as the nineteenth century drew to a close. Having peaked around 1880, the number of congregations fell precipitously thereafter. The continuing downward spiral also brought geographical contraction; in the twentieth century, the churches that remained were concentrated in New England and New York, where the movement had always been best established.[1] The 1961 merger with the Unitarians was a move made partly on the basis of simple denominational erosion; had they not pooled resources with another church, the Universalists might have ceased to exist altogether as a national organization.

The evidence of this study suggests that the movement was already losing its particular appeal and reason for being as early as the middle decades of the nineteenth century. As the generation of preachers that had shared Hosea Ballou's basic insights and outlook began to pass from the scene, Universalism lost its distinctiveness as a popular movement that sought to combine faith and reason, to sustain an objective communal piety; it was already virtually dead in this respect by the time of the 1870 centennial celebration. Readers familiar with well-worn models in the sociology of religion will inevitably see a familiar pattern in this rise and decline of a popular church.[2] But such categories, no matter how carefully refined, cannot make much sense of the profound shifts in eschatological thought that were affecting all of American religious culture in the nineteenth century. By focusing on the Universalist movement, a unique attempt among common people to preach a synthesis of faith and reason, a genuinely popular communal piety, this study has sought not to explain those shifts but to illuminate their meaning for popular religious liberalism generally.

Ballou's *Treatise on Atonement* had provided theological coherence and direction to the emerging Universalist movement at the opening of the nineteenth century. Addressing a culture increasingly split between evangelical piety and liberal rationalism, Ballou advanced what he saw as a reasonable piety that could uphold a religious sense of community. We have seen that his thought reflected and encouraged a popular synthesis of ideals inherited from both Puritan culture and the Democratic Enlightenment, a synthesis that allowed room for radical individual freedom but insisted upon the organic wholeness of society and the necessary interdependence of all persons.

But it is clear that the sensibility represented by Ballou and his followers in the first decades of the century proved increasingly unappealing in the fast-changing society of the antebellum era. By the later antebellum period, the Universalist movement was gaining ground far less on account of its revised Calvinism than because of its Enlightenment call for rationality in religion. A significant number of Americans responded to the Universalist plea that religious belief not offend reason; far fewer embraced Universalism's broader expression of the sovereignty of God. Protestants of many persuasions had chafed against the communal constraints of Jonathan Edwards's organic spiritual vision, and they hesitated to answer his call to "consent to being" as part of a common, sinful humanity. Now, citizens of the new republic increasingly demanded that religion afford a large berth to personal responsibility and virtue. Both Charles Finney's pronouncements about the voluntary nature of sin and conversion and William Ellery Channing's summons to moral improvement manifested a high regard for individual human obligation and potency.

With their belief in transcendent, universal salvation and communion, Universalists sought to recast Edwards's consent to being. In this doctrine, they found ultimate eschatological hope within the context of a modified Calvinism. It was a belief that encouraged faith not in current human power but in the power of God eventually to realize his kingdom. But most Americans in the Methodist age had little use for such a deeply eschatological and organically minded conviction. Ironically, the Brahmin Channing reflected the popular religious mentality far more than the man of the people, Ballou.

Despite the opposition of a number of prominent adherents, Universalist preaching and writing began to reflect the moralism, individualism, and perfectionism that pervaded the main forms of nineteenth-century religious thought. It seems evident that a simple affirmation of the divine restoration of all things could not serve the social purposes that were popularly sought in religious belief. By the middle third of the nineteenth century, the quest for a sense of community in universal redemption was losing its appeal.

Tenuously held together by a single general doctrine, Universalism was increasingly strained by centrifugal tendencies as the nineteenth century progressed. Because much of the popular appeal of the expanding movement lay in the broad scope it allowed for rational critiques of any and all religions, Universalists engaged ever more strongly in polemical attacks on evangelical teachings and on whatever could be denounced as either irrational or unscriptural. Clearly a movement highly attractive to aggressive religious seekers and controversialists, by the 1830s, Universalism had become more notable for its adversarial role than for its positive message.

As the Second Great Awakening lost momentum and as adherents sensed the need for a more active expression of their faith, there was a rush into a wide variety of social reform projects. Contrary to assumptions shared widely even by scholars of American religious history, however, Universalism was not the early home of intense social reformism; we have seen that, in general, denominational involvement in this realm came relatively late and was even halting in some respects. Much of the denomination's growth in this era was fueled by the influx of women, though the evidence has tended not to support the well-known thesis that this "feminization" worked against the true interests of women; we have found instead that the movement made a real contribution to the expansion of women's roles. Also around midcentury, however, the denomination entered a crucial phase of internal debate, as various forms of popular rationalism and social radicalism became so absorbing to many members that some leaders felt the Christian core of Universalism was seriously threatened. The reaction of denominational leaders to this perceived threat helps to explain the remarkably swift end to the earlier ideal of a popular synthesis of reason and faith.

By midcentury, denominational leaders were engaged in a major effort to reform the faults and excesses that they believed were preventing their church from enjoying respectability; they also sought to impose a clear system of church order upon a movement traditionally characterized by extreme distrust of ecclesiastical hierarchy or centralization of any sort. And yet, even as the denomination as a whole became more socially respectable, more educated, more self-consciously inclusive (of women, for example), and more active in various programs of social reform, the sense of common purpose that had inspired early Universalism was disappearing.

In the postbellum era, as the idea of universal salvation became far less controversial amidst the sentimentalized teachings of liberal evangelicalism, Universalists themselves moved ever closer to the broadly shared assumptions of American Protestantism. Most of their leaders adopted theological teachings about human free will that were directly at odds with the earlier piety of Ballou. Our survey of Universalist writings from this period reflects a broad shift away from the eschatological doctrine of divinely effected universal redemption toward a humanistic vision of the infinite potential of every member of the human family. Despite the persistence of a buoyant conviction that the spread of their faith and the progress of humanity were inevitable—a conviction, as George Williams has pointed out, much in evidence at the denominational centennial celebration at Gloucester in 1870—the meaning of Universalism had changed drastically for most of its adherents.

There were, to be sure, Universalist thinkers who sensed danger in the drift toward mainstream liberalism. Indeed, the conservative wing of the movement produced some penetrating critiques of late nineteenth-century American religion, which have gone almost entirely unnoticed despite their significance as precursors of Protestant neo-orthodoxy.[3] But the worries and warnings of scholars and theologians had little effect on a broader cultural movement through which the very concept of salvation was losing meaning.

Fewer and fewer people were willing to see limits placed on the individual's capacity to repent of sin, improve character, or explore the potential of mind and will. Indeed, by the later decades of the century, Americans had become "far less concerned about the theology of free will than about the problem of will power," as Gail Parker so aptly puts it.[4] While the vision of eternal salvation remained spiritually inspiring, it hardly seemed adequate to meet the challenges of modern civilization. New Thought and "mind-cure" movements aimed to alleviate a variety of human afflictions through mental processes.[5] In the popularity of mind cure and in the virtual end of debate over universal salvation, we see the eclipse of American Protestantism's traditional eschatological orientation.[6] People had begun to seek and expect humanly engineered resolutions to the anxieties, conflicts, and pressures of a new age.

By the last decades of the nineteenth century, though many Universalists could still see their church as the leader of liberal Christianity, little remained of the popular synthesis that had originally inspired the movement. The denomination still cherished highly affirmative if vague conceptions of God as love and the brotherhood of all humanity, and in this sense a trace of the early concern for a sense of community persisted. Yet, in these respects, Universalists were hardly different from members of other American churches. The early ideal of a communal, rational, and biblical faith in God's power and intention to redeem all souls had long since waned as the focus of Universalism.

Notes

INTRODUCTION

1. Sydney Ahlstrom and Jonathan Carey, *An American Reformation* (Middletown, 1985), 90.

2. Jack Mendelsohn, *William Ellery Channing, Prophet of Progress* (Boston, 1971), 169.

3. Russell E. Miller, *The Larger Hope: The First Century of the Universalist Church in America, 1770–1870* 2 vols. (Boston, 1979, 1985), 1:800.

4. Mendelsohn, *William Ellery Channing*, 178.

5. Hosea Ballou, *A Candid Examination of Dr. Channing's Discourse on the Evil of Sin* (Boston, 1833), 11.

6. Mendelsohn, *William Ellery Channing*, 203, 217, 221.

7. Ahlstrom and Carey, *An American Reformation*, 90.

8. Hosea Ballou, *A Treatise on Atonement* 1882; (reprint, Boston, 1986), 19.

9. William Ellery Channing, "Unitarian Christianity," in Ahlstrom and Carey, *An American Reformation*, 109. Channing is careful to grant that "intelligent Christians of that class from which we differ" also now "disowned" the idea that Christ's death made God "placable" or "merciful."

10. Ballou, *Treatise*, 99.

11. Channing, "Unitarian Christianity," 99, 109–110.

12. Ballou, *Treatise*, 92.

13. Channing, "Unitarian Christianity," 99–100.

14. Ballou, *Treatise*, 75.

15. Channing, "Unitarian Christianity," 99–100.

16. Ibid., 106.

17. John White Chadwick, *William Ellery Channing* (New York, 1903), 110–111.

18. Andrew Delbanco, *William Ellery Channing* (Cambridge, 1981), 72.

19. Channing, "Unitarian Christianity," 111.

20. Delbanco, *William Ellery Channing*, 72.

21. Ernest Cassara, *Hosea Ballou: A Challenge to Orthodoxy* (Boston, 1961), 148.

22. Ballou, *Treatise*, 125.

23. Henry May, *The Enlightenment in America* (Oxford, 1976), 58–59.

24. Bruce Kuklick, *Churchmen and Philosophers: From Jonathan Edwards to John Dewey* (New Haven, Conn., 1985), 64–65.

25. Delbanco, *William Ellery Channing*, 75.

26. Jonathan Edwards, *The Nature of True Virtue* (1765; reprint, Ann Arbor, Mich., 1960), 61.

27. Arminianism, or what Philip Greven terms the "moderate" Protestant temperament, retained its own "organicism," the "belief that the entire universe, both inanimate and animate, was arranged by God hierarchically in subtly tiered ranks of being, function and virtue." Greven, *The Protestant Temperament* (New York, 1977), 194.

28. The saying that Universalists believed God was too good to damn man and that Unitarians believed man was too good to be damned is attributed to Thomas Gold Appleton (1812–1884), brother-in-law of Henry Wadsworth Longfellow. Jon Butler paired Unitarianism with Universalism as "rationalist liberalism"; see his *Awash in a Sea of Faith* (Cambridge, Mass., 1990), 220. William McLoughlin characterized Universalists as "like the Unitarians, part of the rationalist or anti-Calvinist movement associated with the Enlightenment." McLoughlin, *Soul Liberty: The Baptists' Struggle in New England, 1630–1833* (Providence, 1991), 296. Recently, Daniel Feller characterized Universalism as "Unitarianism's country cousin." Feller, *The Jacksonian Promise* (New York, 1995) 97. Steven Mintz affirmed, "If Unitarianism drew its support largely from genteel, urban Boston, Universalism was its 'lower-class' counterpart, with members in rural, economically marginal areas of New England, though it also gained influence in the Philadelphia area." Mintz; *Moralists and Modernizers* (Baltimore, 1995), 23.

29. Mark A. Noll's book *A History of Christianity in the United States and Canada* (Grand Rapids, Mich., 1992) gives only passing mention to the Universalist movement.

30. Russell Miller's excellent and comprehensive two-volume institutional history of Universalism, *The Larger Hope*, should encourage scholars to focus more attention on the denomination. It is surely not for want of materials that students of American religious history have taken scant notice of Universalism. Universalists were more prolific than most groups in an age marked by an outpouring of religious literature. Periodicals, tracts, books, and pamphlets comprise the 2,278 items cataloged by Richard Eddy in his 1886 bibliography, which covers the period from 1753 to 1886. Eddy's two-volume work *Universalism in America*, in which the bibliography was published, stood until recently as the primary resource for study of the movement; scholars still rely heavily on his carefully organized list of publications. Eddy laid extensive groundwork for historians seeking to analyze the role of Universalism in American religious history. Unfortunately, the field lay almost entirely unexploited for close to a century. Only during the last quarter of the twentieth century have historians begun to mine the rich sources left by nineteenth-century Universalists. Alan Seaburg's fine survey, "Recent Scholarship in American Universalism: A Bibliographic Essay," *Church History* 41 (Dec. 1972), 513–523, gives a good view of research on Universalist topics.

31. In a classic statement about the cultural and theological transition from Jonathan Edwards to Lyman Beecher, relevant to the development of Universalism, Reinhold Niebuhr observed that:

> When God's sovereignty has become a law and the living relation a mechanical one, the dialogue between God and man is dissolved into a statement of incompatible doctrines. Man, it is said, is completely determined; man, it is said, is completely free. The dialectic becomes a debate in which men shout their dogmas at one another, and sometimes make slight concessions, such as that God does not wholly determine man or that man is not quite free; and such concessions are called "improvements in divinity." What could be truly said of a living process becomes untrue or unintelligible when it is asserted of the petrified product.

Niebuhr, *The Kingdom of God in America* (New York, 1937), 175.

32. Louise L. Stevenson, *The Victorian Homefront* (New York, 1991), 33.

33. Andrew Delbanco, *The Death of Satan* (New York, 1995).

CHAPTER ONE

1. Joseph Conforti, *Samuel Hopkins and the New Divinity Movement* (Grand Rapids, Mich., 1981), 58–61.

2. Arthur Brown, *William Ellery Channing* (New York, 1961), 53; Perry Miller, "The Marrow of Puritan Divinity," in Miller, *Errand into the Wilderness* (Cambridge, 1956), 83–84. As Harry Stout has observed, for Chauncy, "conversion was more a matter of duty than emotion. Above all else, he insisted, 'Salvation by *Grace*, through *Christ*, is the Way of *Obedience*.' " Stout, *The New England Soul: Preaching and Religious Culture in Colonial New England* (New York, 1986), 203. While Edwards rejected the Arminian implications of federal theology, he continued to employ the covenant scheme. Man remained in a powerless state, but the ultimately inscrutable God he confronted in the covenant was also a God who chose to come into the world through Christ. The covenant was thus, for Edwards, an understandable and even desirable mitigation of a divine rule that might otherwise be conceived as arbitrary and utterly inhumane. See Conrad Cherry, *The Theology of Jonathan Edwards* (Gloucester, Mass., 1974), 113–116. The tendency to value human initiative and moral action was, for Edwards, symptomatic of a greater problem: at the root of his quarrel with Arminian assumptions was his conception of history. He argued that Arminians, with their emphasis on freely decided human actions, made the world a confused and directionless place. See Perry Miller, *Jonathan Edwards* (New York, 1949), 313–314.

3. Bruce Kuklick, "The Two Cultures in Eighteenth-Century America," in Barbara Oberg and Harry Stout, *Benjamin Franklin, Jonathan Edwards and the Representation of American Culture* (New York, 1993), 108–111. Kuklick insightfully observes in his comparison of Franklin and Edwards:

> The wrong thing in Edwards has attracted his champions—the sinner. They have consequently attributed to Edwards the angst-ridden substantial self that has been very much a part of twentieth-century life. Commentators have not recognized that it was repellent to Edwards. The soul-searching that some people found attractive in the modern period is not the Edwardsean ideal but the end to which the self of a man like Franklin must be driven. The self of the Edwardsean saint, as B. F. Skinner wrote in another context, was beyond freedom and dignity. (111)

4. Robert W. Jenson, *America's Theologian: A Recommendation of Jonathan Edwards* (New York, 1988), 54.

5. Ibid., 60.

6. Alan Heimert, *Religion and the American Mind* (Cambridge, 1966), 101–113.

7. Allen C. Guelzo, *Edwards on the Will: A Century of American Theological Debate* (Middletown, Conn., 1989), 132–135.

8. Gerald McDermott, *One Holy and Happy Society: The Public Theology of Jonathan Edwards* (University Park, Pa., 1992), 98–101. McDermott quotes Sang Hyun Lee, *The Philosophical Theology of Jonathan Edwards* (Princeton, N.J., 1988), 109: "A thing *is* only as it is related to other things."

9. Daniel Walker Howe, "Franklin, Edwards, and the Problem of Human Nature," in Oberg and Stout, *Franklin, Edwards and American Culture*, 87. Alan Heimert argued that, for Edwards and his disciples, a "beatific vision" of perfect brotherhood was the only true basis for relationships among human beings. Equality was, for them, an aesthetic imperative. Heimert, *Religion and the American Mind*, 307–308. Heimert emphasized that Edwards's *Two Dissertations: I. Concerning the End for Which God Created the World; II. The Nature of True Virtue* (New York, 1985) pointed to the "equality" of all nature and art. Yet Howe notes that, in *Charity and Its Fruits* (New York, 1851), Edwards maintained that, in a good society, Christians "will not desire that all should be on a level; for they know it is best that some should be above others and should be honored and submitted to as such." Howe, "Franklin, Edwards, and Human Nature," 87. Gerald McDermott comments:

> Edwards was a hierarchialist of sorts. He believed that God's original design was for there to be "heads, princes or governors to whom honor, subjection and obedience should be paid." Yet he never elaborated on the gradations among humans as liberal parsons often did, and waxed eloquent instead on the beauty of equality. His heavenly hierarchy was based on holiness and fairly inverted New England's social hierarchy.

McDermott, *One Holy and Happy Society*, 153. "Just as God must be understood as a holy society," writes Janice Knight of Edwards, "so human beings cannot be considered as unitary; each saint is part of a dynamic community of believers, a society to be enlarged over time and particularly by seasons of awakening." Knight, *Orthodoxies in Massachusetts: Rereading American Puritanism* (Cambridge, 1994), 208.

10. Jonathan Edwards, *A Humble Attempt to Promote Explicit Agreement and Visible Union of God's People in Extraordinary Prayer*, quoted in Roland Delattre, *Beauty and Sensibility in the Thought of Jonathan Edwards* (New Haven, Conn., 1968), 211.

11. Richard Rabinowitz, *The Spiritual Self in Everyday Life* (Boston, 1979), 51, 61, 63. Conrad Cherry asserts that "Hopkins transformed Edwards's universe of natural images into a world of moral facts, his symbolic understanding of faith into discrete acts of obedience, the dynamism of being in general into the fixed structures of moral government." Cherry, *Nature and Religious Imagination from Edwards to Bushnell* (Philadelphia, 1980), 82.

12. Kuklick stresses that the New Divinity saw individuals as "real in the nature of things," a view much different from that expressed by Edwards in *Original Sin* (Boston, 1758). Kuklick, *Churchmen and Philosophers: From Jonathan Edwards to John Dewey* (New Haven, Conn., 1985), 63.

13. William Breitenbach, "Unregenerate Doings: Selfishness and Selflessness in New Divinity Theology," *American Quarterly* 34, no. 5 (Winter 1982), 479–502. New Divinity

believers charged that, if the understanding, as well as the heart, was depraved, a human being was saddled with a natural inability, "a *cannot* [that is] independent of a *will not.*"

14. Guelzo, *Edwards on the Will*, 132–135.

15. New Divinity theologians such as Hopkins and Nathanael Emmons were engaged in a deliberate effort to accommodate Calvinist thought to Enlightenment ideas; they acknowledged that God must be reasonable and that human happiness was important to God's glory. See Kuklick, *Churchmen and Philosophers*, 52. Kuklick also writes, "The God of the covenant had limited himself, but he need not have done so. The God of the New Divinity was confined by his benevolent character. The limitations on his sovereignty were intrinsic rather than adventitious" (61). Williams College president Edward Dorr Griffen took a leading role among New Divinity theologians in criticizing Calvinists for their inattention to human moral agency. Indeed, for all practical purposes, he set aside the doctrine of election as a hindrance to the cause of evangelicalism. David Kling, *A Field of Divine Wonders* (University Park, Pa., 1993), 84, 94–95.

16. Stephen Berk, *Calvinism versus Democracy* (Hamden, Conn., 1974), 172.

17. Henry May, *The Enlightenment in America* (New York, 1976), 58–59.

18. Conrad Wright, *The Beginnings of Unitarianism In America*, (Boston, 1955) 8; Heimert, *Religion and the American Mind*, 5–6. John Corrigan locates antecedents of Arminian liberalism in a group of Boston-area "catholick" Congregational clergymen, who "did not conceive of regeneration essentially as annihilation of the sinful self . . . but, rather, as the resuscitation of the faculties through grace." They envisioned God as a "benevolent father" rather than as a "chastening judge." Corrigan, *The Prism of Piety* (New York, 1991), 103.

19. Wright, *The Beginnings of Unitarianism*, 165–166.

20. John Corrigan, *The Hidden Balance* (Cambridge, 1987), 46.

21. Ibid., 26.

22. Wright, *The Beginnings of Unitarianism*, 199.

23. Heimert, *Religion and the American Mind*, 47. Robert J. Wilson indicates that "even Chauncy did not approach the explicit intellectual elitism which permeated Gay's description of the various degrees of sanctification." Wilson, *The Benevolent Deity: The Rise of Rational Religion in New England, 1696–1787* (Philadelphia, 1984), 181.

24. Quoted in Heimert, *Religion and the American Mind*, 252–262. Heimert argued that liberals affected a neoclassical posture in order to "dissociate themselves from the orthodoxy and vulgarity of American Protestantism."

25. May, *The Enlightenment in America*, 58.

26. Berk, *Calvinism versus Democracy*, 172.

27. Michael Wigglesworth, "The Day of Doom," in *The Poems of Michael Wigglesworth*, ed. Ronald A. Bosco (Lanham, N.Y., and London, 1989), 62.

28. David Stannard, *The Puritan Way of Death* (New York, 1977), 154.

29. Ibid., 150, 156.

30. Charlotte Irwin, "The Pietist Origins of American Universalism," master's thesis, Tufts Univ., 1966.

31. Stephen Marini, *Radical Sects of Revolutionary New England* (Boston, 1982), 6–7, 156, 72–73, 137–138. Marini sees the radical evangelicals as "seekers who followed the dictates of their own spiritual gifts into schismatic dissent from normative New England congregationalism" (11). He stresses the influence of Whitefield, who "provided a common vocabulary that combined the languages of the Bible, the marketplace and the human emotions." Marini contends that the sectarians (i.e., Shakers, Free Will Baptists, and Universalists):

propounded a benevolent God, human perfectability, universal nonpenal atonement and free grace for all believers. The mature sectarian theologies moved beyond defiance of Calvinism on particular doctrines to construction of alternative systems that circumvented and invalidated its internal logic. (137)

He sees them as "apparently Arminian in teaching yet unambiguous in their rejection of rationalism." Calvinists themselves, of course, were coming to accept "free grace for all believers," and a clear gulf existed between Arminianized Shakers and Free Will Baptists and the Universalists (138).

32. Paul I. Chestnut, "The Universalist Movement in America," Ph.D. diss., Duke Univ., 1974, 109–111.

33. George Hunston Williams, "American Universalism: A Bicentennial Essay," *Journal of the Universalist Historical Society* 9 (1971), 23; Russell Miller, *The Larger Hope*, (Boston, 1979, 1985), 1:3–156; Ernest Cassara, *Universalism in America* (Boston, 1971), 7.

34. Hosea Ballou 2nd, "Dogmatic and Religious History of Universalism in America," *Universalist Quarterly Review* 5 (Jan. 1848), 81.

35. Richard Eddy, *Universalism in America* (Boston, 1886), 1:106–109; Chestnut, "The Universalist Movement," 14.

36. Wayne Clymer, "The Life and Thought of James Relly," *Church History* 11 (1942), 193–216.

37. James Relly, *Union; or, A Treatise on the Consanguinity and Affinity between Christ and His Church* (London, 1759; first American ed., Boston, 1779).

38. Abel Thomas, *A Century of Universalism* (Philadelphia, 1872), 258–260.

39. Miller, *The Larger Hope*, 1:21.

40. Chestnut, "The Universalist Movement," 20.

41. Ibid., 22–26.

42. Miller, *The Larger Hope*, 1:35.

43. Elhanan Winchester, *The Universal Restoration, Exhibited in Four Dialogues between a Minister and His Friend* (Philadelphia, 1843), XV. Sir George Stonhouse [Sir James Stonhouse] first published this work as Universal Restitution (London, 1761).

44. Miller, *The Larger Hope*, 1:39.

45. Chestnut, "The Universalist Movement," 57.

46. Ballou 2nd, "Dogmatic and Religious History," 96.

47. Chestnut states that eighteenth-century Calvinists embraced the idea that Christ died for all men, thus all were capable of accepting or rejecting salvation ("The Universalist Movement," 141–144); Miller, *The Larger Hope*, 43.

48. Ballou 2nd, "Dogmatic and Religious History," 99.

49. Chestnut, "The Universalist Movement," 146–147.

50. Cassara, *Universalism in America*, 14.

51. Eddy, *Universalism in America*, 143–144, 217–218.

52. Joseph Huntingdon, *Calvinism Improved* (New London, Conn., 1796), 59. Huntingdon wrote that faith provided assurance and enjoyment of the fact of salvation, "but faith does not create the benefit, or change the divine purpose, or make any alteration in the previous certainty of anything in the universe" (59). Huntingdon's entire belief rested on human dependence on God. "If I recede in the least from this idea," he confessed, "I fall into complete atheism" (74). Nathaniel Stacy, an early preacher of universal salvation, contended that the sovereignty of God meant "his ability to accomplish his *will*, to do his pleasure and purposes in spite of all opposition." *Memoirs of the Life of Nathaniel Stacy* (Columbus, Pa., 1850), 472–473.

53. Stephen Marini, "The Origins of New England Universalism: Daughter of the

New Light," *Journal of Unitarian Universalist History* 24, (1997), 31–63. Marini notes that Edwards "strove mightily" to fuse the tenets of predestination, election, and limited atonement "to the inherently subjective experience of the New Birth," but:

> Separate Baptists practiced a style of homiletical and theological expression notable for its rejection of the Enlightenment philosophical methodologies employed by Edwards and the New Divinity. Instead, Separate Baptists approached doctrinal questions through a biblical hermeneutic informed by their spiritual experience of the New Birth. They bequeathed that hermeneutic to rural Universalists, the great majority of whom were Separate Baptist converts. (69)

54. Ibid., 70–71.

55. Ibid., 70. Marini cogently states his disagreement with Peter Hughes's claim that "early Universalists eschewed tendentious systematic doctrinal disputes and instead employed independent-minded 'common sense' to discover universal salvation." See Hughes, "The Origins of New England Universalism: A Religion without a Founder," *Journal of Unitarian Universalist History* 24 (1997), 64–75.

56. Eddy, *Universalism in America*, 167, 258–259, 265, 353. Shippie Townsend answered criticism from Samuel Mather in *Some Remarks on a Pamphlet Intitled* All Men Will Not Be Saved for Ever (Boston, 1783).

57. William McLoughlin, *New England Dissent, 1630–1833* (Cambridge, 1971), 721–722.

58. Guelzo, *Edwards on the Will*, 141.

59. Huntingdon, *Calvinism Improved*, 78–82.

60. Ibid., 83.

61. Chestnut, "The Universalist Movement," 121. Even Chauncy professed a somewhat attenuated belief in original sin. See H. Shelton Smith, *Changing Conceptions of Original Sin* (New York, 1955), 37–59.

62. Huntingdon, *Calvinism Improved*, 111–112. Eighteenth-century Universalists had some difficulty explaining how God could be both sovereign and admit sin into the world. Huntingdon, for instance, could not admit that an all-powerful God was responsible for sin; he blamed the devil and evil men. Yet he also acknowledged that sin was the possession of God, who is "wholly without limitation with regard to his absolute power in all things moral as well as *natural*" (112). In a faith that rested on divine omnipotence, sin somehow had to be part of God's plan. Many early Universalists experienced similar problems reconciling the existence of sin with divine goodness. See Chestnut, "The Universalist Movement," 120–129. But for the first generation of believers, the idea of universal salvation made Calvinist piety reasonable; for their purposes, this was enough.

63. Joseph Young, *Calvinism and Universalism Contrasted in a Series of Letters to a Friend* (New York, 1793), 33.

64. Ibid., 66.

65. Ibid., 122.

66. Huntingdon, *Calvinism Improved*, x.

67. Ibid., xi.

68. Young, *Calvinism and Universalism Contrasted*, 45. Chestnut points out that Young "was one of the first Universalists to denounce Calvinism by name." Chestnut, "The Universalist Movement," 129.

69. Huntingdon, *Calvinism Improved*, 133–134.

70. Heimert, *Religion and the American Mind*, 537–538.

71. Miller, *The Larger Hope*, 1:39; Benjamin Rush, *Letters*, ed. L. H. Butterfield, 2 vols. (Princeton, 1951), 1:583–584.

72. May, *The Enlightenment in America*, 207–211. John M. Kloos, Jr. writes that while Jonathan Edwards "professed natural ability but moral inability," Rush "posited a natural and collective inability, while, at the same time, he worked to recover a moral ability in the republic." He notes further:

> an extraecclesiastical religiosity finally characterized the doctor's piety. He called himself a Christocrat, by which he meant a Christian republican, one whose religious beliefs required an ethical attention to matters beyond the boundary of the sect or local church. Kloos, *A Sense of Deity* (Chicago, 1991), 84, 88.

73. Charles Cohen, *God's Caress: The Psychology of Puritan Religious Experience* (New York, 1986), 5. In conversion psychology, Cohen remarks, "the perception of God's love to oneself inspired a reciprocal ardor toward Him and a renewed affection for other worldlings" (160).

74. Gordon E. Geddes, *Welcome Joy: Death in Puritan New England* (Ann Arbor, Mich., 1981), 6.

75. Ibid., 8. Geddes recognizes that the "whole framework" of dying was inherited from the late Middle Ages. It:

> remained individualized and spiritualized even though certain features were dropped (such as purgatory and prayers for the dead) and others modified. . . . At death the organic and the communal faded to a formalized background as little connected to the event at hand. (35)

76. May, *The Enlightenment in America*, 274.

77. Rabinowitz, *The Spiritual Self in Everyday Life*, xxvii. What Perry Miller saw as a crucial underlying support for the church covenant in Puritan society—"a deep and wordless sense of the tribe, of the organic community"—was clearly giving way. Miller, *The New England Mind: The Seventeenth Century* (New York, 1937), 440.

78. Helena M. Wall, *Fierce Communion: Family and Community in Early America* (Cambridge, Mass., 1990), 11–12.

79. Ibid., 128.

80. Ibid., 130–133.

81. Stephen Watts, *The Republic Reborn: War and the Making of Liberal America, 1770–1820* (Baltimore, 1987), 113.

82. Lucy Barns, *The Female Christian* (Portland, Maine, 1809), 67.

83. Richard Brown, *Knowledge Is Power: The Diffusion of Information in Early New England* (New York, 1989), 294–296. See also William Gilmore, *Reading Becomes a Necessity of Life: Material and Cultural Life in Rural New England, 1780–1835* (Knoxville, Tenn., 1989), 350–354.

84. Timothy Hall addresses the growing practice of itinerancy and "the transformation of eighteenth-century consciousness from localism to the emergence of an intercolonial and transatlantic 'imagined community.'" Itinerant ministers:

> linked the widely scattered members of the community by providing local assemblies a personal, representative contact with distant, anonymous groups of awakened brethren. In so doing they offered a new model of the church and its surrounding social world: a mobile, dynamic, expansive, potentially unbounded community held together voluntarily by a common spirit among individual members of every locale.

Hall, *Contested Boundaries: Itinerancy and the Reshaping of the Colonial American Religious World* (Durham, N.C., 1994), 5–7.

85. Marini, *Radical Sects of Revolutionary New England*, 30–31. In her important study of Oneida County, New York, Mary P. Ryan concludes, "If anything, frontier circumstances exaggerated the importance of family in society beyond what even a Puritan social theorist would advise." Ryan, *Cradle of the Middle Class* (Cambridge, 1981), 51.

86. Marini, *Radical Sects of Revolutionary New England*, 39.

87. Randolph Roth, *The Democratic Dilemma: Religion, Reform and the Social Order in the Connecticut River Valley of Vermont* (Cambridge, 1987), 68.

88. Ibid., 66.

89. Ronald Schultz, "God and Workingmen: Popular Religion and the Formation of Philadelphia's Working Class, 1790–1830," in Ronald Hoffman and Peter J. Albert, eds., *Religion in a Revolutionary Age* (Charlottesville, Va., 1994), 150. Schultz comments on the themes of Universalist hymns, for example:

How sweet is the union of souls
In harmony, friendship and love
Lord help us, this union to keep
In *union* God grant we may meet

This was written in 1808, a time when masters and journeymen were being relentlesssly driven apart by the new manufacturing economy, a time during which the Democratic-Republican party was dividing itself into opposing manufacturing and working-class wings. It would have been difficult for many Philadelphia workingmen to separate the union of Christian fellowship from early craft unions.(150)

90. Ibid., 152–155.

91. Miller, *The Larger Hope*, 1:21–33. Roth, *Democratic Dilemma*, 65. Of a sick woman who imagined she was tormented in hell by demons, Brown wrote, "It brought forcibly to my mind the misbelief of such doctrines as that of endless misery that was [sic] being installed in the minds." Quoted in Blanche B. Bryant and Gertrude E. Baker, eds., *The Diaries of Sally and Pamela Brown, 1832–1838*, 2nd ed. (Springfield, Vt., 1979), 48.

92. See Whittemore's autobiography, *The Early Days of Thomas Whittemore* (Boston, 1858). On Whittemore, see also Miller, *The Larger Hope*, 1:295ff.

93. For much of the information in this and the following two paragraphs, I relied extensively on Ernest Cassara's fine biography, *Hosea Ballou: A Challenge to Orthodoxy* (Boston, 1961), 1–21. See also Miller, *The Larger Hope*, 1:100–103; and Oscar Safford, *Hosea Ballou* (Boston, 1889), 15–39. Orestes Brownson recorded that "both physically and intellectually" nature was "bountiful" to Ballou. "She gave him a tall, athletic frame, symmetrical and finely moulded, handsome features and an air of dignity and authority...." "The Convert," in Henry F. Brownson, ed. *The Works of Orestes A. Brownson* (Detroit, 1884) 5:24.

94. Hosea Ballou, *A Treatise on Atonement* (1882; reprint, Boston, 1986), 82–83. I have chosen a reprint of Alonzo Ames Miner's 1882 edition of the *Treatise* because Miner added chapters and an index to Ballou's 1832 revision of his original 1805 work. In his introduction to the 1986 reprint, Ernest Cassara points out that there were two significant changes in Ballou's thinking between 1805 and 1832. Ballou had originally been an "Arian," asserting that Christ was the "first-created spirit." In 1832, he asserted that Christ was a "man—but with a divine mission." The second important change concerned

punishment after death. Ballou was still uncertain about the issue when the first edition was published; with the second edition, he became a convinced ultra-Universalist, denying any punishment in the afterlife. See xix–xxii.

95. David R. Williams, "Horses, Pigeons and the Therapy of Conversion: A Psychological Reading of Jonathan Edwards's Theology," *Harvard Theological Review* 74 (1981), 335–352.

96. William Breitenbach, "Piety *and* Moralism: Edwards and the New Divinity," in Nathan Hatch and Harry Stout, eds., *Jonathan Edwards and the American Experience* (Oxford, 1988), 184.

97. Ballou, *Treatise*, 188.

98. Ibid., 121.

99. Hosea Ballou, *Select Sermons Delivered on Various Occasions, from Important Passages of Scripture* (Boston, 1832), 98. Ballou, in some respects, shared the perspective of William Hart, minister at the First Church of Saybrook, Connecticut, and an opponent of Edwards, who spoke not of a mystical love imparted by God but rather of "a spirit of equitable friendly regard to the whole family of God." Quoted in Conrad Edick Wright, *The Transformation of Charity in Postrevolutionary New England* (Boston, 1992), 46.

100. Ballou, *Treatise*, 48–49. Ballou was clearly influenced by Charles Chauncy, who held that the connection between sin and misery, virtue and happiness, needed to be made more clear. Cassara, *Hosea Ballou: A Challenge to Orthodoxy*, 28.

101. Breitenbach, "Piety *and* Moralism," 183.

102. Jenson, *America's Theologian*, 60.

103. Breitenbach, "Piety *and* Moralism," 183–184.

104. Quoted in Clyde Holbrook, *The Ethics of Jonathan Edwards* (Ann Arbor, Mich., 1973), 58.

105. Although written in 1738, this work was not published until 1851. Edwards, *Charity and Its Fruits*, 229, quoted in Holbrook, *Ethics of Jonathan Edwards*, 56. Joseph Conforti helpfully explains differences in the thought of Edwards and Samuel Hopkins. For Edwards:

> Self-love, like the will, was a faculty common to all members of the human race. The converted as well as the unconverted were moved by it to desire their own happiness. The essential difference was that the regenerate, having gained a new disposition of the heart, identified their interest and happiness with the love of Being in general. . . . Regeneration disposed the faculty of self-love to relish, delight and seek eternal harmony with God. . . . Hopkins countered by arguing that a Christ-like disposition for self-denial, rather than an inclination flowing from self-love, was the hallmark of true virtue. (120–121)

In particular, "Edwards saw true virtue as essentially a matter of right affections," while "Hopkins viewed it as right actions." Hopkins was "attempting to furnish a corrective to the increasingly fashionable theological notion of self-love." Self-love ethical theories, New Divinity believers held, "were contributing to the failure of communal ideals" (121–123). Conforti, *Samuel Hopkins and the New Divinity Movement*, 109–124.

106. Ballou, *Treatise*, 33. With this assertion, Ballou reflected the influence of rationalists such as Chauncy, who actually possessed a much more pessimistic view of human nature than evangelical Calvinists. Rationalists doubted that more than a few people could transcend self-interest, while Calvinists believed conversion conferred a new and "gracious" nature, a nature capable of acting out of "disinterested benevolence" rather than self-interest. William McLoughlin, *Revivals, Awakenings and Reform: An*

Essay on Religion and Social Change in America, 1607–1977 (Chicago, 1978), 77. To be sure, New Divinity believers, as Mark Valeri makes clear, acknowledged the universal human search for happiness. Joseph Bellamy stated that it was "natural" to seek happiness as a result of regeneration:

All mankind are in pursuit of this. They propose some good to themselves in whatever they do, either present or future, and they have been searching after that which is happifying, or, that which if we are possessed of will make us happy, and have found it to be the favour of God.

Quoted in Valeri, *Law and Providence in Joseph Bellamy's New England* (New York, 1994), 31.

107. Ballou, *Treatise*, 36. Ballou might also have inquired, as historian Joseph Conforti recently has, whether benevolence could be disinterested when it was linked, as it so often was in the nineteenth century, to the pursuit of personal perfection. Conforti, *Jonathan Edwards, Religious Tradition and American Culture* (Chapel Hill, N.C., 1995), 86.

108. Daniel Walker Howe comments that Edwards thought of true virtue as an involuntary emotion rather than a deliberate decision. "True virtue overcame the limitations of self and opened the door to the world of love." Howe, "Franklin, Edwards and the Problem of Human Nature," in Oberg and Stout, *American Culture*, 89. Wholehearted acceptance of the doctrine of universal salvation also demanded that the believer look beyond the self.

109. Ballou, *Treatise*, 34.

110. Breitenbach, "Unregenerate Doings," 490–491.

111. Ann Douglas has argued that "man has displaced God on center stage in Ballou's vision." This broad characterization of Ballou's work is simply not sustained by a close reading of the *Treatise* and Ballou's other writings. Douglas, *The Feminization of American Culture* (New York, 1977), 121–126. Hans Hofman's reflections on Reinhold Niebuhr are relevant here. Niebuhr's interest is

explicitly centered on man. . . . But we must immediately add that it does not mean that his view of the world is man-centered. Whoever takes man seriously must see that man's problem is precisely that he has lost the sense of his destined goal and with it true insight into his own nature.

Hofman, *The Theology of Reinhold Niebuhr* (New York, 1956), 145.

112. Ballou, *Treatise*, 126–129.

113. H. Richard Niebuhr observed that, for Edwards, the quest for honor and praise, "is man's pettiness, his perversity, his pustulant sickness." Niebuhr, "The Anachronism· of Jonathan Edwards," in William Stacy Johnsons ed., *H. Richard Niebuhr, Theology, History and Culture: Major Unpublished Writings* (New Haven, Conn., 1996), 126. Ballou's thought, in fact, is not incompatible with the view expressed by Edwardsean Joseph Bellamy in *True Religion Delineated* (Boston, 1750). Obviously, Ballou would have rejected Bellamy's insistence on "unmitigated love for God" and divine law that extended to the doctrine of eternal punishment. But Ballou, like Bellamy, was concerned with "the release of souls from the bind of selfishness." Bellamy distinguished between the natural, or selfish, good and the moral good, which "deemed others as divine creations, not objects for profit but 'cordial friends' worthy of care, compassion and charity." For Ballou, "moral good" was prompted by a belief in universal salvation. See Valeri, *Law and Providence in Joseph Bellamy's New England*, 91–101.

114. Mark A. Noll, "Jonathan Edwards and Nineteenth-Century Theology," in *Jon-*

athan Edwards and the American Experience, 278. H. Richard Niebuhr nicely stated Edwards's view of the human condition: "The will is as its strongest motive is and its strongest motive is self-interest and so man is determined and cannot by any new freedom at his disposal change his determination by self-interest." See Niebuhr, *Theology, History and Culture,* 130.

115. Ballou, *Treatise,* 147.

116. Ibid., 53.

117. Ibid., 102–104.

118. Ibid., 98–99.

119. Ibid. 92, 111–118, 188–191.

120. Ibid., 119–124.

121. Marini, *Radical Sects of Revolutionary New England,* 146–147.

122. Ballou, *Treatise,* 136.

123. Cassara, *Hosea Ballou: A Challenge to Orthodoxy,* 71–73.

124. Ballou, *Treatise,* 136.

125. Geddes, *Welcome Joy,* 6. Geddes observes:

> Eschatology concerned with the fate of the soul at death is of necessity individualized and spiritualized. But the eschatology of the truly last things — of the great last judgment, when death and the devil are consigned to eternal perdition, of the resurrection of the body and its reunion with the soul, and of the consummation of the marriage of the Lamb of God to his bride, the completed church — this eschatology pictures a total and communal fulfillment. (6)

The Puritans inherited a medieval eschatology that

> focused on the event of death as the most crucial experience. Death brought the individual immortal soul, regarded as the essential person, to a personal judgment before God and then to complete salvation, purgation or damnation. The resurrection, the last judgment and the completion of the church were treated as formal appendages to these earlier events occurring for each soul. They were indeed felicitous but not essential. (6)

126. Cassara, *Hosea Ballou: A Challenge to Orthodoxy,* 54.

127. Kerry S. Walters, *The American Deists* (Lawrence, Kans., 1992), 1–46.

128. Ballou, *Treatise,* 226–228.

129. Hosea Ballou, *Nine Sermons on Important Doctrinal and Practical Subjects* (Philadelphia, 1835), 177–179.

130. Rabinowitz, *The Spiritual Self in Everyday Life,* 61.

131. Kling, *A Field of Divine Wonders,* 41.

132. Noll, "Jonathan Edwards and Nineteenth-Century Theology," 278–279.

133. Conforti, *Samuel Hopkins and the New Divinity Movement,* 122.

134. Although his teaching differed significantly from Ballou's, the American Reformed theologian John Williamson Nevin (1803–1886) also noted and opposed the increasing subjectivism of American religious faith, maintaining, "The order of all true supernatural teaching is, the objective first, and the subjective or experimental afterwards, as something brought to pass only by its means." Quoted in Richard E. Wentz, *John Williamson Nevin: American Theologian* (New York, 1997), 137.

135. Jenson, *America's Theologian,* 115.

136. As James Hoopes points out, "In Edwards's metaphysics people did not have a substantial personal identity but were constituted in the mind of God." Thus, "the question of justice did not apply to relations between God and man any more than to

relations between men and their thoughts, fantasies, and dreams." Ballou, apparently, did not share Edwards's metaphysics, but his theological thought was similarly unpreoccupied by questions of justice. Hoopes, "Calvinism and Consciousness from Edwards to Beecher," in Hatch and eds., *Jonathan Edwards and the American Experience*, 214.

137. Miller, *The New England Mind: The Seventeenth Century*, 64–88.

138. Henry May, *The Divided Heart* (New York, 1991), 140.

139. Donald Meyer, *The Democratic Enlightenment* (New York, 1976), 191.

140. Mark Noll makes the point that John Witherspoon:

advocated the new moral philosophy at the expense of an older practical theology that stretched back from Edwards through the Puritan William Ames and John Calvin to Augustine. From the newer perspective, Witherspoon could treat virtue as a subject of natural scientific inquiry rather than as a product of divine grace.

Princeton and the Republic, 1768–1822: The Search for a Christian Enlightenment in the Era of Samuel Stanhope Smith (Princeton, N.J., 1989), 47.

141. Meyer, *Democratic Enlightenment*, 221.

CHAPTER TWO

1. Richard Rabinowitz, *The Spiritual Self in Everyday Life* (Boston, 1979), 68. For its first opponents in the late eighteenth and early nineteenth centuries, Charles P. Hanson observes, "Universalism bore an alarming resemblance to Catholic doctrine in two different respects: the criteria for church membership and the punishment that awaited sinners." Such critics believed that "by rejecting predestination and the concept of the chosen few, the Universalists had abandoned the Puritan attempt to restrict church membership to the outwardly righteous. If anyone who felt like joining a Universalist congregation could do so, then this was no better than the Catholic practice of inviting those who sinned six days a week to worship and confess on Sunday." Moreover, when the prominent minister Charles Chauncy proposed the notion of temporary, rather than eternal, punishment he seemed to be embracing a "popish" doctrine of purgatory. Hanson, *Necessary Virtue: The Pragmatic Origins of Religion in New England* (Charlottesville, Va., 1998), 169–170.

2. Nathan Hatch, "The Puzzle of American Methodism," *Church History* 63, no. 2 (June 1994), 179.

3. David Kling, *A Field of Divine Wonders* (University Park, Pa., 1993), 238.

4. Russell Miller, *The Larger Hope* (Boston, 1979), 1:163. Orestes Brownson wryly observed that a certain Universalist minister "was a tall, majestic person, of grave and venerable aspect, a chaste and dignified speaker, and the best sermonizer I ever knew among Universalists. But he had too refined and cultivated a taste to be a popular Universalist preacher, and finally, I believe, followed my example, and associated with the Unitarians." "The Convert," in *The Works of Orestes Brownson*, 5:30.

5. Sydney Ahlstrom, *A Religious History of the American People* (Garden City, N.Y., 1975), 1:584.

6. George Rogers, *The Pro and Con of Universalism* (1838; reprint, Cincinnati, 1871), 27–28.

7. Ibid., 75.

8. Stephen R. Smith, *Historical Sketches and Incidents, Illustrative of the Establishment and Progress of Universalism in the State of New York* (Buffalo, 1843), 100.

9. Miller, *The Larger Hope*, 1:56, 67.

10. Ibid. The Winchester Profession built upon an earlier Rule of Faith, which had

been adopted by the Philadelphia Convention in 1790 and by the New England Convention in 1794. The Rule of Faith was a slightly longer document; it included references to Jesus, the "Mediator," and the Holy Ghost, which were dropped in the far more important Winchester Profession. See Miller, *The Larger Hope*, 1:46.

11. William McLoughlin, *Isaac Backus and the American Pietistic Tradition* (Boston, 1967), 153.

12. Ibid., 153–154.

13. Ibid.

14. Hosea Ballou, *A Treatise on Atonement* (1882; reprint, Boston, 1986), 229.

15. See William McLoughlin, *New England Dissent, 1630–1833* (Cambridge, 1971), vol. 2, for a good discussion of Universalist interest in disestablishment.

16. Ibid., 934.

17. Nathan Hatch, *The Democratization of American Christianity* (New Haven, Conn., 1989), 99–101.

18. Nathan O. Hatch, "The Demand for a Theology of the People," *Journal of American History* 67, no. 3 (1980), 545–576.

19. Hatch, *Democratization of American Christianity*, 171–173.

20. Thomas Whittemore, *Plain Guide to Universalism* (Boston, 1840), 290.

21. Monitor, "Faith and Hope," *Candid Examiner* 2, no. 9 Montrose, Pa. (Oct. 9, 1826), 65–66.

22. George Hunston Williams, "American Universalism: A Bicentennial Essay," *Journal of the Universalist Historical Society* 9 (1971), 12.

23. John Bodo, *The Protestant Clergy and Public Issues* (Princeton, N.J., 1954), 50–60.

24. Sidney Mead, *The Lively Experiment* (New York, 1963), 97, 145. In contrast to Universalism's emphasis on divine will, Cynthia Lyerly notes that "One of the enduring aspects of early Methodism was its expansion of human agency. Converts from all walks of life found in the church a sense of power and control over their own destiny." Lyerly, *Methodism and the Southern Mind* (New York, 1998), 184.

25. It is true that many evangelicals subscribed, like Universalists, to Jacksonian ideals. Indeed, one well-known scholar, who acknowledges that Universalists "tended to be Jacksonian Democrats," also suggested that "Finney's theology was the Christian counterpart of Jacksonian democracy" and points out that conservative figures, such as Lyman Beecher, feared the egalitarian tendencies of the revival. McLoughlin, *New England Dissent*, 1231; and McLoughlin, *Modern Revivalism* (New York, 1959), 100–101, 130–131. Whatever egalitarian feelings they had in common with Universalists, evangelicals condemned the movement more intensely over the years of the Second Great Awakening. See Whitney Cross, *The Burned-Over District* (Ithaca, N.Y., 1950), 43–44.

26. J. R. Pole, *The Pursuit of Equality in American History* (Berkeley, Calif., 1978), 146–147.

27. George M. Marsden, *The Soul of the American University: From Protestant Establishment to Established Nonbelief* (New York, 1994), 51.

28. Donald H. Meyer, *The Instructed Conscience* (Philadelphia, 1972), 54.

29. Mark A. Noll, *Princeton and the Republic, 1768–1822: The Search for a Christian Enlightenment in the Era of Samuel Stanhope Smith* (Princeton, N.J., 1989), 208–209.

30. Meyer, *The Instructed Conscience*, 51–60.

31. William McLoughlin, *Revivals, Awakenings and Reform: An Essay on Religion and Social Change in America, 1607–1977* (Chicago and London, 1978), 118.

32. Joel Hawes wrote that the "moral government of God" was one of "law and

motive," administered through "reward and punishment." Hawes, *Reason for Not Embracing the Doctrine of Universal Salvation* (Hartford, 1827), 115.

33. James Davis, *Universalism Unmasked; or, The Spurious Gospel Exposed* (Philadelphia, 1837), 64.

34. Timothy Merritt, *A Discussion of Universal Salvation* (New York, 1836), 104. In a course of lectures delivered in response to the Universalist minister Thomas J. Sawyer, the Reverend Stephen Remington, pastor of a Methodist church in New York City, maintained that "if God has made man so destitute of moral freedom, which is the power to perform or not to perform right or wrong actions, then man must be as destitute of moral holiness as the bee, which acts from instinct or the necessary laws of its own nature." Universalism, he concluded, "destroys man's moral agency." Remington, *Anti-Universalism; or, Universalism Shown to Be Unscriptural* (New York, 1837), 26, 132.

35. Seth Crowell, *Strictures on the Doctrine of Universal Salvation Wherein the Doctrine Is Disproved on the Principle of the Moral Government of God* (New York, 1821), 24–27, 74–112.

36. Jacob Tidd, *A Correspondence, in Part Attempted To Be Suppressed by Hosea Ballou, an Editor of the Universalist Magazine* (Boston, 1823), 44–46.

37. Karen Halttunen, *Confidence Men and Painted Women: A Study of Middle-Class Culture in America, 1830–1870* (New Haven, Conn., 1982), 48.

38. Charles Finney, *Memoirs* (New York, 1876), 48–51. Adam Empie, a distinguished Episcopalian minister, pointed out, "It is *not true* that sin is *always fully* punished in this world, and that holiness is always *rewarded*." Empie, *Remarks on the Distinguishing Doctrine of Modern Universalism* (New York, 1824), 25. An 1833 pamphlet from the American Tract Society agreed and insisted that, since men often did not receive their due on earth, "It is strange . . . that there should be no future retribution." *A Strange Thing* vol. 4, no. 119. Joel Parker, the president of Union Theological Seminary in New York, argued that "something more than salutary chastisement is required of strict justice." Otherwise, "all the threatenings of God's word amount to simply this: if you sin, you shall be put under the influence of the best possible means to reclaim you and make you happy" (41). Despite his insistence that justice required the eternal punishment of some, Parker went to great lengths to indicate how few would go to hell. Hell was merely the "sink of the universe," a dark speck in the bright Universe." Parker, *Lectures on Universalism* (New York, 1841), 164.

39. "Endless Punishment, a Result of Character," *New Englander* (May 1851), 186–197.

40. As late as 1860, Joseph Thompson, pastor of the Broadway Tabernacle Church in New York City, could still pay lip sevice to the idea that God's rule was beyond the grasp of human reason. In an anti-Universalist work dedicated to his teacher, Nathaniel Taylor, Thompson asserted, "Our nature demands a God the dignity and purity of whose nature is not impaired by any effeminate weakness arising out of the claim of *relationship*." Yet the pastor clung to little more than the memory of the authoritative Calvinist God. He needed to believe in God as a moral governor, who ruled in accordance with the "requirements of our moral nature."

Critics such as Thompson, who denounced Universalism as "rationalistic infidelity," were, of course, seeking in their own way to subject faith to the scrutiny of reason. Thompson's main concern was explaining the existence of evil in the world and reconciling it with divine power and purpose. Atheism attributed it to mere chance or fate, and a dualistic system proposed that man was not powerful enough to overcome evil. Both of these systems were most unsatisfactory. As a third possibility, Thompson cited the obviously Calvinist (but not so labeled) beliefs of a character in Harriet Beecher Stowe's *The Minister's Wooing* (Boston, 1859). But the notion that evil could have originated in a God who was merely "exercising sovereignty" or some "mysterious plan in nature not connected with a moral administration" could not be entertained. Thompson, *Love and Penalty; or, Eternal Punishment Consistent with the Fatherhood of God* (New York, 1860), 1–10, 41–79, 348–349.

41. Philemon Russell, *A Series of Letters to a Universalist* (Exeter, N.H., 1842), 5. Nathan George of the Maine Conference of the Methodist Episcopal church noted that Universalists "come to the blasphemous conclusion that a holy God sins" and "charge him with the grossest acts of cruelty toward his creatures, to say nothing of punishing them for what they cannot avoid." George, *Universalism Not of the Bible* (New York, 1856), 215.

42. Edwin Hatfield, *Universalism as It Is; or, Textbook of Modern Universalism* (New York, 1841), 141.

43. John Borland, *Observations on the Moral Side of Man and the Demerit of Sin* (Sherbrooke, Canada, 1848), 18–21. It was not uncommon for opponents to charge Universalism with Jesuitism. See, for example, John Power, *An Exposition of Universalism* (Cincinnati, 1843), 297.

44. Parsons Cooke, *Modern Universalism Exposed* (Lowell, Mass., 1834), 224–230.

45. Timothy Dwight, *Duration of Future Punishment* (New York, n.d., no. 181), 12. As Seth Crowell put it, "If wicked men are made to believe . . . that salvation is infallibly certain, they will have no motive sufficiently powerful to induce them to oppose the corrupt propensities of their nature." Crowell, *Strictures*, 114.

46. Merritt, *Discussion on Universal Salvation*, 307–311.

47. *The Universalist; or, A Word in Season* (Philadelphia, n.d, no. 251).

48. Lyman Beecher, *Sermon against the Doctrine of Universal Salvation Delivered at the New Calvinistic Meeting House, Dorchester, Massachusetts* (Boston, 1830), 17. Parsons Cooke agreed, observing that "dissolute and immoral men" were "specifically inclined toward Universalism." Cooke, *Modern Universalism Exposed*, 228–229.

49. N. Levings, *Anti-Universalism* (Troy, N.Y., 1840), 30.

50. Miller, *The Larger Hope*, 1:196.

51. Power, *Exposition of Universalism*, 282.

52. Origen Bacheler, *Address on the Subject of Universalism* (Boston, 1830), 11–12.

53. "Universalism," *Quarterly Christian Spectator* 5, no. 2 (June 1833), 266–290. Some southern opponents of Universalism clearly believed that the doctrine posed a particular danger to their social and economic system. Although the South as a whole remained inhospitable toward the movement, Universalist congregations had begun to appear there, especially in the Carolinas and Georgia. Miller, *The Larger Hope*, 1:742. North Carolinian Adam Empie charged in 1825 that the Universalist was an "incendiary" who preached "a doctrine calculated to throw society into combustion." He further warned that, if Universalism were *"fully preached in all its bearings"* to the slaves and the lower classes, "woeful experience will soon teach you whether it is calculated to make men better or worse." Empie, *Remarks*, 21, 23.

54. John S. Thompson, *Universalism Vindicated and the Refuter Refuted* (1825), 13.

55. Abel Thomas, *Autobiography of Abel Thomas* (Boston, 1852), 328.

56. J. Aiken, *Review of "The Serpent Uncoiled; or, The Full-Length Portrait of Universalism"* (Indianapolis, Ind., 1848), 41–42.

57. Hosea Ballou 2nd, *Letters to the Rev. Joel Hawes* (Boston, 1833). John Boyden agreed in 1843 that "partial" salvation "addresses itself to our self-esteem, and flatters our

vanity, self-righteousness and self-distinction." Boyden, *Dangerous Tendency of Partialism* (Providence, 1843), 16.

58. Thomas, *Autobiography of Abel Thomas*, 51.

59. Russell, *Series of Letters*, 17.

60. Thomas J. Sawyer, *Review of "Universalism as It Is" by E. R. Hatfield* (New York, 1841), 234–235, 263–264.

61. Hosea Ballou, "In My Father's House Are Many Mansions," *Universalist Quarterly* 1 (Jan. 1844), 128–136.

62. Rev. G. W. Skinner, "Universalists as a Christian Sect," *Universalist Quarterly* 21 (Jan. 1864), 103–111.

63. By midcentury, southern arguments against Universalist theology were enmeshed in a general suspicion of northern political and economic motives. The Reverend L. Pierce used Universalism as a symbol of northern "liberal principles," which he believed were contemptuous of the Constitution and southern rights. He published a summary of his side in a debate held in Americus, Georgia, with Universalist C. F. R. Shehane. Pierce complained that the principle expressed in the Declaration of Independence — that God created all men equal — had been interpreted in too "unqualified" a sense. This newly imported belief had deeply disturbing implications, and Pierce was candid about his own reaction. "The views entertained by Universalists about the final equality of men are too agrarian for me," he concluded, for Universalism "leaves the lines of separation between the pure and the vile much like the colors of the rainbow, hard to tell where one ends and the other begins." And in morals, "this is ruin. There must be an impassable gulf or all is lost." Pierce, *Universalism Examined and Condemned* (Savannah, Ga., 1851), 41, 45.

64. Gregory A. Wills notes that, among nineteenth-century Southern Baptists as well, "democratic religion meant a startlingly different kind of populism." These Baptists:

> rejected much of the individualism that rose in tandem with the populist republicanism that swept the young nation. They honored their clergy, they were unashamedly authoritarian, they were stubbornly creedal, and they defended orthodox Calvinism.

Wills, *Democratic Religion: Freedom, Authority and Church Discipline in the Baptist South, 1785–1900* (New York, 1997), vii.

65. Miller, *The Larger Hope*, 1:118.

66. Richard Eddy, *Universalism in America* (Boston, 1886), 2:323–326. It is noteworthy that Whittemore's own sentiments were, like Ballou's, ultra-Universalist. His bias toward this position may have affected his survey.

67. Miller, *The Larger Hope*, 1:111–123. Miller includes a detailed account of the restorationist controversy.

68. Eddy, *Universalism in America*, 2:333–335.

69. Bernard Whitman, *Friendly Letters to a Universalist* (Cambridge, 1833), 289–326.

70. Charles Hudson, "Restorationism," in *Religious Denominations in the United States: Their Past History, Present Condition and Doctrine*, ed. Israel Daniel Rupp (Philadelphia, 1861), 581. Hudson insisted that only a system of limited future punishment could "reconcile the attributes of justice and mercy, and secure to the Almighty a character worthy of our imitation."

71. Ibid., 556–559.

72. Charles Hudson, *A System of Divine Truth* (Providence, 1828), 9.

73. Ibid.

74. Hosea Ballou, *An Examination of the Doctrine of Future Retribution* (Boston, 1834).

75. Hosea Ballou, *Nine Sermons on Important Doctrinal and Practical Subjects* (Philadelphia, 1835), 40.

76. Hosea Ballou, "Definite Theology," *Universalist Quarterly* 1 (Oct. 1844), 408–420.

77. Hosea Ballou, "Effect of Our Present Conduct on Our Future State," *Universalist Quarterly* 2 (Jan. 1845), 39–51.

78. Hosea Ballou, "Relation of Our Present Character to the Future," *Universalist Quarterly* 2 (July 1845), 312–320.

79. Miller, *The Larger Hope*, 1:119–120.

80. Indeed, in 1819, Ballou reprinted in toto Priestley's argument for a unitarian theology in the *Universalist* magazine. Ernest Cassara, *Hosea Ballou: A Challenge to Orthodoxy* (Boston, 1961), 134–135. See also Paul K. Conkin, "Priestley and Jefferson: Unitarianism as a Religion for a New Revolutionary Age," in Ronald Hoffman and Peter J. Albert, *Religion in a Revolutionary Age* (Charlottesville, Va., 1994), 209–307.

81. John Passmore, "Joseph Priestley," in Paul Edwards, ed., *Encyclopedia of Philosophy* (New York, 1967), 6:453.

82. Ballou, *Examination of the Doctrine of Future Retribution*, 191–197.

83. Walter Balfour, *Letters on the Immortality of the Soul* (Charlestown, Mass., 1829), viii, 343.

84. Henry Grew, *Report of the Discussion at Brunswick, Rensselaer Co., N.Y., between Revs. John R. Kendall and C. F. Lefevre* (Troy, N.Y., 1834), 13.

85. Norman T. Burns, *Christian Mortalism from Tyndale to Milton* (Cambridge, Mass., 1972), 34.

86. M. Hill, *The System of American Universalism Exhibited and Exposed* (Portland, Maine, 1844), 6.

87. *A Debate on the Doctrine of Universal Salvation Held in Cincinnati from March 24, to April 1, 1845 between Rev. E. M. Pingree, Pastor of the First Universalist Church of Louisville, Ky., and Rev. N. L. Rice, Pastor of Central Presbyterian Church, Cincinnati, O.* (Cincinnati, 1845), 419, 270–271, 121.

88. Hosea Ballou, *A Voice to Universalists* (Boston, 1849), 47.

89. Ernest Cassara, *Universalism in America* (Boston, 1971), 27.

90. Hosea Ballou 2nd, "Analogy between the Present State and the Future," *Universalist Quarterly* 4 (Apr. 1847), 113–128.

91. M. D., "On the Resurrection," *Universalist Quarterly* 4 (July 1847), 249–270.

92. A. M., "Restoration," *Universalist Quarterly* 4 (Oct. 1847), 329–338.

93. Hosea Ballou 2nd, "Condition of Man after Death," *Universalist Quarterly* 10 (Jan. 1853), 29–51.

94. Wilbur Fisk, quoted in Merritt, *Discussion on Universal Salvation*, 282.

95. Cassara, *Universalism in America*, 161–165.

96. Miller, *The Larger Hope*, 1:809.

97. W. E. M., "The Present Equalities of Life Consistent with a Present Retribution," *Universalist Quarterly* 4 (Oct. 1847), 338–346.

98. O. D. M., "The Divine Law and Divine Justice," *Universalist Quarterly* 6 (Apr. 6 1849), 160–168.

99. E. G. Brooks, "Hosea Ballou," *Universalist Quarterly* 27, n.s. 7 (July 1870), 419.

100. See, for example, Lewis Perry, *Radical Abolitionism: Anarchy and the Government of God in Antislavery Thought* (Ithaca, N.Y., 1973), 137.

101. Undated fragment from a sermon by Emerson, cited in Kenneth Walker Cameron, *Index-Concordance to Emerson's Sermons* (Hartford, Conn., 1963), 2:604.

102. "Compensation," in Ernest Rhys, ed., *Emerson's Essays: First and Second Series* (New York, 1906), 58.

103. William A. Clebsch, *American Religious Thought* (Chicago, 1973), 103, 106.

104. Ibid., 102.

105. Emerson, "Compensation," 67.

106. Stephen Whicher, *Freedom and Fate* (Philadelphia, 1953), 23.

107. Ibid., 139.

108. E. W. Emerson, ed., *The Complete Works of Ralph W. Emerson*, 12 vols. (Boston, 1903–1904), 6:241.

109. Whicher, *Freedom and Fate*, 140. David Robinson also calls attention to the "pietistic" quality of the superseding of the ego; selflessness was "the final criterion" that Emerson proposed "to measure the progress of self-culture." Robinson, *Apostle of Culture: Emerson as Preacher and Lecturer* (Philadelphia, 1982), 155.

110. Robert D. Richardson, *Emerson: The Mind on Fire* (Berkeley, Calif., 1995), 258.

111. Stephen E. Whicher, Robert E. Spiller, and Wallace E. Williams, eds., *The Early Lectures of Ralph W. Emerson*, 3 vols. (Cambridge, 1959–1972), 2:11, 17.

112. Ahlstrom, *Religious History of the American People*, 2:40. Commenting on the evolution of theology in antebellum New England, Philip Gura writes that Congregationalists like James Marsh "struggled with ideas so provocative that, often unknown to them, their theological formulations replaced the doctrinal elements of their theology with the *poetic*, thus revealing to their followers new dimensions of religious experience." Gura, *The Wisdom of Words: Language, Theology and Literature in the New England Renaissance* (Middletown, Conn., 1981), 39.

113. Daniel Howe, *Making the American Self: Jonathan Edwards to Abraham Lincoln* (Cambridge, Mass., 1997), 205.

114. Richardson, *Emerson: The Mind on Fire*, 375.

115. Robinson, *Apostle of Culture: Emerson as Preacher and Lecturer*, 136. See also "Emerson's Divinity School Address," in Stephen E. Whicher, ed., *Selections from Ralph Waldo Emerson* (Boston, 1960), 107.

116. Ahlstrom, *Religious History of the American People*, 2:40–42.

117. Richardson, *Emerson: The Mind on Fire*, 96.

118. Ibid., 529. Despite Whitman's comment, Emerson's apparent disdain for the spiritual sensibility expressed in Universalism almost certainly reflects the difficulties of communicating across social boundaries even in that self-consciously democratic age. The sage of Concord remained ever a patrician; Whicher observes that Emerson's humanism evolved into an ethics of culture "for the superior man, for the well-born soul." Emerson's *The Conduct of Life* (1860) was a book for and about "the best people." Whicher, *Freedom and Fate*, 163.

119. Theodore Parker, *Theodore Parker's Experience as a Minister and Some Account of His Early Life and Education for the Ministry* (Boston, 1859), 50.

120. Theodore Parker, "Duties of the Church," delivered at the Melodeon, July 25, 1852, quoted in the *Trumpet* 25 (July 31, 1852), 30.

121. John Edward Dirks, *The Critical Theology of Theodore Parker* (Westport, Conn., 1948), 133.

122. Miller, *The Larger Hope*, 1:130. Ernest Cassara notes that a group of young Universalist ministers were impressed with Parker and started to deny scriptural miracles. A resolution passed by a "solid majority" of the Boston Association in 1847 "sought to avoid the imposition of a creed," but defined the standard for service as a Christian minister as belief in the "Bible account of life, teachings, miracles, death and resurrection of the Lord Jesus Christ." Cassara, *Universalism in America*, 168.

123. Hosea Ballou 2nd, *Universalist Quarterly* 9 (Apr. 1852), 138–144.

124. The Universalist minister O. F. Safford reflected in "Ralph Waldo Emerson and Hosea Ballou," *Universalist Quarterly* 41, n.s. 21 (Oct. 1884), 418, that:

> Transcendentalism magnifies individualism, and there its mission ends. In its day, as a protest against the yoke of a medieval theology, its mission was manifestly good. But as a finality, disintegration of this sort is not good.

125. Mary Kupiec Cayton, "The Making of an American Prophet: Emerson, His Audiences and the Rise of the Culture Industry in America," *American Historical Review* 92 (1987), 597–620.

126. Gail Thain Parker, *Mind Cure in New England from the Civil War to World War I* (Hanover, N.H., 1973), 59–60. Parker asserts, "It is hard to find anything in the New Thought creed which Emerson did not say first" (58).

127. Lawrence Levine, *Highbrow/ Lowbrow: The Emergence of Cultural Hierarchy in America* (Cambridge, Mass., 1988), 149.

128. Neil Harris, *Humbug: The Art of P. T. Barnum* (Chicago, 1983), 78.

129. Levine, *Highbrow/Lowbrow*, 100–101.

CHAPTER THREE

1. R. Laurence Moore includes a chapter on "The Market for Religious Controversy" in his book *Selling God: American Religion in the Marketplace of Culture* (New York, 1994), 118–145. He writes that, in antebellum America, "religious controversy became a species of paid amusement for Americans" and that "disputes about religion and morals provided public stimulation and liveliness." Nothing illustrates this point more clearly than the widespread controversy over universal salvation and its implications for society. The many debates over universal salvation, however, were often not paid but were free "amusements."

2. Richard Eddy, *Universalism in America* (Boston, 1886), 2:479. Although Eddy's bibliography was not quite exhaustive, his listing was certainly complete enough to demonstrate clear trends. The figure for the decade of the 1880s is my estimate. The actual figure is likely to be lower rather than higher; Eddy lists some ninety works for the six years between 1880 and 1885; if that rate had continued through 1889, the total would have been 150.

3. Lewis Todd, *A Defence, Containing the Author's Renunciation of Universalism* (Erie, Pa., 1834), 18–23.

4. Origen Bacheler, *Address on the Subject of Universalism* (Boston, 1830), 14.

5. Nathaniel Stacy, *Memoirs of the Life of Nathaniel Stacy* (Columbus, Pa., 1850), 218–219.

6. Stephen R. Smith, *Historical Sketches and Incidents, Illustrative of the Establishment and Progress of Universalism in the State of New York* (Buffalo, 1843), 21–22.

7. Thomas Whittemore, *The Early Years of Thomas Whittemore: An Autobiography* (Boston, 1859), 131.

8. George Rogers, *Memoranda of the Experience, Labor, and Travels of a Universalist Minister* (Cincinnati, 1845), 77.

9. See, for example, Joseph Young, *Calvinism and Universalism Contrasted in a Series of Letters to a Friend* (New York, 1793), and Charles Prentiss, *Calvin and Hopkins v. the Bible and Common Sense* (Boston, 1819).

10. Writing in 1803, Elisha Andrews, a minister from Templeton, Massachusetts,

pointed out that sin occupied a minor role in the Universalist drama, as did the requirement of repentance. Thus it was a

> delusive and soul-ruining doctrine, because it cries Peace, where there is no peace, and leads the sinner to hope for the favor of God, where it cannot be found; and tends to soothe them into a state of eternal sleep, while in a state of enmity toward God and exposed to his displeasure.

Andrews, *A Candid Examination of the Moral Tendency of the Doctrine of Universal Salvation* (Boston, 1803), 91–145.

John Kelly offered a standard objection to Universalism, noting that "those . . . who argue the salvation of all men on the supposition that the universal benevolence of the Deity require it, must deny the existence of this benevolence, while sin and misery remain, or they must deny the present will, or power of the Deity, to banish them." Kelly, *Additional Reasons against Universalism: or, Divine Benevolence Vindicated in the Distribution of Future and Everlasting Rewards and Punishments* (Haverhill, Mass., 1815), 23.

11. Bacheler, *Address on the Subject of Universalism*. Bacheler wrote that Universalists were held together primarily by a "mutual and cordial hatred of experimental religion" (21–22).

12. Andrew Royce, *Universalism: A Modern Invention Not According to Godliness* (Windsor, Conn., 1838), 184–185.

13. Samuel Bartlett, *Lectures on Modern Universalism: An Exposure of the System, from Recent Publications of Its Standard Authors* (Manchester, N.H., 1856), 179.

14. Nathan George, *An Examination of Universalism* (Boston, 1846), 215.

15. Bacheler, *Address on the Subject of Universalism*, 21–22.

16. Parsons Cooke, *Modern Universalism Exposed* (Lowell, Mass., 1834), 245–246.

17. Todd, *A Defence, Containing the Author's Renunciation of Universalism*, 89–105. Eventually, however, Todd was drawn back to the Universalist fold and issued a tract entitled *Moral Justice of Universalism* (Erie, Pa., 1845).

18. Russell Miller, *The Larger Hope* vol. 1 (Boston, 1979). Matthew Hale Smith's instability and eventual insanity were later attributed to a brain tumor. His father, Elias, had helped found the "Christian Connection" in 1802. Like his son, Elias found religious truth in a number of denominations, including Universalism. See Michael G. Kenney, *The Perfect Law of Liberty: Elias Smith and the Providential History of America* (Washington, D.C., 1994).

19. Matthew Hale Smith, *Universalism Examined, Renounced* (Boston, 1842), 62–63.

20. Matthew Hale Smith, *Universalism, Not of God* (New York, 1847), 195.

21. Orestes Brownson, "The Convert," in Henry F. Bronson, ed., *The Works of Orestes Brownson* (Detroit, 1884), 5:38–40.

22. Whittemore, *The Early Years*, 268, 319. For further evidence of Universalist feistiness, see T. D. Cooke and A. B. Grosh, *The Kingdom Shut* (Utica, N.Y., 1839).

23. Smith, *Historical Sketches and Incidents*, 144–145, 180–181.

24. Hosea Ballou 2nd, "Review of the Denomination of Universalists in the United States," *Expositor and Universalist Review* 3 (Mar. 1839), 77–105.

25. Stephen F. Farley, *A Solemn Protest against Universal Salvation. A Sermon, Delivered in Claremont, N.H.* (Claremont, N.H., 1816), 1–23.

26. Russell Streeter, *Familiar Conversations between Inquirer and Universalist* (Woodstock, Vt., 1835), 213.

27. Thomas Whittemore, *An Examination of Dr. Beecher's Sermon on Universalism*

(Boston, 1830), 9; and John G. Adams, *Memoir of Thomas Whittemore* (Boston, 1878), 33–34.

28. Jacob Ide, ed., *The Works of Nathanael Emmons*, 6 vols. (Boston, 1842), 1:259ff., 314–316, 260; 2:426.

29. See, for example, *The Danvers Discussion: A Report on the Discussion at Danvers, Massachusetts, between M. D. Brahman and Thomas Whittemore* (Boston, 1834), 42; and Thomas J. Sawyer, *Review of "Universalism as It Is" by E. R. Hatfield* (New York, 1841), 234–235.

30. Sylvanus Cobb, *Autobiography of the First Forty-one Years of the Life of Sylvanus Cobb* (Boston, 1867), 40.

31. *An Address from, the Berean Society of Universalists in Boston to the Congregation of the First Church in Weymouth, in Answer to a Sermon Delivered in Said Church, December 18, 1808, by their Pastor, Rev. Jacob Norton, A. M., Entitled "The Will of God Respecting the Salvation of All Men Illustrated"* (Boston, 1809), 56–57.

32. "To the Editor of the *Gospel Advocate*," *Gospel Advocate* 2, no. 42 (Buffalo, N.Y., Oct. 29, 1824), 332.

33. Russell Streeter, *Latest News from Three Worlds, Heaven, Earth and Hell, as Reported at a Four-Day Meeting in Shirley, Massachusetts* (Boston, 1832), 42–56. Streeter challenged that, if Fisher could point to any Calvinist church that did not contain these beliefs in its creed, he would forfeit a thousand dollars and stop preaching universal salvation.

34. Ibid., 59–61.

35. Ibid., 32–35. Universalists pointed out that a favorite revival theme was that "the whole scheme of divine grace in the salvation of sinners might be resisted and defeated by the sinner himself." God respected man's "free agency" and refused to violate it even to save him. Revivalists regularly called on subjects to "make their calling and election sure." But a correspondent in a Universalist paper wondered how any man could make his election any more sure than God before the world was created. "Impious thought!" he exploded. "To the Editor of the *Gospel Advocate*," *Gospel Advocate* 2, no. 42 (Oct. 29, 1824), 332.

36. Menzies Rayner, *Six Lectures on Revivals of Religion Delivered in the Universalist Church in Portland* (Portland, Maine, 1834), 25–29. Rayner, who had been pastor of an Episcopal church in Monroe, Connecticut, resigned in 1827 to become pastor of the Universalist church in Hartford. His farewell discourse was an argument in favor of a belief in universal salvation and was published as *Universal Grace: A Doctrine Worthy of All Acceptation* (Hartford, 1827).

37. "Gill Measures of Heaven," *Candid Examiner* 2, no. 8 (Sept. 25, 1826), 63–64. In an 1845 oral debate with L. N. Rice, a Presbyterian minister, E. M. Pingree, a Universalist minister, maintained that "Presbyterians do not, generally, know that their own creed teaches. They do not understand their own Confession of Faith. I suspect that Mr. Rice does not know as much about it as I do. I judge this audience will soon suspect the same." *A Debate on the Doctrine of Universal Salvation Held in Cincinnati from March 24, to April 1, 1845 between Rev. E. M. Pingree, Pastor of the First Universalist Church of Louisville, Ky., and Rev. N. L. Rice, Pastor of Central Presbyterian Church, Cincinnati, O.* (Cincinnati, 1845), 252.

38. Jacob Frieze, *Two Discourses Delivered in the Universalist Church in Pawtucket on Sunday, August 30, 1829 on the Subject of Religious Excitements* (Pawtucket, R.I., 1829), 5–11. Frieze was the first person to organize a Universalist church in North Carolina, in Kenansville, in 1827.

39. "Scriptural Illustrations, No. 1," *Gospel Advocate* 3, no. 40 (Oct. 14, 1825), 314–316.

40. Streeter, *Latest News*, 98.

41. "Tricks of Revivalists Exposed," *Sentinel and Star in the West* (Cincinnati, May 21, 1831), 238.

42. "Effect of Religious Mania," *Sentinel and Star in the West* (Jan. 22, 1831), 115.

43. "Horrible Effects of a Four Day's [sic] Meeting," *Sentinel and Star in the West* (Oct. 1, 1831), 392.

44. *Trumpet and Universalist Magazine* 15 (Boston, Mar. 15, 1834), 150; and 22 (July 4, 1840), 7.

45. "Suicide," *Candid Examiner* 2, no. 15 (Jan. 8, 1827), 119.

46. Rayner, *Six Lectures*, 107–116.

47. Frieze, *Two Discourses*, 12–13.

48. Stacy, *Memoirs*, 85.

49. Ibid., 218. Since their itinerant ministers often followed the same paths, Methodists and Universalists had frequent exposure to each others' preaching and much opportunity for sectarian wrangling. The Reverend Nathaniel Gunnison complained about his mission to Cape Cod in the late 1830s that the Methodists were "insolent and abusive" and "traduced" the characters of Universalists. Gunnison, *The Autobiography of the Rev. Nathaniel Gunnison* (Brooklyn, N.Y., 1910).

50. Rogers, *Memoranda*,

51. D. J. Mandell, *Adventures of Search for Life: A Bunyanic Narrative* (Portland, Maine, 1838), 45–53.

52. Bernard Weisberger, *They Gathered at the River* (Boston, 1958), 154–155.

53. "Original Anecdote," *Gospel Advocate* 1, no. 29 (Aug. 1, 1823), 232; and "For the *Gospel Advocate*," *Gospel Advocate* 1, no. 32 (Aug. 22, 1823), 256.

54. *Gospel Advocate* (Jan. 21, 1825), 11–13.

55. Hosea Ballou, *Select Sermons Delivered on Various Occasions from Important Passages of Scripture* (Boston, 1832), 168–171. Women were easy prey at revivals, a Universalist writer hastened to add, not because of any constitutional weakness of mind but rather because they possessed "finer feelings." Frieze, *Two Discourses*, 19. In a letter to the editor, George Armstrong wryly noted that, at an 1830 Chillicothe, Ohio, Presbyterian revival, there was much consternation over the failure to convert any more than fifteen women and one small boy. See *Sentinel and Star in the West* (Dec. 4, 1830), 52.

56. "On the Arrogant Pretensions of the Orthodox Clergy," *Christian Telescope and Universalist Miscellany* 3, no. 2 (Providence, R.I., Aug. 19, 1826), 9–10.

57. "Clerical Impudence, No. 1," *Gospel Advocate* 3, no. 2 (Jan. 21, 1825), 11–12; and "Clerical Impudence, No. 2," *Gospel Advocate* 3, no. 3 (Jan. 28, 1825), 19–20.

58. Abel C. Thomas, *Autobiography of Abel C. Thomas* (Boston, 1852), 349.

59. Rogers, *Memoranda*, 106–107.

60. Donald Scott, *From Office to Profession* (Philadelphia, 1978), 44–51.

61. Curtis Johnson, *Islands of Holiness: Rural Religion in Upstate New York, 1790–1860* (Ithaca, N.Y., 1989), 55.

62. Streeter, *Latest News*, 41, 97; "Clerical Impudence, No. 2," *Gospel Advocate* 3, no. 3 (Jan. 28, 1825), 19–20.

63. Scott, *From Office to Profession*, 44–45.

64. "From the Kingston (U.C.) Patriot," *Sentinel and Star in the West* (Feb. 5, 1831), 115.

65. "Missionary Societies," *Christian Telescope and Universalist Miscellany* 1, no. 22

(Jan. 1, 1825), 37. A letter to an editor of the *Christian Telescope* expressed amazement at the formation of a "Rag Bag Society" in New York to collect and sell rags for the missionary box. This had to be *"the last thing* that could be thought of to draw money from [the] credulous and unthinking for the pretended purpose of saving souls." "Another Plan," *Christian Telescope and Universalist Miscellany* 1, no. 22 (Mar. 19, 1825), 130. Another anecdote concerned a minister accepting IOUs for the missionary box. "Missionary Cause," *Gospel Advocate* 2, no. 17 (May 7, 1824), 136.

66. "Money Answereth All Things," *Christian Telescope and Universalist Miscellany* 3, no. 1 (Aug. 12, 1826), 2. A two-part series in the same periodical on "Domestic Missions" observed that, despite their use of Arminian notions to lure converts, missionaries never actually denied the tenets of election and reprobation. "Domestick Missions," 1, no. 23 (Jan. 8, 1825), 89.

67. T. G. Farnsworth, *Sermon before the First Universalist Society*, Haverhill, Massachusetts, April, 1829 (Boston, 1829), 13–14.

68. William McLoughlin, "Revivalism," in Edwin Gaustad, *The Rise of Adventism* (New York, 1974), 138–141.

69. William McLoughlin, "Pietism and the American Character," *American Quarterly* 17, no. 2 (1965), 168.

70. Perry Miller, "From Covenant to Revival," in *Nature's Nation* (Cambridge, Mass., 1967), 11, 17.

71. John L. Hammond, *The Politics of Benevolence* (Norwood, N.J., 1979), 199–207.

72. McLoughlin, quoted in Gaustad, *Rise of Adventism*, 138–141.

73. Nathan Hatch, *The Democratization of American Christianity* (New Haven, Conn., 1989), 173. George Marsden observes, "The individuals who made up the interlocking directorship of the 'benevolent empire,' as well as their constituencies, were predominantly Presbyterians and Congregationalists." Marsden, *The Evangelical Mind and the New School Presbyterian Experience* (New Haven, Conn., 1970), 19.

74. Miller, *The Larger Hope*, 1:177–178.

75. See, for example, "Church and State," *Christian Telescope and Universalist Miscellany* 1, no. 42 (May 21, 1825), 165–168. In a chapter on "Artisan Republicanism," Sean Wilentz quotes Thomas F. King's 1821 Independence Day speech to an assembly of craftsmen. King, a Universalist shoemaker, decried "ecclesiastical despotism" as "the most cruel—the most unrelenting kind of despotism that ever tormented man." King, *An Oration Delivered on the 4th of July, 1821, before the Tammany, Hibernian, Stone Cutters', Tailors' and Cordwainers' Societies in the Mulberry Street Church* (New York, 1821), 5–7, quoted in Wilentz, *Chants Democratic* (New York, 1984), 84.

76. Joshua Lawrence, "Missionary Craft," *Sentinel and Star in the West* (Dec. 18, 1831), 66–67.

77. "National Tract Society," *Christian Telescope and Universalist Miscellany* 1, no. 34 (Mar. 26, 1825), 135.

78. "American Tract Society," *Christian Telescope and Universalist Miscellany* 1, no. 37 (Apr. 26, 1825), 146.

79. See, for example, "The 'Rev.' Edwin Ray," *Sentinel and Star in the West* (Oct. 1, 1831), 389. This article criticized a Methodist clergyman for cooperating with Presbyterian missionaries. The writer observed that Methodists were an "enlightened body . . . opposed to the aspiring ambition of the presbyterian clergy."

80. "Bigotry and Priestcraft Exposed," *Christian Telescope and Universalist Miscellany* 2, no. 41 (May 13, 1826), 162–163; "Secretary Yates and the New York Tract Society," *Gospel Advocate* 3, no. 10 (Mar. 18, 1825), 77–78; and "J. W. Yates and His Coadjutors," *Gospel Advocate* 3, no. 11 (Mar. 25, 1825), 82–84.

81. "Sabbath Schools," Christian Telescope and Universalist Miscellany 1, no. 35 (Apr. 2, 1825), 140.

82. "On Sunday Schools," *Gospel Advocate* 2, no. 30 (Aug. 6, 1824), 234; and "A New Scheme, Sunday Schools, etc.," *Gospel Advocate* 3, no. 26 (July 8, 1825), 207–208.

83. "The Conductors of Papers," *Sentinel and Star in the West* (Dec. 11, 1830), 61; and "American Sunday School Union," *Sentinel and Star in the West* (June 25, 1831), 279.

84. Miller, *The Larger Hope*, 1:275–286.

85. "Petitioners for Stopping the Mail," *Sentinel and Star in the West* (Nov. 20, 1830), 33; and "For the *Sentinel and Star in the West*" (Dec. 4, 1830), 52–53.

86. "The Cat Out of the Wallet," *Sentinel and Star in the West* (Apr. 16, 1831), 196–198; (Apr. 23, 1831), 204–207; (Apr. 30, 1831), 210–211; (May 7, 1831), 220; and (May 14, 1831), 228–230.

87. "Present State of Christianity in the United States," *Christian Telescope and Universalist Miscellany* 3, no. 1 (Aug. 12, 1826), 1–3. See also "From the *Universalist Magazine*," *Gospel Advocate* 3, no. 37 (Sept. 23, 1825), 293–294.

88. Zelotes Fuller, *The Threshing Instrument: A Discourse Delivered at the Second Universalist Church, Philadelphia, November 30, 1828* (Philadelphia, 1828), 4–5, 6–7; and *A Discourse Delivered at the Second Universalist Church, Philadelphia, October 11, 1829* (Philadelphia, 1829), 14–15.

89. Johnson Mewhinney, "Brother Mewhinney's Communication," *Sentinel and Star in the West* (July 9, 1831), 289–291.

90. Neil Harris, *Humbug: The Life of P. T. Barnum* (Chicago, 1973), 17–18. In his autobiography, Barnum wrote that he was upset by "the dangers of sectarian interference which were then apparent in political affairs." P. T. Barnum, *Struggles and Triumphs* (New York, 1981), 73.

91. "Universalism—Its Views of Human Nature," *Universalist Miscellany* 3 (Boston, 1846), ed. O. A. Skinner and E. A. Chapin, 401.

92. "The Position, Duty, and Prospects of Universalists," *Universalist Miscellany* 6 (Boston, 1849), 384.

93. See Ray Billington, *The Protestant Crusade* (Chicago, 1964), 32–135, on the anti-Catholic forces of the age. It is curious that Jenny Franchot's *Roads to Rome: The Antebellum Protestant Encounter with Catholicism* (Berkeley, Calif., 1994) includes no reference to Universalism and does not mention Orestes Brownson's important early Universalist affiliation.

94. "Romish and Protestant Church Uniting," *Gospel Advocate* 3, no. 14 (Apr. 15, 1825), 107–108; and "Romish and Protestant Churches Uniting, No. 2," *Gospel Advocate* 3, no. 17 (May 5, 1825), 129–130.

95. Russell Miller includes a detailed section on Universalist opposition to sectarian schools in *The Larger Hope*, 1:369–370.

96. "Dr. Beecher and the Catholics," *Sentinel and Star in the West* (Feb. 9, 1831), 133.

97. Quoted in Miller, *The Larger Hope*, 1:176.

98. Thomas, *Autobiography*, 184–185.

99. "Occasional Sermon Delivered before Maine Convention of Universalists, Bangor, June 24, 1846," *Gospel Banner* 12, no. 1 (Augusta, Maine, July 25, 1846), 1.

100. Miller, *The Larger Hope*, 1:787–788.

101. Quoted in Perry Miller, *The Life of the Mind in America* (New York, 1965), 73–84.

102. George Rogers, *Tales from Life, Designed to Illustrate Certain Religious Doctrines Which Prevail at the Present Day* (Boston, 1841), 15–22.

103. George Rogers, *Adventures of Triptolemus Tub, Comprising Startling Disclosures Concerning Hell, Its Magnitude, Morals, Employments, Climate, etc., All Very Satisfactorily Authenticated* (Boston, 1846), 11–16, 31–32, 84–85, 118.

104. *Gospel Banner* 12, no. 2 (Jan. 16, 1847), 102.

105. Edward Beecher, *The Conflict of Ages; or, The Great Debate on the Moral Relations between God and Man* (Boston, 1853).

106. Robert Meredith, *The Politics of the Universe* (Nashville, Tenn., 1986), 132.

107. Major Universalist criticisms of Beecher include Moses Ballou, *The Divine Character Vindicated: A Review* (Redfield, N.Y., 1854); Thomas Starr King, "The Conflict of Ages: A Review," *Universalist Quarterly* 11 (Jan. 1854), 34–72; and Hosea Ballou 2nd, "The Great Moral Conflict," *Universalist Quarterly* 12 (Apr. 1855), 113–132. Marie Caskey observes "Whatever hopes Beecher may have entertained of unifying Calvinism behind his views, he met with tremendous hostility from all the nominally Calvinist camps, while other evangelicals were equally baffled or offended by *The Conflict of Ages.*" Caskey, *Chariot of Fire: Religion and the Beecher Family* (New Haven, Conn., 1978), 136.

108. Miller, *The Larger Hope*, 1:164–165.

109. Thomas J. Sawyer, "The Importance and Necessity of Doctrinal Preaching," *Universalist Quarterly* 6 (July 1849), 221–238.

110. J. S. L., "Qualifications of the Minister," *Universalist Quarterly* 7 (July 1850), 221–232.

111. Otis A. Skinner, "Ecclesiastical and Denominational Organization," *Universalist Quarterly* 7 (Jan. 1850), 43–60.

112. E. F., "The Righteous and the Wicked," *Universalist Quarterly* 12 (July 1855), 299–309.

113. Skinner, "Ecclesiastical and Denominational Organization," *Universalist Quarterly* 7 (Jan. 1850), 43–60.

114. Quoted in Miller, *The Larger Hope*, 1:150–151.

115. M. B., "Attractions of the Pulpit," *Universalist Quarterly* 12 (July 1855), 254–266.

116. A. D. M., "Martineau's 'Endeavors after the Christian Life,' " *Universalist Quarterly* 3 (Jan. 1846), 58–78.

117. Hosea Ballou 2nd, "The Millennium; or, The Golden Age to Come," *Universalist Quarterly* 6 (Apr. 1847), 144–153.

118. E. T., "Changes in the Religious Views of Universalists," *Universalist Quarterly* 6 (Jan. 1849), 5–15.

119. E. A. Branch, *The Sentimental Years* (New York, 1934), 153.

120. M. G., "The Unwritten History of Universalism," *Universalist Quarterly* 5 (July 1848), 274–275.

121. George H. Emerson, "The Movement to Revive Calvinism," *Universalist Quarterly* 16 (Apr. 1859), 171–181.

122. Thomas Baldwin Thayer, *Theology of Universalism* (Boston, 1862), 20, 26.

123. Rev. J. Smith Dodge, "God's Dealing with New England," *Universalist Quarterly* 23, n.s. 3 (Jan. 1866), 5–16.

124. O. W. W., "The Man, Calvin," *Universalist Quarterly* 8 (July 1851), 255–271.

125. "Sermons on Theism, Atheism and Popular Theology by Theodore Parker," *Universalist Quarterly* 10 (Oct. 1853), 422–426.

126. Otis Skinner, "Relations of Mercy to Divine Government," *Universalist Quarterly* 13 (July 1856), 243–257.

127. B. P., "The Growth of Religious Thought," *Universalist Quarterly* 19 (Oct. 1862), 418–426.

128. George Emerson, "The Movement to Revive Calvinism," *Universalist Quarterly* 16 (Apr. 1859), 172. Clearly, Stephen Mintz did not acquaint himself with Universalist belief, or he would not have recently repeated a common misperception: "Sharing the Unitarians' optimistic view of human destiny and the innate goodness of human nature, the Universalists also downplayed theology and stressed conscience and benevolence." Mintz, *Moralists and Modernizers* (Baltimore, 1995), 23.

129. Amos Alonzo Miner, "Character and Its Predicates," *Universalist Quarterly* 10 (July 1853), 248–274.

130. Hosea Ballou 2nd, "The Faith Requisite to Christian Fellowship," *Universalist Quarterly* 3 (Oct. 1846), 366–393.

131. See Daniel Howe, *The Unitarian Conscience: Harvard Moral Philosophy, 1805–1861* (Middletown, Conn., 1970), 156.

132. See Walter Houghton, *The Victorian Frame of Mind* (New Haven, Conn., 1957).

133. "The Ministry," *Universalist Quarterly* 4 (Oct. 1847), 377–392.

134. Daniel Howe observes, "Although the difference in religious outlook between the Harvard Unitarians and their Puritan ancestors was pronounced, the difference between them and their American Calvinist contemporaries was much less great." Howe, *Unitarian Conscience*, 105.

135. Hosea Ballou, "Definite Theology," *Universalist Quarterly* 1 (Oct. 1844), 408–420.

136. See, for example, the following articles: "Attractions of the Pulpit," *Universalist Quarterly* 12 (July 1855); and Amos Alonzo Miner, "Progressive Character of the Reformation," *Universalist Quarterly* 14 (Apr. 1857), 140–150.

137. Rev. I. C. Knowlton, "The Fatal Defect," *Universalist Quarterly* 23 n.s. 3 (Jan. 1866), 29–44.

138. See, for example, *Universalist Quarterly* 14 (July 1857), 327. Under "Literary Notices" is a review of Unitarian George Ellis's book, *A Half-Century of Unitarian Controversy* (Boston, 1857). The reviewer finds it odd that the book makes no mention of Hosea Ballou, "the first who publicly taught the doctrine of Divine Unity." See also the notice about Henry Bellows's correspondence with a European on liberal Christianity in America. Bellows, too, failed to mention the Universalists; he observed that Unitarianism was "the *only* scholarly form of Liberal Christianity in America," and he continued:

> It is not too much to say that amid all the present blind and unconscious tendencies, the only church in America that has studied the past and the future, that lives from its thought and knowledge, that consciously represents the freest, and yet most religious tendencies of the age, is the Unitarian Church.

With resignation and dry wit, the Universalist editor commented, "Pleasant, this consciousness of standing not only alone in one's glory, but at such immense distance from all others." "General Review," *Universalist Quarterly* 26, n.s. 6 (Oct. 1869), 503.

139. D., "The Broad Church," *Universalist Quarterly* 19 (Oct. 1862), 362–371.

140. Ibid., 386–400.

141. Rev. B. Peters, "The Great Issue; or, Universalism the Fate of the Future," *Universalist Quarterly* 22, n.s. 2 (Oct. 1865), 488–508.

142. James D. Bratt, "The Reorientation of American Protestantism, 1835–1845," *Church History* 67, n.s. 1 (Mar. 1998), 68–69. Bratt asserts:

American Protestant theology for a century had addressed questions rising out of revivalism's confluence with the Enlightenment: the proper place of reason and the affections in the conversion process, the relative roles of human agency and divine decree within that process, and—reflecting upon both these questions— the (tri)unity of God.

CHAPTER FOUR

1. Quoted in Paul Goodman, *Towards a Christian Republic: Antimasonry and the Great Transition in New England, 1826–1836* (New York, 1988), 39, 41.

2. Steven C. Bullock, *Revolutionary Brotherhood* (Chapel Hill, N.C., 1996), 137–139, 163–173, 197. Masons had long presided at ceremonies opening public buildings, but the shift to Masonic rituals sanctifying churches is striking. The calling of a popular organization, albeit an avowedly Christian one, to consecrate a church building suggests a need to link the church with the more dynamic currents of society. It could have also signified the attempt to draw men into the life of churches, attendance at which was increasingly dominated by women.

3. Ibid., 176–177.

4. Dorothy Ann Lipson, *Freemasonry in Federalist Connecticut* (Princeton, N.J., 1977), 129.

5. Kathleen Smith Kutolowski, "Freemasonry and Community in the Early Republic: The Case for Antimasonic Anxieties," *American Quarterly* 34 (1982), 552–553.

6. Goodman, *Towards a Christian Republic*, 202, 276.

7. Jacob Frieze, *An Address Delivered before the Grand Lodge of Rhode Island at the Annual Festival of St. John the Baptist, East Greenwich, R.I.* (Providence, R.I., 1831), 6.

8. Walter Ferris, *Five Sermons by Rev. Walter Ferris . . . to Which Is Subjoined a Festival Sermon by Brother Hosea Ballou* (Randolph, Vt., 1807), 99; and Thomas Whittemore, *Life of Rev. Hosea Ballou; with Accounts of His Writings, and Biographical Sketches of His Seniors and Contemporaries in the Universalist Ministry* (Boston, 1854), 1:271n.

9. Hosea Ballou, *An Oration, Pronounced at Windsor, before . . . Vermont Lodge, on the 27th December, A. L. 5808 . . .* (Windsor, Vt., 1809), 3–4.

10. Paul Dean, *An Address Delivered before the Fraternity at Fall River, Troy, Mass., . . .* (Boston, 1825), 5–7.

11. Ballou, *An Oration, Pronounced at Windsor*, 3.

12. Randolph Roth, *The Democratic Dilemma: Religion, Reform and the Social Order in the Connecticut River Valley of Vermont, 1791–1850* (New York, 1987), 155.

13. Goodman, *Towards a Christian Republic*, 137–139.

14. A. R. Abbott, "Our Helps and Hindrances," *Universalist Quarterly* 16 (Jan. 1859), 37–60.

15. Ibid., 26–37.

16. J. S. L., "Qualifications of a Minister," *Universalist Quarterly* 7 (July 1850), 226–228.

17. L. C. B., "Position and Duties of the Universalist Denomination," *Universalist Quarterly* 8 (Jan. 1851), 29–36. Addressing the Maine Convention of Universalists in June 1840, Darius Forbes insisted that the time for controversy was past and that Universalists needed "different weapons to sustain" the interests of the denomination (7–8). Universalists needed more organization and "more and competent ministers." He asserted:

I believe also that we have been too lax in our attentions to the literary and theological attainment of candidates for the ministry. I know it was so [with] myself. I believe, in our present circumstances, no young man should be admitted to the ministry until he has acquired a respectable literary education, and taken a regular course in theology (10–11). Forbes, *Duties of Universalists* (Augusta, Maine, 1840), 7–11.

18. See Russell Miller, *The Larger Hope* (Boston, 1979), 1:438–471.

19. It is worth noting that Hosea Ballou and other ministers of his generation had opposed the establishment of theological seminaries in the 1840s. Many of them were former Baptists, and they believed ministerial education to be unnecessary—and even corrupting. See Ernest Cassara, *Universalism in America* (Boston, 1971), 17.

20. Miller, *The Larger Hope*, 1:488.

21. Ibid., 487–491.

22. Ibid., 488. Chapin was a prolific author; probably his best known and most influential work is *Humanity in the City* (New York and Boston, 1854). A brief summary of his early reforming outlook can be found in an oration published as *The Idea of the Age* (New York, 1842).

23. See Horace Greeley, *Recollections of a Busy Life* (New York, 1868), 84; and Glyndon Van Deusen, *Horace Greeley* (Philadelphia, 1953), 124.

24. Philip English Mackey, "An All-Star Debate on Capital Punishment, 1854," *Essex Institute Historical Publications* 110 (July 1974), 191n, quoted in Miller, *The Larger Hope*, 1:499.

25. General observations on Universalism, penal reform, and other branches of social reform are offered by George Hunston Williams, "American Universalism: A Bicentennial Essay," *Journal of the Universalist Historical Society* 9 (1971), 57–60.

26. Louis P. Masur, *Rites of Execution: Capital Punishment and the Transformation of American Culture* (New York and Oxford, 1989), 67–69, 86; Philip English Mackey, *Hanging in the Balance: The Anti-Capital Punishment Movement in New York State, 1776–1861* (London and New York, 1982), 214; and Miller, *The Larger Hope*, 1:501–502.

27. Mackey, *Hanging in the Balance*, 250–279.

28. Masur, *Rites of Execution*, 130–135. I have used the edition of Spear's work published in 1851, which is listed as the thirteenth: Charles Spear, *Essays on the Punishment of Death* (Boston and London, 1851).

29. Spear, *Essays*, 80.

30. Mackey, *Hanging in the Balance*, 215; Masur, *Rites of Execution*, 138.

31. G. W. Quimby, *The Gallows, the Prison and the Poor-House: A Plea for Humanity* (Cincinnati, 1856); Miller, *The Larger Hope*, 1:499–508.

32. See Mackey, *Hanging in the Balance*, esp. 214.

33. Miller, *The Larger Hope*, 1:516–519.

34. See Sylvanus Cobb, *Autobiography of the First Forty-One Years* (Boston, 1867).

35. On this theme generally, see Miller, *The Larger Hope*, 1:514–533.

36. The suggestion is made by Williams, "American Universalism," 50.

37. Ibid., 51.

38. John R. McKivigan, *The War against Proslavery Religion: Abolitionism and the Northern Churches, 1830–1865* (Ithaca, N.Y., and London, 1984), 51.

39. McKivigan, *The War against Proslavery Religion*, appendix, 201–220; see also Miller, *The Larger Hope*, 1:584, 617.

40. McKivigan, *The War against Proslavery Religion*, 173–174.

41. Miller, *The Larger Hope*, 1:610–614.

42. McKivigan, *The War against Proslavery Religion*, 174; Miller, *The Larger Hope*, 1:617.

43. McKivigan, *The War against Proslavery Religion*, 179.

44. Miller, *The Larger Hope*, 1:616.

45. Blanche Glassman Hersh, *The Slavery of Sex: Feminist Abolitionists in America* (Urbana, Ill., Chicago, and London: 1978), 141.

46. Miller, *The Larger Hope*, 1:598–608. Miller points out that there were certainly some slaveholding Universalists in the South, though it is impossible to determine how many.

47. Ibid., 617.

48. McKivigan, *The War against Proslavery Religion*, 53.

49. Miller, *The Larger Hope*, 1:611.

50. Ibid., 586–587.

51. Ibid., 626.

52. Ibid., 619

53. Ibid., 575.

54. The term is from Williams, "American Universalism," 44.

55. Sheila Skemp, *Judith Sargent Murray: A Brief Biography with Documents* (Boston, 1998), 19–31, 111–112.

56. E. R. Hanson, *Our Women Workers* (Chicago, 1881), vi.

57. Miller, *The Larger Hope*, 1:546–547.

58. Carroll Smith-Rosenberg, *Disorderly Conduct: Visions of Gender in Victorian America* (New York, 1985), 129.

59. Mary A. Livermore, *The Story of My Life* (Hartford, Conn., 1897), 395.

60. Miller, *The Larger Hope*, 1:535.

61. Hanson, *Our Women Workers*, 400.

62. Miller, *The Larger Hope*, 1:333.

63. Ibid., 536–547.

64. Antoinette Brown Blackwell (1825–1921) was ordained in 1852 by the Congregational church of South Butler, New York, without the concurrence of the Congregational General Conference.

65. Miller, *The Larger Hope*, 1:546–549, 557–559. Chapin was also the first American woman to receive an honorary D.D. (1893).

66. Ibid., 540.

67. A Universalist Spokesman, Quoted in William Leach, *True Love and Perfect Union: The Feminist Reform of Sex and Society* (New York, 1980), 278.

68. Miller, *The Larger Hope*, 1:558.

69. Leach, *True Love and Perfect Union*, 278.

70. Miller, *The Larger Hope*, 1:558.

71. See Miller, *The Larger Hope*, 1:542. In 1851. The charter was changed in 1857 to Lombard University, four years after it had been authorized to offer college level instruction (462).

72. Ann Douglas, *The Feminization of American Culture* (New York, 1977).

73. Miller, *The Larger Hope*, 1:560–564.

74. Douglas, *Feminization of American Culture*, 233.

75. Miller, *The Larger Hope*, 1:334.

76. Rev. Mrs. Jenkins, "The Perfectibility of Human Character," *Ladies Repository* 41 (May 1869), 378–379. The *Ladies' Repository* stands in marked contrast to the magazines discussed in Judith Levett Dye's dissertation, "For the Instruction and Amusement of Women: The Growth, Development and Definition of American Magazines for Women" (University of Pennsylvania, 1977). Patricia Oker, in *Our Sister Editors: Sarah J. Hale and the Tradition of Nineteenth-Century Women Editors* (Athens, 1995), writes

of the "gendered separatism" of women's magazines of the era but does not recognize the *Ladies' Repository* as a significant exception to her characterization of women editors.

77. "The Need for Training Women," *Ladies Repository* 40 (Oct. 1868), 313–314; Nellie Day, "A Statue in Every Block of Marble" 34 (Dec. 1865), 335–336; "Women as Orators" 32 (Mar. 1864), 420–421; "Women-Physicians" 38 (Oct. 1867), 307–308; Mrs. Julia A. Carney, "Housekeeping vs. Writing" 49 (June 1873), 442–448; E. M. Bruce, "Quantity or Quality?" 53 (Feb. 1874), 144.

78. Henrietta Bingham, "Every Man His Own Tailor," *Ladies Repository* 45 (Jan. 1871), 70–72.

79. Mrs. N. T. Munroe, "Man's Work and Women's Work," *Ladies Repository* 29 (Feb. 1861), 345–349; Mrs. N. T. Munroe, "Sewing" 45 (Feb. 1871), 99–103; Mrs. N. T. Munroe, "History of a Church" 50 (Oct. 1873), 288–294.

80. Sarah L. Joy, "Our Settlement of a Vexed Question," *Ladies Repository* 44 (Sept. 1870), 220–223.

81. George S. Weaver, *The Christian Household* (1854; reprint, New York, 1878), 159–160.

82. George S. Weaver, *Aims and Aids for Girls and Young Women on the Various Duties of Life* (New York, 1856), 83–84.

83. Smith-Rosenberg, *Disorderly Conduct*, 134.

84. Ibid., 158.

85. Ann Braude, *Radical Spirits: Spiritualism and Women's Rights in Nineteenth-Century America* (Boston, 1989), 2.

86. For a broad characterization of a selected group of such women, see Hersh, *The Slavery of Sex*, 141.

87. On the notion that most feminists were, in fact, working for such a balance, see Leach, *True Love and Perfect Union*, 7, 290.

88. Miller, *The Larger Hope*, 1:534–573.

89. On Livermore, see Miller, *The Larger Hope*, 1:567–573. Livermore's autobiography, *The Story of My Life*, is a remarkable document of the late nineteenth century; naturally, the author's interpretations of her experiences from forty or fifty years earlier must be used with care. Despite her fame during the nineteenth century, Livermore's name is notably absent from Douglas's *Feminization of American Culture*.

90. Miller, *The Larger Hope*, 1:538–539, 549.

91. Ibid., 539.

92. Gail Parker, *The Oven Birds: American Women on Womanhood* (Garden City, N.Y., 1972), 3.

93. Henrietta Bingham, "Editors' By-Hours," *Ladies' Repository* 52 (Dec. 1874), 470–472.

94. Ibid.

95. Miller, *The Larger Hope*, 1:573.

96. Braude, *Radical Spirits*, 201.

97. Ibid.

98. The early religious experience of Elizabeth Cady Stanton, a leading nineteenth-century feminist, is instructive here. As R. Laurence Moore points out, Stanton's stern Calvinist upbringing prompted her thought about the unjust relation of the sexes. She most resented an arbitrary God, not mistreatment because she was a girl. Moore, "What Children Did Not Learn in School: The Intellectual Quickening of Young Americans in the Nineteenth Century," *Church History* 68, no. 1 (Mar. 1999), 50.

99. Universalist clergyman A. D. Mayo, who became a strong supporter of reform, reflected this shift, declaring in 1847, "Never can the immortal soul be exhausted; it

must live and move onward forever." Illustrating his belief in the potential of women, he wrote, "Look at that delicate girl, raised in the midst of luxury" and see how she responds when her character is tested by misfortune. "She girds herself to meet the world, and with a strong arm, bends all circumstances to her will . . . to become a lofty, self-sustaining spirit, equal to every calamity." Mayo was married to Sarah Edgerton Mayo (1819–1848), a poet and editor of several Universalist periodicals. A. D. Mayo, *The Balance; or Moral Arguments for Universalism* (Boston, 1847), 70–72.

CHAPTER FIVE

1. Russell Miller, *The Larger Hope* (Boston, 1979); Whitney Cross, *The Burned-Over District* (Ithaca, N.Y., 1950), 324–326. Cross notes that both mesmerism and phrenology "reinforced Universalist doctrines and suggested that natural laws rather than whimsical miracles embodied God's purpose for humanity." Also see J. William Broadway, "Universalist Participation in the Spiritualist Movement of the Nineteenth Century," *Proceedings of the Unitarian Universalist Historical Society* 19 (1981), 1–15. This article colorfully documents Universalist involvement in spiritualism but offers little in the way of analysis.

2. "The Great Harmonia, Concerning the Seven Mental States. By Andrew Jackson Davis," *Universalist Quarterly* 9 (July 1852), 326–327.

3. Albert Post, *Popular Freethought in America* (New York, 1943), 226.

4. Ibid., 195.

5. Herbert Hovenkamp, *Science and Religion in America, 1800–1860* (Philadelphia, 1978), 44–46. Hovenkamp includes a good discussion of antebellum belief in natural theology and the changing nature of religious education.

6. John Davies, *Phrenology: Fad and Science* (New Haven, Conn., 1955), 3–63.

7. T. J. Sawyer, "Influence of Cerebral Organization on Religious Opinions and Belief," *American Phrenological Journal and Miscellany* 3, no. 10 (July 1841), 433–451.

8. Davies, *Phrenology*, 67.

9. "Remarks on the Religious Bearing of Phrenology," *American Phrenological Journal and Miscellany* 2, no. 10 (July 1840), 468–472.

10. "Adaption of Religion to the Nature of Man," *American Phrenological Journal and Miscellany* 3, no. 10 (July 1841), 526–527.

11. Davies, *Phrenology*, 66–75.

12. Cross, *The Burned-Over District*, 325; Davies, *Phrenology*, 62, 74.

13. "The Great Harmonia, Concerning the Seven Mental States. By Andrew Jackson Davis," *Universalist Quarterly* 9 (July 1852), 326–327.

14. Joseph A. Warne, "Phrenology in Relation to Fatalism, Necessity and Human Responsibility," *American Phrenological Journal and Miscellany* 1, no. 10 (July 1839), 345–351; 1, no. 12 (Sept. 1839), 478–487.

15. "From the Edinburgh Phrenological Journal," "On the Harmony between Philosophy and Religion," *American Phrenological Journal and Miscellany* 2, no. 11 (Aug. 1840), 497–510.

16. George Weaver, *The Open Way* (Cincinnati, 1870), 212.

17. George Weaver, *Lectures on Mental Science according to the Philosophy of Phrenology* (New York, 1852), 18–23, 60–63, 273.

18. "On the Abuse or Perversion of Certain Faculties in Religion," *American Phrenological Journal and Miscellany* 3, no. 11 (July 1841), 517–522.

19. Sawyer, "Influence of Cerebral Organization," 433–451. In her 1998 dissertation, "Between the Enlightenment and Public Protestantism: Religion and the American

Phrenological Movement" (Univ. of California, Santa Barbara), Lisle Dalton Woodruff rightly observes that "modern American religious historians tend to neglect the study of phrenology altogether" (235). She describes American phrenology as a "mixed tradition that drew upon the resources of two more or less distinctive symbolic resources—the Enlightenment and American public Protestantism" (240). Yet at no point does she mention Universalism or the strong connections between phrenology and that movement.

20. "The Great Harmonia, Concerning the Seven Mental States. By Andrew Jackson Davis," *Universalist Quarterly* 9 (July 1852), 326–327.

21. Robert C. Fuller, *Mesmerism and the American Cure of Souls* (Philadelphia, 1982), 1–15.

22. Ibid., 16–47.

23. Ibid., 78–81. Fuller cites no evidence to support his contention that "many former revivalists transferred their fervor to what they considered more progressive religious causes." His assertion that, in particular, "spiritualism, Universalism and Swedenborgianism all drew from the ranks of those seeking to sustain their earlier religious enthusiasms through ever more daring departures from the mainstream tradition" mistakenly implies that Universalism was a nonchristian and very unorthodox faith.

24. Ibid., 69, 80.

25. John Bovee Dods, *Thirty Short Sermons* (Boston, 1842), 230–331.

26. John Bovee Dods, *The Philosophy of Electrical Psychology* (New York, 1850), 35.

27. John Bovee Dods, *Six Lectures on the Philosophy of Mesmerism* (New York, 1847), 8–9.

28. Dods, *Six Lectures on the Philosophy of Mesmerism*, 42–43.

29. R. Laurence Moore, *In Search of White Crows* (New York, 1977), 29. The spiritualist's words are quoted in Ann Braude, *Radical Spirits: Spiritualism and Women's Rights in Nineteenth-Century America* (Boston, 1989), 5.

30. Dods, *Six Lectures on the Philosophy of Mesmerism*, 40.

31. Dods, *The Philosophy of Electrical Psychology*, 110–111.

32. Dods, *Philosophy of Electrical Psychology*, 100–119.

33. John Bovee Dods, *Immortality Triumphant* (New York, 1852), 29–31.

34. Ibid., 102–143.

35. Dods, *Six Lectures on the Philosophy of Mesmerism*, 8–65. Mesmerism offered "new fields of action" for people to "roam at large and find ample gratification of all their sympathies and Christian feelings" (28).

36. Ibid., 74.

37. J. O. Barrett, *The Spiritual Pilgrim: A Biography of James M. Peebles* (Boston, 1872), 44.

38. John Bovee Dods, *Spirit Manifestations Examined and Explained* (New York, 1854), contains Dods's criticism of contemporary spiritualism. It may well be that Dods was "read out" of Universalism because of his spiritualist/materialist teachings and that this work was a later recantation.

39. Miller, *The Larger Hope*, 1:226.

40. See E. Douglas Branch, *The Sentimental Years* (New York, 1934), 362–379; and Moore, *In Search of White Crows*, 49.

41. Frank Podmore, *Mediums of the Nineteenth Century* (New Hyde Park, N.Y., 1963), 1:217.

42. Moore, *In Search of White Crows*, 6–7.

43. Slater Brown, *The Heyday of Spiritualism* (New York, 1970), 114; William Harlan Hale, *Horace Greeley, Voice of the People* (New York, 1950), 123–124; and Glyndon Van Deusen, *Horace Greeley: Nineteenth-Century Crusader* (Philadelphia, 1953), 152–153.

44. R. P. Ambler ed., *Spirit Messenger* (Feb. 15, 1851), 222.

45. R. P. Ambler, *Elements of Spiritual Philosophy* (Springfield, Mass., 1851), 13–76.

46. R. P. Ambler, *The Spiritual Teacher* (New York, 1852), 45–144; see also Brown, *The Heyday of Spiritualism*, 73–75.

47. Miller, *The Larger Hope*, 1:127. The links between Adin Ballou's restorationism and his perfectionism are suggested by Jerry V. Caswell, " 'A New Civilization Radically Higher than the Old': Adin Ballou's Search for Social Perfection," *Journal of the Universalist Historical Society* 7 (1967–1968), 70–96.

48. Adin Ballou, *An Exposition of the View Respecting the Principal Facts, Causes and Peculiarities Involved in Spirit Manifestations* (Boston, 1852), iii–93.

49. See, for example, Woodbury Fernald, *A Discourse Delivered in the First Universalist Church, Cabotville, Massachusetts, January 14, 1838* (Portsmouth, 1838); and his *Universalism against Partialism* (Boston, 1840).

50. "Eternity of Heaven and Hell. By Woodbury M. Fernald," *Universalist Quarterly* 13 Jan. 1856, 103–104.

51. Brown, *The Heyday of Spiritualism*, 53.

52. J. G. F, "Swedenborg," *Universalist Quarterly* 14 (Oct. 1857), 329–338.

53. Woodbury Fernald, *Eternity of Heaven and Hell* (n.p., n.d.).

54. Woodbury Fernald, *God and His Providence* (Boston, 1859), 42–44, 127–128, 88–89. Bret E. Carroll underscores the deterministic element in spiritualism. Spirits gradually and inevitably progressed, albeit at different rates, as spiritualism "bound the individual in a moral universe whose architecture included no discernible ceiling but an emphatically impenetrable floor." Carroll, *Spiritualism in Antebellum America* (Bloomington, Ind., 1997), 77–79.

55. Fernald, *God and His Providence*, 196, 289.

56. Brown, *The Heyday of Spiritualism*, 73–75.

57. Gibson Smith, *Lectures on Clairmativeness; or, Human Magnetism* (New York, 1845). Andrew Jackson Davis noted that after Smith delivered his lectures, his Poughkeepsie church, "being in quest of respectability and popularity, refused to extend as cordially as before the right hand of fellowship." Davis, *The Magic Staff* (New York, 1864), 279.

58. Brown, *The Heyday of Spiritualism*, 77–83.

59. William Fishbough's introduction to Andrew Jackson Davis, *The Principles of Nature* (New York, 1847), iii.

60. Brown, *The Heyday of Spiritualism*, 73–75.

61. Moore, *In Search of White Crows*, 66–67, 86.

62. Fishbough, introduction to Davis, *The Principles of Nature*, iv.

63. Davis, *The Magic Staff*, 160–162. Davis's thinking was also influenced by Emerson and the Transcendentalists, for whom he showed open admiration.

64. Ibid., 336–337.

65. Davis, *The Principles of Nature*. 154–155, 489–490, 514–515, 633–636.

66. Robert Delp, "Andrew Jackson Davis: Prophet of American Spiritualism," *Journal of American History* 54 (June 1967), 43–56.

67. Andrew Jackson Davis, *The Great Harmonia* (Boston, 1850), 3:360.

68. Ibid., 13. See also Catherine L. Albanese, "On the Matter of Spirit: Andrew Jackson Davis and the Marriage of God and Nature," *Journal of the American Academy of Religion*, 60, no. 1 (1992), 1–17.

69. Davis, *The Great Harmonia*, 1:215.

70. Ibid., 102–188.

71. James Turner, *Without God, Without Creed: The Origins of Unbelief in America* (Baltimore, 1985), 78–89.

72. Woodbury Fernald, *Univercoelum and Spiritual Philosopher* (Dec. 4, 1847), 2–8.

73. *Univercoelum and Spiritual Philosopher* (Apr. 8, 1848), 299.

74. *Univercoelum and Spiritual Philosopher* (Dec. 18, 1847), 37.

75. William Fishbough, *Univercoelum and Spirit Philosopher* (Oct. 14, 1848), 289.

76. William Fishbough, *Univercoelum and Spiritual Philosopher* (Jan. 15, 1848), 114–117.

77. *Univercoelum and Spiritual Philosopher* (Feb. 12, 1848), 161.

78. Woodbury Fernald, *Univercoelum and Spiritual Philosopher* (Dec. 2, 1848), 9.

79. *Univercoelum and Spiritual Philosopher* (Feb. 17, 1849), 185.

80. *Univercoelum and Spiritual Philosopher* (Apr. 1, 1848), 280.

81. William Fishbough, *Macrocosm and Microcosm* (New York, 1852), vi–127.

82. S. B. Brittan, *Man and His Relations* (New York, 1864), 134–219.

83. *Univercoelum and Spiritual Philosopher* (Dec. 11, 1847), 23.

84. *Univercoelum and Spiritual Philosopher* (Jan. 1, 1848), 75.

85. S. C. Hewitt, *Messages from the Superior State, Communicated through John Murray Spear, Containing Important Instructions to the Inhabitants of the earth* (Boston, 1852), 82–109.

86. E. E. Guild, *Univercoelum and Spiritual Philosopher* (Jan. 22, 1848), 117.

87. A. B. Grosh, *Univercoelum and Spiritual Philosopher* (Sept. 16, 1848), 248.

88. R. P. Ambler, *Univercoelum and Spiritual Philosopher* (Oct. 21, 1848), 329.

89. S. B. Brittan, *Univercoelum and Spiritual Philosopher* (Oct. 14 1848), 314.

90. E. E. Guild, *Univercoelum and Spiritual Philosopher* (Feb. 5, 1848), 152.

91. *Univercoelum and Spiritual Philosopher* (May 6, 1848), 148.

92. *Univercoelum and Spiritual Philosopher* (Feb. 5, 1848), 155. Bret E. Carroll cites the case of Uriah Clark, who:

> left the Universalist fold because he preferred the democratized salvation of "genuine Universalism, in its broadest, truest, eclectic sense" to "the organized sect" with its "enforcement of creeds, authorities, tests, books, and formula that interfere with individual freedom, and would enslave the soul to certain standards of alleged infallible judgment."

Carroll, *Spiritualism in Antebellum America*, 45.

93. Thomas Lake Harris, *Univercoelum and Spiritual Philosopher* (Nov. 25, 1848), 400. In 1857, A. D. Mayo, who had been a Universalist clergyman before becoming a preacher in the Independent Liberal church, delivered a penetrating critique of the state of contemporary religion and the promise of spiritualism:

> A faith that truly expresses the life of a people is active; but with the vigor of advancing power and health, not with the neuralgic energy witnessed in the fluctuations of the American church. The church is not content nor self-sustained; but, under an outside show of strength and confidence, it carries a timorous heart that quakes daily before the portents of American society. It is afraid of every living, characteristic development in our time; afraid of science, afraid of German theology, afraid of the best literature of the day, afraid of the socialists, the reformers, the spiritualists, the infidels—afraid of its own noblest men and women. (16)

Even Unitarianism and Universalism had not "arrived at a theological creed" that satisfied their followers, "nor is it desirable that they should." "They are gradually melting into each other, and blending with the other elements of advanced theological opinion in the land" (22). Mayo viewed the advent of spiritualism as a hopeful sign, a rebellion against "the materialism of our society that has brought the popular faith in immortality to a very low ebb." He continued:

> The tipping tables and rattling wainscots will, in good time, be left with other prodigies in the hands of curious men of scientific leisure for experiment; but this great cry of the popular heart after a rational faith in immortality will shiver numberless churches, and burst the bonds of many a man now enfolded in materialism or petrified into theological marble. *We shall learn out of it what it means in the nineteenth century to believe in the immortality of the soul.* (21)

Mayo, *Theology in America* (Albany, 1857).

94. Frances H[arriet Whipple] Green McDougall, *Biography of Mrs. Semantha Mettler, the Clairvoyant* (New York, 1853), 41. While still a preacher in Bridgeport, Brittan converted Mettler to the Universalist faith; she never recovered her "Orthodox equilibrium" after hearing Brittan's sermon (36).

95. Barrett, *The Spiritual Pilgrim*, 55–56. In a letter to Peebles, the spiritualist wife of a Universalist minister noted that denominational matters no longer interested her, since "*the scale* seems to me an ascending one" (123, 150–151).

96. S. B. Brittan, *Univercoelum and Spiritual Philosopher* (Sept. 16, 1848), 249.

97. *Univercoelum and Spiritual Philosopher* (June 17, 1848), 43.

98. Thomas Lake Harris, *Univercoelum and Spiritual Philosopher* (Sept. 30, 1848), 282. Harris abruptly separated himself from Davis when he became aware of Davis's practice of free love:

> He revolted violently against all naturalistic forms of spiritualism, against pantheism and the many secular gospels of progress and utopian reform current in his day. He turned unequivocally Christian. In the face of his earlier Universalism, he now believed in the literal reality of hell and damnation.

Essentially, Harris preached that there were two spiritualisms, the lower and the higher. The latter, Christian spiritualism, grew out of his Swedenborgianism and "was the work of the Divine Spirit and lifted man into the heavens." Herbert Schneider, *A Prophet and a Pilgrim* (New York, 1942), 21–22.

99. Davis, *Principles of Nature*, 586.

100. *Spirit of the Age* (July 7, 1849), 8–10.

101. *Spirit of the Age* Aug. 4, 1849), 76.

102. Miller, *The Larger Hope*, 1:204–207.

103. John Murray Spear, *The Educator* (Boston, 1857), 238–257, 634–640. See also Emma Hardinge, *Modern American Spiritualism: A Twenty Years' Record of the Communion between Earth and the World of the Spirits*, 4th ed. (New York, 1870), 217–229; Frank Podmore, *Modern Spiritualism: A History and a Criticism*, 2 vols. (London, 1902), 1:298–299; and E. W. Capron, *Modern Spiritualism: Its Facts and Fanaticisms, Its Consistencies and Contradictions* (Boston, 1855), 220–225.

104. Braude, *Radical Spirits*, 47.

105. Barrett, *The Spiritual Pilgrim*, 52, 55, 302. During his ministry at a Universalist church in Elmira, New York, from 1853 to 1855, Peebles maintained a congenial relationship with the Reverend Thomas K. Beecher, a Congregationalist and half brother of Henry Ward Beecher. Peebles wryly observed that "both of us were considered by the denominations to which we respectively belonged a little 'shaky,' theologically" (36).

106. Miller, *The Larger Hope*, 1:231.

107. Braude, *Radical Spirits*, 47–48; Miller, *The Larger Hope*, 1:226.

108. Braude, 4; see also Lewis Perry, *Radical Abolitionism: Anarchy and the Government of God in Antislavery Thought* (Ithaca, N.Y., 1973), esp. 218–219.

109. John Greenleaf Adams, *Memoir of Thomas Whittemore* (Boston, 1878), 173.

110. Miller, *The Larger Hope*, 1:230.

111. Bret Carroll comments that the spiritualist universe "was an interactive social network in which individual existence could not be understood apart from the social whole, nor selfhood separated from the influence of others." Carroll, *Spiritualism in Antebellum America*, 77.

112. Hovenkamp, *Science and Religion in America*, 55–56.

113. Ibid., 46–54.

114. Andrew Jackson Davis, *The Approaching Crisis, Being a Review of Dr. Bushnell's Course of Lectures on the Bible, Nature, Religion, Skepticism and the Supernatural* (Boston, 1869), 200–202.

115. Davis, *The Magic Staff*, 483–490. Davis stingingly condemned "a party calling themselves *Liberal Christians*" as a paradox and dangerous "solecism." He wrote, "To receive the totality of any one record as the only 'Word of God,' is equivalent to the total rejection of every other record" (445).

116. "The Great Harmonia, Being a Philosophical Revelation of the Natural, Spiritual, and Celestial Universe. By Andrew Jackson Davis," *Universalist Quarterly* 8 (Oct. 1851), 427–428; "The Great Harmonia, Concerning the Seven Mental States. By Andrew Jackson Davis," *Universalist Quarterly* 9 (July 1852), 326–327.

117. "Nature and the Supernatural, as Together Constituting the One System of God. By Horace Bushnell," *Universalist Quarterly* 16 (Apr. 1859), 203–204.

118. George H. Emerson, "The Divine Personality," *Universalist Quarterly* 14 (July 1857), 311–316.

119. A. M., "Miracles," *Universalist Quarterly* 15 (Apr. 1858), 142–158.

120. George H. Emerson, "Rationalistic Theology," *Universalist Quarterly* 17 (Jan. 1860), 5–22.

121. Adin Ballou, *Autobiography of Adin Ballou, 1803–1890, Containing an Elaborate Record and Narrative of His Life from Infancy to Old Age*, ed. William S. Haywood (Lowell, Mass., 1896), 379, 500; Adin Ballou, *An Exposition of Views Respecting the Principal Facts, Causes, and Peculiarities Involved in Spirit Manifestations, Together with Interesting Phenomenal Statements and Communications* (Boston, 1853). In this earlier work Ballou asserted that spiritualism would reaffirm "fundamental truths and duties" (15).

122. Rev. A. St. John Chambre, "Lecky's History of Rationalism," *Universalist Quarterly* 23, n.s. 3 (Oct. 1860), 473–485.

123. "Nature and the Supernatural," *Universalist Quarterly* 16 (Apr. 1859), 203–204.

124. Hosea Ballou 2nd, "Fourierism and Similar Schemes," *Universalist Quarterly* 2 (Jan. 1845), 52–76.

125. Miller, *The Larger Hope*, 1:153.

126. *Report of Addresses at a Meeting Held in Boston, May 30, 1867 to Consider the Conditions, Wants and Prospects of Free Religion in America. Together with the Constitution of the Free Religious Association There Organized* (Boston, 1867), 53. On the subject in general, see Stow Persons, *Free Religion: An American Faith* (Boston, 1947).

127. *Free Religion: Report of Addresses*, 10.

128. Ibid.

129. Ibid., 48.

130. Miller, *The Larger Hope*, 2:154–155.

131. Ibid., 66–67.

132. Barrett, *The Spiritual Pilgrim*, 44–45.

133. Miller, *The Larger Hope*, 2:71.

134. Ibid., 75. On the Bisbee trial, see also Mary F. Bogue, "The Minneapolis Radical Lectures and the Excommunication of the Rev. Herman Bisbee," *Journal of the Universalist Historical Society* 7 (1967–1968), 3–69.

135. Stephen Gottschalk, *The Emergence of Christian Science in American Religious Life* (Berkeley, Calif., 1973), 199.

136. Winthrop Hudson, *Religion in American Life* (New York, 1965), 197.

CHAPTER SIX

1. James Turner, *Without God, Without Creed: The Origins of Unbelief in America* (Baltimore, 1985), 63.

2. No religious development in late postbellum America illustrates this point more clearly than the rise of Christian Science. Stephen Gottschalk comments that people:

> were receptive to a religion which claimed that Christian promises were to be realized in the present; which offered demonstration instead of doctrine; and which taught that symbols of religious truth could be replaced by the discernment and demonstration of the spiritual fact of being.

Gottschalk, *The Emergence of Christian Science in American Religious Life* (Berkeley, Calif., 1973), 291.

3. Charles Cashdollar, *The Transformation of Theology: Positivism in Protestant Thought in Britain and America* (Princeton, N.J., 1989), 446.

4. Turner, *Without God, Without Creed*. Turner indicates that unbelief spread because church leaders "committed religion functionally to making the world better in human terms and intellectually to modes of knowing God fitted only for understanding this world" (267).

5. Ann Rose, *Victorian America and the Civil War* (Cambridge, 1992), 18.

6. Colleen McDannell, *The Christian Home in Victorian America* (Bloomington, Ind., 1986), 154.

7. Allan Nevins, *The Emergence of Modern America, 1865–1878* (New York, 1927), 225.

8. McDannell, *The Christian Home*, 130.

9. Sidney Mead, *The Lively Experiment* (New York, 1963), 179. R. Laurence Moore observes that children in the early decades of the nineteeenth century were far more influenced by their exposure to religious debate than were their later century counterparts. Religious controversy ceased to play a major role in the intellectual formation of children toward the end of the century. Moore, "What Children Did Not Learn in School: The Intellectual Quickening of Young Americans in the Nineteenth Century," *Church History* 68, no. 1 (Mar. 1999), 42–61.

10. *The Universalist Centennial, Held in Gloucester, Massachusetts, September 20th, 21st, 22nd, 1870* (Boston, 1870), 94.

11. William McLoughlin, *The Meaning of Henry Ward Beecher* (New York, 1970), 180. Charles G. Finney's sermons reflect the changing times; his stress was on "victory over the world," not on sin, death, or the devil. Finney, *Victory over the World: Revival Messages* (Grand Rapids, Mich., 1966), 11–17.

12. Geoffrey Rowell, *Hell and the Victorians* (Oxford, 1974), 14–16. Although Rowell's work deals with the decline of hell in Britain, it has important relevance to American

religious history as well, since no similar work is extant on the changing conceptions of hell in late nineteenth-century America. James H. Moorhead asserts that the growth of a capitalist economy and the need for continued expansion and consumption mitigated against a static view of death. See his "As Though Nothing at All Had Happened: Death and the Afterlife in Protestant Thought," *Soundings* (Winter 1984), 466. See also Boyd Hilton, *The Age of Atonement* (New York, 1988), on the growing belief in universal salvation in Britain, where, Hilton asserts, "The emasculation of Godly terrors can be seen as a failure of middle-class nerve" (276–277).

13. Richard Rabinowitz, *The Spiritual Self in Everyday Life* (Boston, 1979), 238.

14. Charles Cashdollar, "The Social Implications of the Doctrine of Divine Providence: A Nineteenth-Century Debate in American Theology," *Harvard Theological Review* (1978), 280–81, 283.

15. Mead, *The Lively Experiment*, 169.

16. Louise Stevenson, *The Victorian Homefront* (New York, 1991), 150.

17. McLoughlin, *The Meaning of Henry Ward Beecher*, 6.

18. Rabinowitz, *The Spiritual Self in Everyday Life*, 192.

19. Stanley French, "The Cemetery as Cultural Institution: The Establishment of Mount Auburn and the 'Rural Cemetery' Movement," in *Death in America*, ed. David Stannard (Philadelphia, 1975), 69–91. Colleen McDannell emphasizes that the cemetery was not a "secularized space" for the Victorians. "Walking through the cemetery provided security, not a sense of dread. Victorian landscapes were visited by many people because they emphasized that Christianity was about immortality and not judgment," *Material Christianity* (New Haven, Conn., 1995), 128.

20. Elizabeth Stuart Phelps, *The Gates Ajar* (New York, 1868). McDannell writes that "Heaven was not the opposite of this life; it was the continuation and perfection of what made this life good. Love, family, friendship, work, progress, conversation—all these familiar earthly involvements continued in the next life." *Material Christianity*, 128.

21. Harriet Beecher Stowe, *Uncle Tom's Cabin* (New York, 1978), 353.

22. Jon Butler, *Softly and Tenderly Jesus Is Calling* (Brooklyn, N.Y., 1991), 153.

23. Rose, *Victorian America and the Civil War*, 38. Writing about Victorian England, John Morley comments, "It is difficult for modern men, most of whom were born with doubt, to conceive of the horror death brought to men born with faith." Morley, *Death, Heaven and the Victorians* (Pittsburgh, Pa., 1971), 103.

24. Robert W. Habenstein and William M. Lammers, *The History of American Funeral Directing* (Milwaukee, Wis., 1955), 389–444.

25. Noted in Phillipe Ariès, "The Reversal of Death," in Stannard, ed., *Death in America*, 152.

26. Margaret Deland, *John Ward, Preacher* (Boston, 1888), 447. One of the characters in Deland's book asserts, "I think belief in eternal damnation is a phase in spiritual development" (180).

27. Daniel Calhoun, *The Intelligence of a People* (Princeton, N.J., 1973), 259–261.

28. Gottschalk, *The Emergence of Christian Science in American Religious Life*, 8–9. Christian Science is a form of Christian Universalism that explicitly embraces the belief in a probation after death. Mary Baker Eddy wrote, "Resurrection from the dead . . . must come to all sooner or later," and "Universal salvation rests on progression and probation, and is unattainable without them." Quoted in Gottschalk, *The Emergence of Christian Science in American Religious Life*, 94–95.

29. T. J. Jackson Lears notes, "As heaven became less an urgent necessity than a pleasant inevitability, the intense yearning for salvation waned. To many late Victorians,

the depth of emotional life seemed shallower, the contours of spiritual life softer, than ever before." Lears, *No Place of Grace: Antimodernism and the Transformation of American Culture, 1880–1920* (New York, 1981), 44.

30. Paul Carter, *The Spiritual Crisis of the Gilded Age* (DeKalb, Ill., 1971), 58–59.

31. An "orthodox minister of the gospel" contended in 1876 that "a cloud of impenetrable mystery hides the ultimate lot of the wicked" and insisted that "we can't be certain of the endlessness of future punishment, however sure we are that it exists." Orthodox churches, he maintained, are "inconsistent and unsatisfactory" on the subject, as "restorationists" continue to point to our "embarrassed, uncertain, divergent and apparently transitional views." See James Morris Whiton, *Is Eternal Punishment Endless?* (Boston, 1876), viii–101.

32. John G. Adams, *Fifty Notable Years* (Boston, 1882), 309.

33. Ira V. Brown, *Lyman Abbott, Christian Evolutionist: A Study in Religious Liberalism* (Cambridge, 1953), 128–138. Brown comments that the conflict over a second probation had important implications for missionary activity. Some members of the American Board of Commissioners for Foreign Missions felt that to deny that the unrepentant were destined for everlasting hell would "cut the nerve" of missions. Others, however, argued that this idea had itself badly hurt missions, since it offended non-christian populations. "If no man could be saved who had not heard of Christ, and if death were the limit of probation, then all their ancestors were in irredeemable misery. They positively refused, missionaries reported, to accept a 'Gospel' of which this was a cardinal doctrine" (132).

34. Bruce Kuklick, *Churchmen and Philosophers: From Jonathan Edwards to John Dewey* (New Haven, Conn., 1985) 222.

35. Editorial, "Two Noteworthy Opinions," *Andover Review* 10 (1888), 320–321.

36. Daniel Merriman, "Belief in Endless Punishment Requisite to the Ordination of a Minister," *Congregational Quarterly* (Apr. 1873), 225–247.

37. Noah Porter, "The Doctrine of Eternal Punishment," *North American Review* 126 (1878), 323–357.

38. Quoted in Brown, *Lyman Abbott, Christian Evolutionist*, 135–136.

39. Noted the Reverend J. T. Tucker, "The impression of the whole treatment of this subject in the New Testament is against the fact of grace beyond death." Tucker, "Probation beyond Death," *Congregational Review* (July 1870), 342.

40. Daniel Day Williams, *The Andover Liberals* (New York, 1941), 28.

41. Samuel C. Bartlett, *Future Punishment* (Boston, 1875), 59–60. See also Charles Marsh Mead, *The Soul Here and Hereafter* (Boston, 1879). Mead, a professor at Andover Theological Seminary, argued that "a future perpetual punishment of the impenitent" was "clearly taught" by the Bible (409).

42. Samuel Barrows, *The Doom of the Majority of Mankind* (Boston, 1883), v. Indeed, all attempts to change the creed of the Presbyterian church in the last quarter of the nineteenth century met with complete failure. To quiet dissenters, some Presbyterians in the 1890s proposed inserting a footnote in their creed to express the mercy of God. See William R. Hutchinson, *The Modernist Impulse in American Protestantism* (Cambridge, 1976), 69. For most believers, though, the creed itself was becoming about as important as the footnote.

43. Austin Phelps, *My Study* (New York, 1886), 95, 118, 140.

44. Edward Cornelius Towne, *The Question of Hell: An Essay in New Orthodoxy by a Puritan* (New Haven, Conn., 1873), 87.

45. William G. T. Shedd, *The Doctrine of Endless Punishment* (New York, 1886), 154–155, 162.

46. Robert Withers Memminger, *Present Issues: Facts Observable in the Consciousness of the Present Age* (Philadelphia, 1873), 160–194.

47. Horace Bushnell, *The Vicarious Sacrifice* (New York, 1866), 340.

48. Quoted in Luther Tracy Townsend, *The Intermediate World* (Boston, 1878), 237–238. A Unitarian journal published a two-part article by "an Orthodox minister of the Gospel" asking, "Is there any limit to man's probation?" The article concluded that there was "an abyss of sin so deep as to be beyond the reach even of God's arm." There are:

> some phenomena of sin which are absolutely horrible, more so than anything that was ever painted in the most lurid Hell. . . . And though it may linger for years, the point at which it falls may be far along in eternity, ages after the body has deceased, what can the end be but a consummation of that most significant of scriptural phrases, so awfully suggestive in its very vagueness, . . . a state of spiritual death.

J. C. K., "Is There Any Limit to Man's Probation?" *Monthly Religious Magazine* (Apr.–May 1867), 346–347.

49. William R. Huntingdon, *Conditional Immortality* (New York, 1878), 121–142.

50. See Rowell, *Hell and the Victorians*, 180–207, for a fuller discussion of annihilationism (or conditionalism) in Britain and America.

51. Quoted in Carter, *The Spiritual Crisis of the Gilded Age*, 60.

52. See A. A. Miner, *Old Forts Taken: Five Lectures on Endless Punishment and Future Life* (Boston, 1878); and I. C. Knowlton, *Through the Shadows* (Boston, 1885).

53. M. J. Steere, *Footprints Heavenward; or, Universalism: The More Excellent Way* (Boston, 1862), 397–398. Steere observed that preachers now had difficulty lighting the fires of revival because people no longer sensed any "danger" from divine wrath.

54. A. J. Patterson, "A Hundred Years," *Universalist Quarterly* 31, n.s. 11 (Jan. 1874), 92.

55. "General Review," *Universalist Quarterly* 33, n.s. 13 (Oct. 1876), 500. An editor of the *Quarterly* in 1874 was similarly encouraged by "the struggles of the churchmen of all sects to shake off the horrible nightmare of *absolutely endless* punishment." *Universalist Quarterly* 31, n.s. 11 (Jan. 1874), 97.

56. "General Review," *Universalist Quarterly* 35, n.s. 15 (Apr. 1878), 228–229.

57. "General Review," *Universalist Quarterly*, 38, n.s. 18 (July 1881), 364.

58. "The Future of The Impenitent," *Universalist Quarterly* 39, n.s. 19 (Apr. 1882), 235–237.

59. "Progressive Orthodoxy," *Universalist Quarterly* 43, n.s. 23 (July 1886), 63–74.

60. George Emerson, *The Doctrine of Probation Examined with Reference to Current Discussion* (Boston, 1883), 161–168.

61. T. J. Sawyer, "The Grounds of Endless Punishment Considered," *Universalist Quarterly* 31, n.s. 11 (July 1874), 306–328.

62. "General Review," *Universalist Quarterly* 33, n.s. 13 (Jan. 1876), 101.

63. A. C. Barry, "The New Orthodoxy," *Universalist Quarterly* 38, n.s. 18 (July 1881), 294–308; G. M. Harmon, "The Restoration of Humanity," *Universalist Quarterly* 39, n.s. 19 (July 1882), 328–338.

64. S. S. Hebbard, "The New Orthodoxy," *Universalist Quarterly* 42, n.s. 22 (Jan. 1885), 17–31.

65. Olympia Brown, "Folly Is Set in Great Dignity," "If Ye Then Be Risen on Christ," "Neither Shall They Say," and "Come See the Works of the Lord," unpublished manuscripts, Schlesinger Library, Harvard University.

66. Phebe Hanaford, "No Night There," *The Ladies Repository* 36 (July 1866), 65–67; "Death and Victory" 37 (Apr. 1867), 270.

67. *Manford's Monthly Magazine* (Chicago–St. Louis, June 1866), 17–18; (Nov. 1866), 161–165.

68. George Quimby, *Heaven: Our Home* (Augusta, Maine, 1875), 209.

69. Ibid., 213.

70. "General Review," *Universalist Quarterly* 24, n.s. 4 (July 1867), 379.

71. Phineas T. Barnum, *Why I Am a Universalist* (Boston, 1895), 9.

72. Donald H. Meyer, *The Instructed Conscience* (Philadelphia, 1972), 38–42.

73. Ibid., 55.

74. "The Divine Efficacy and Moral Harmony of the Universe; Proved from Reason and Scripture. By a Pastor," *Universalist Quarterly* 11 (Apr. 1854), 215–217. The author also emphasized the need to retain the "*moral* responsibility of man" and the "*moral* worthiness of God."

75. E. F., "The Will," *Universalist Quarterly* 12 (Jan. 1855), 57–69.

76. George H. Emerson, "The Authority and Sphere of Consciousness," *Universalist Quarterly* 13 (July 1856), 277–295.

77. Hosea Ballou 2nd, "The Doctrine of Necessity," *Universalist Quarterly* 15 (Oct. 1858), 346–373.

78. Hosea Ballou 2nd, "The Doctrine of Necessity," *Universalist Quarterly* 16 (July 1859), 329–359. Ballou 2nd also sought to attack I. D. Williamson by pointing out:

> If we adopt this obsolete position, we cannot then object to the doctrine of *imputed* sin and righteousness or to *original* sin; to the notion of our having been *created* sinners; nor to our being really guilty of all the misconduct practiced in this world. (352)

This doctrine, surely, Universalists had discarded long ago.

79. T. J. Sawyer, "Dr. Williamson's Rudiments," *Universalist Quarterly* 28, n.s. 8 (Jan. 1871), 59–81; (Apr. 1871), 133–150.

80. Elbridge Gerry Brooks, *Our New Departure* (Boston, 1874), 21–22, 34, 55–56.

81. H. I. Cushman, "Drifts in Religious Thought," *Universalist Quarterly*, 40, n.s. 20 (Jan. 1883), 22–33; H. I. Cushman, "Catholic Universalism," *Universalist Quarterly* 45, n.s. 25 (Apr. 1888), 147–160. Despite his desire to move out of "Ballou's ruts," Brooks believed it was "doubtful whether the reckonings of the future will assign even to Luther a place so eminent among the great theological leaders and discoverers of our race" as Hosea Ballou. Elbridge Gerry Brooks "Hosea Ballou," *Universalist Quarterly* 27, n.s. 7 (Oct. 1870), 389–420.

82. Meyer, *The Instructed Conscience*, 55.

83. Sydney Ahlstrom, "The Scottish Philosophy and American Theology," *Church History* 29 (1955), 269.

84. On Edwards, see Morton White, *Science and Sentiment in America* (New York, 1972), 40.

85. Obadiah H. Tillotson, *The Divine Efficiency and Moral Harmony of the Universe* (Boston, 1854), 35–119.

86. "J. W. T.," "What is Will?" *Universalist Quarterly* 12 (Apr. 1855), 202–204.

87. "J. W. T.," "Divine Sovereignty," *Universalist Quarterly* 16 (Jan. 1859), 86–94.

88. I. D. Williamson, *Rudiments of Theological and Moral Science* (Boston, 1870), 73–169.

89. Ibid.

90. Defending Williamson against his critics, O. D. Miller insisted that, to realize

its distinct purpose, the denomination had to commit itself to certain theological positions. Miller explicitly rejected the epistemological basis of Williamson's necessitarianism, which he explained, had been influenced by Henry Longueville Mansel's *The Limits of Religious Knowledge* (1858). Drawing upon Kant and William Hamilton, Miller tried to demonstrate human nescience and the resulting need for total reliance on biblical authority. Adducing a variety of arguments from sources as diverse as Hegel and American philosopher Laurens Hickok, Miller opposed the tendency to reject reason entirely in theological matters; this was to "abandon one half of the grounds of Universalism itself." But, for all that, Miller's defense of necessitarianism was essentially Kantian and thus not new in any basic way: he saw freedom as a matter of consciousness, of feeling, but insisted that all volition is ultimately determined by external motives. Rational freedom, Christian freedom, was perfectly consistent with the doctrine of necessity.

In Miller's eyes, Williamson was the first Universalist to appreciate fully that "the true [Universalist] doctrine of the atonement finds its only logical basis in the doctrine of necessity." Williamson showed that "God necessitates the act; he also necessitates the conscious intent on man's part." The larger divine purpose is always "unselfish, rational, one with universal reason and one with the universal aim of history"; sinfulness exists only in ephemeral, irrational human intent. Miller concluded that the doctrine of necessity served to illustrate in a rational, logical way the Universalist view that all punishment was remedial: man does not "deserve" punishment in the sense of the old theories of satisfaction, but simply "needs" punishment as part of a universal plan. O. D. Miller, "Dr. Williamson and His Reviewer," *Universalist Quarterly* 28, n.s. 8 (July 1871), 289–318.

91. Meyer, *The Instructed Conscience*, 57.

92. Williamson, *Rudiments*, 290–292. A number of Universalists, while not eager to plunge into philosophical debate, saw no need to dwell on moral responsibility and moral freedom. Pointing out reproachfully that the Unitarians viewed Universalism as a "forcing of salvation," a *Quarterly* writer in 1858 asked rhetorically, Does God "not annul our free-will when he sits in his incomprehensible wisdom interweaving the actions of his creatures in one harmonious issue?" Quoting from the English Unitarian F. D. Maurice, he expressed infinite faith in God to overcome a resistant human will. J. C. P., "Hope, Sympathy, Destiny," *Universalist Quarterly* 15 (July 1858), 278–293. A similar article in the next issue concluded simply that, in "practical life," the truths of divine sovereignty and human freedom "play harmoniously, though speculative subtlety may bring them into apparent collision." Emphasizing Universalism's single commitment to the power of redeeming goodness, the commentator asserted, "Decrees and free-will do not come into any fatal collision on a platform as broad as ours." E. W. R., "Speculative and Practical Universalism," *Universalist Quarterly* 15 (Oct. 1858), 329–346.

93. T. J. Sawyer, "Dr. Williamson's Rudiments," *Universalist Quarterly* 28, n.s. 8 (Apr. 1871), 133–150.

94. R. O. Williams, "Our New Departure," *Universalist Quarterly* 32, n.s. 12 (July 1875), 281–300.

95. A. D. Mayo, "The Prospect of Liberal Christianity," *Universalist Quarterly* 34, n.s. 14 (July 1877), 334–356.

96. A. D. Mayo, "Prophecies of the Hour Concerning the Liberal Christian Church," *Universalist Quarterly* 36, n.s. 16 (Oct. 1879), 409–424.

97. Charles W. Biddle, "Abstract Religion and the Personal Christ," *Universalist Quarterly* 46, n.s. 26 (Apr. 1889), 158–173.

98. S. S. Hebbard, "The New Orthodoxy," *Universalist Quarterly* 42, n.s. 22 (Jan. 1885), 17–31.

99. W. H. Ryder, "Punishment, Forgiveness, Salvation," *Universalist Quarterly* 36, n.s. 16 (Oct. 1879), 388–407.

100. L. W. Ballou, "More Questions," *Universalist Quarterly* 43, n.s. 23 (July 1886), 298–303.

101. E. C. Sweetser, "A Study of the Atonement," *Universalist Quarterly* 44, n.s. 24 (July 1887), 279–292. See also J. Coleman Adams, "New Problems in Our Church Work," *Universalist Quarterly* 37, n.s. 17 (Oct. 1880), 463–474. Adams asserted that Universalism needed a "more lucid and positive assertion of the nature of Sin, its heinousness, its perversion of the Spirit's normal life and its corruption of the very tissues, so to speak, of the soul." Universalist dissenters worried that a strain of "latent sentimentalism" would eventually destroy the denomination if it were not eliminated.

102. W. C. Stiles, "Universalism and Sin," *Universalist Quarterly* 37, n.s. 17 (Jan. 1880), 51–65; "Universalism and Punishment" (July 1880), 327–343. H. Richard Niebuhr also asserted, "Radically and critically used, the conviction that all men are sinners implies logically for the Christian believer that therefore all men are equal." Niebuhr, "The Idea of Original Sin in American Culture," in William Stacy Johnson, ed., *Theology, History and Culture: Major Unpublished Writings* (New Haven, Conn., 1996), 178.

103. S. S. Hebbard, "The Sacrifice of Christ," *Universalist Quarterly* 38, n.s. 18 (July 1881), 313–329.

104. A. St. John Chambré, "The Polity of the Universalist Church," *Universalist Quarterly* 33, n.s. 13 (Oct. 1876), 471–487.

105. Kenneth Cauthen, *The Impact of American Religious Liberalism* (New York, 1962), 9–10.

106. Reinhold Niebuhr, *Does Civilization Need Religion?* (New York, 1929), 176.

107. Discussing Niebuhr's belief in *The Theology of Reinhold Niebuhr* (New York, 1956), Hans Hofman writes, "In the rise of the secular idea of the 'autonomous self' . . . the Biblical teaching of the value of the individual is accepted; but man's relatedness to God and fellowmen, the essential condition of true individuality is denied" 177. "From God, life flows out and touches man and leads him into society. True community is impossible without true relatedness to God. It is equally impossible that true relatedness should not create true community" (163).

108. Jackson Lears observes:

> Liberal Protestants sought to exorcise the last vestiges of shadow and magic from their creeds, to create a clean, well-lighted place where religion and rational optimism could co-exist in harmony. The triumph of what was called "modernism" in theological circles signalled the submergence of religion in secular modes of thought.

No Place of Grace, 23.

109. Quoted in Mead, *The Lively Experiment*, 175.

110. Richmond Fisk, "The Successful Christian Ministry," *Universalist Quarterly* 28, n.s. 8 (Oct. 1871), 427–443.

111. G. M. Harmon, "Certain Phases of Our Growth," *Universalist Quarterly* 38, n.s. 18 (Apr. 1881), 151–157

112. *Manford's Monthly Magazine* (Jan. 1867), 232–234.

113. *Manford's Monthly Magazine* (Mar. 1867), 296.

114. Horace Greeley, *Recollections of a Busy Life* (New York, 1868), 71.

115. Turner, *Without God, Without Creed*, 129.

116. Mead, *The Lively Experiment*, 152.

117. Rose, *Victorian America and the Civil War*, 18.

118. Karen Lystra, *Searching the Heart: Women, Men and Romantic Love in Nineteenth-Century America* (New York, 1989), 8, 31, 247.

119. Clifton E. Olmstead, *Religion in America Past and Present* (Englewood Cliffs, N.J., 1961), 112.

120. Ibid., 112–113.

121. McDannell, *The Christian Home in Victorian America*, 154.

122. Butler, *Softly and Tenderly Jesus Is Calling*, 152.

123. Patricia Bonomi, *Under the Cope of Heaven* (New York, 1986), 219. Rabinowitz notes that an "older pattern of grace" marked by the "imitation of Christ" was by the mid–nineteenth century overtaking "the Reformation ideal of personal progression through sin and redemption." *The Spiritual Self in Everyday Life*, 183.

124. Butler, *Softly and Tenderly Jesus Is Calling*, 129.

125. Quoted in Brown, *Lyman Abbott, Christian Evolutionist*, 148.

126. See Robert W. Jenson, *America's Theologian: A Recommendation of Jonathan Edwards* (New York, 1988), 183–184, for a good discussion of the "de-eschatologizing" of Western Christianity.

127. Richmond Fisk, "The Successful Christian Ministry," *Universalist Quarterly* 28, n.s. 8 (Oct. 1871), 427–443.

CONCLUSION

1. Edwin Gaustad, *A Documentary History of Religion in America* (Grand Rapids, Mich., 1993), 133. My study does not seek to analyze the history of Universalism beyond the late nineteenth century. The details of denominational history in the period after 1870 are readily available in the second volume of Russell Miller, *The Larger Hope* (Boston, 1979), and George Hunston Williams, "American Universalism: A Bicentennial Essay," *Journal of the Universalist Historical Society* 9 (1971), 1–94 sorts out some of the broader intellectual trends among Universalists in the later era. Miller makes it clear that the major theme of his second volume is one of decline.

2. I have in mind here, above all, the categories of Max Weber, especially the concepts of "charisma" and "routinization," which have undergone many permutations but which retain influence in many studies of the history of religion. See Weber, *On Charisma and Institution Building: Selected Papers*, ed. S. Eisenstadt (Chicago and London, 1968).

3. The New Psychology reflected the emphasis on a dynamic will, with John Dewey maintaining, "The will . . . [is] a living bond connecting and conditioning *all* mental activity." Quoted in George Cotkin, *Reluctant Modernism: American Thought and Culture, 1880–1900* (New York, 1992), 33. E. Brooks Holifield writes that the:

> emphasis on the will endured throughout the late nineteenth century. . . . But the dethronement of the will in the post-Freudian era, combined with the revolt against moralism in Protestant theology, helped to revive older notions of sin as distrust or as false pride rooted in anxiety.

Holifield, *A History of Pastoral Care in America* (Nashville, Tenn., 1983), 352. Conservative Universalists in the late nineteenth century had clearly anticipated this revival.

4. Gail Parker, *Mind Cure in New England* (Hanover, N.H., 1973), 24.

5. Ibid., 133.

6. T. J. Jackson Lears notes that many troubled Americans sought solace

not from ministers but from mind-curists and mental hygienists whose cures for nervousness frequently lacked a supernatural dimension. References to salvation dropped from view; psychological well-being became—though often only implicitly—an entirely secular project.

No Place of Grace: Antimodernism and the Transformation of American Society, 1880–1920 (New York, 1981), 55.

Index

Abbott, A. R., 80, 83
Abbott, Lyman, 131–132, 146
abolitionism. *See* antislavery
Adams, J. Coleman, 194n
Adams, John G., 131
Ahlstrom, Sydney, 32, 50, 51, 140
Aiken, J., 41
Allen, Ethan, 27, 98
Ambler, R. P., 108–110, 117
American Red Cross, 94
American Sunday School Union. *See* Sunday Schools
American Tract Society, 67, 165n
American Woman's Suffrage Association, 93, 94
Amherst College, 68
Andover Theological School (Seminary), 65, 131, 132, 190n
Andrews, L. F. W., 87
Anglicans/Anglicanism. *See* Episcopalians
annihilationism, 131, 133, 191n
Anthony, Susan B., 93, 94
anticlericalism, Universalist, 64–67

antinomianism, 19
antislavery, 85–88, 93, 120
Aquinas, Thomas, 29
Arminianism: antecedents of, 155n; and eighteenth-century Universalism, 15, 16, 18, 19; Hosea Ballou's opposition to, 28, 30; as opposed to Edwardseanism, 10, 12–13, 58, 153n; and "organicism," 152n; and radical sectarians, 156n; used by missionaries, 174n. *See also* moralism
atheism/atheists: linked to sentimentalism, 135; mesmerism as a weapon against, 106, 108; phrenology defended against charge of, 101; spiritualism and the danger of, 124; spiritualism as an antidote to, 110, 116; spread of, 188n; Universalism associated with, 39–40, 45–46, 56, 86, 165n
atonement: Anselmic view of, 4, 5, 17; Hosea Ballou on, 27–29; New Divinity on, 11. *See also* Jesus Christ